PRAISE FOR *When Women Were*

"Shedding new insight on a much de[...]
keen and well-researched arguments f[...]
the clergy."

—*Body, Mind & Spirit*

"A powerful work of synthesis. Torjesen is nothing short of brilliant in tracing the connection between the church's move from private to public spheres and the corresponding move to suppress women's leadership. . . . The cumulative effect of the book's argument is to make more rationally urgent than ever the removal of this scandal."

—Elizabeth A. Johnson, author of *She Who Is*

"Helps lift the veil of deceit that has concealed, for almost two thousand years, the powerful roles played by women in the early Christian communities."

—Eva C. Keuls, University of Minnesota,
author of *The Reign of the Phallus*

"Karen Jo Torjesen's sophisticated yet accessible analysis presents a powerful challenge to those who reject women's ordination on biblical grounds."

—Elizabeth Schüssler Fiorenza, Harvard University,
author of *In Memory of Her*

"Provocative in argument and engagingly written, *When Women Were Priests* is bound to stimulate discussion."

—Elizabeth A. Clark, co-editor, *Women and Religion*

"Will contribute to the growing public awareness of the reality of women clergy in the first millennium of the church's history, and the moral imperative toward women clergy in the third."

—Matthew Fox, author of *Sheer Joy*

"Absolutely first rate!"

—Jouette M. Bassler, associate editor, *The HarperCollins Study Bible*

"Brilliantly lays bare the historic roots of the church's prejudice against women. A powerful, revealing, insightful book."

—Rt. Rev. John S. Spong, Bishop of Newark;
author of *Born of a Woman*

"Torjesen's research and analysis bolster the already persuasive case that women managed households both domestic and ecclesial in the early centuries of Christianity, and will do so again to everyone's benefit."

—Mary E. Hunt, co-director of the
Women's Alliance for Theology, Ethics and Ritual (WATER)

"An entirely fresh approach to a vexed and uncertain question."

—Dr. Rowan Williams, Bishop of Monmouth

"Torjesen calls contemporary Christian theologians to extricate the essential teachings of the gospel from the current patriarchal gender system, restoring women to equal partnership in Christian life."

—*National Catholic Reporter*

# When Women  Were Priests

**WOMEN'S LEADERSHIP IN THE
EARLY CHURCH AND THE SCANDAL
OF THEIR SUBORDINATION
IN THE RISE OF CHRISTIANITY**

## Karen Jo Torjesen

HarperOne
*An Imprint of HarperCollinsPublishers*

HarperOne

HarperCollins books may be purchased for educational, business, or sales promotional use. For information, please e-mail the Special Markets Department at SPsales@harpercollins.com.

HarperCollins Web site: http://www.harpercollins.com

HarperCollins®, 📖 ®, and HarperOne™ are trademarks of HarperCollins Publishers.

Interior design by Jaime Robles

FIRST HARPERCOLLINS PAPERBACK EDITION PUBLISHED IN 1995

Library of Congress Cataloging-in-Publication Data

Torjesen, Karen Jo.
    When women were priests : women's leadership in the early church and the scandal of their subordination in the rise of Christianity / Karen Jo Torjesen — 1st ed.
        p. cm.
    Includes bibliographical references and index.
    ISBN: 978-0-06-068661-1
    ISBN-10: 0-06-068661-8
    1. Women in Christianity—History—Early church, ca. 30–600.
    2. Women clergy—History.  I. Title.
BR195.W6T67 1993
262'.14'082—dc20                                    91-58916

        15 16  RRD(H)  20 19 18 17

# Contents

FOR MARGO L. GOLDSMITH

*a patron of women*

*a friend of scholars*

*a founder of the Women's Studies in Religion program at Claremont*

# Preface

■■■■

Too often the notion of scholarship is that of unique individuals cloistered in libraries, putting their own creative thoughts into writing. The understood goal of such scholarship is, apparently, to produce the definitive statement on an issue. But the truth is that virtually all scholarship is collaborative—ideas are tested and reworked in dialogues with colleagues, through questions from students, and during conversations with friends—and feminist scholarship is a particularly collaborative enterprise, sustained by conversations that pose new questions, sharpen insights, and inspire bold connections.

This work comes out of many conversations and intends to be one voice in a larger discussion of religion, power, and women. It chronicles a history of conversations. The most important theoretical parts of my work are the results of collaboration. Chapter 2, on the public and private gender system in the early Christian era, co-authored with Virginia Burrus, whom I first met at the University of Göttingen, Germany, is a prime example. Our joint investigation into the Greco-Roman gender system spanned two continents and five years. In the interest of gaining a broader perspective on ancient beliefs about gender we pooled our expertise, hers in classical authors and mine in Patristic writers. Her early use of the public-private model to interpret gender conflict in the Apocryphal Acts (later published as *Chastity as Autonomy*) became the basis for our elaboration of the complex public–private dichotomies of Greco-Roman antiquity.

My conversation partner in the exploration of the ancient Greco-Roman honor-shame system of values was K. C. Hansen, an Old Testament scholar who lived in the cabin next to mine on Mt. Baldy, California, above Claremont. He introduced me to the anthropological literature on the Mediterranean system of values that associates masculinity with honor and femininity with shame.

Chapter 7, "The Penetrator and the Penetrated," draws on many conversations with my Claremont colleague Ann Taves. Her research interests sparked a fruitful dialogue between American religious history and psychology. Our introductory course on women's studies in religion explored the ways the concepts of the sacred, the self, and society mirror each other. This helped me understand how Greek attitudes toward woman and sexuality found their way into the Greek theory of the self, in which the lower part of the self was characterized as female, sexual, and dangerous.

The idea that patterns of social relationships exercise a profound influence on the formulation of abstract concepts has been a recurring theme in my conversations with Karen King, a scholar of *pre-christian* gnostic Christianity. Our interest in the gender systems implicit in ancient texts was enlivened by our trip to India and our encounters with the gender systems there. Karen and I have long struggled to understand how social categories like gender become symbols for divine realities.

My conversations with the women and men who attended my public lectures, the women who participated in retreats, and my own students have given me the courage to publish the insights gained during this process. This book is an expression of thanks to them.

I owe an enormous debt to those who have transcribed my tapes and helped edit my manuscript: Ellen Sun and Henry Sun, Stephanie Dumoski, and, most of all, Laura Ammon and Randy Reed, who checked footnotes and provided helpful suggestions. My friends Ann Ownbey and Margo Goldsmith read early drafts, offered helpful critiques, and kept inquiring discreetly about my progress.

I am grateful for research grants from the National Endowment for the Humanities and the American Council of Learned Societies. I also want to thank the librarians of the Honnold Library and the Library of the School of Theology at Claremont for their help in securing books not available in their excellent libraries.

I would also like to express my gratitude to the late John Hollar for the idea of publishing a collection of essays and to John Loudon of Harper San Francisco for his new vision of the integrated book that the essays have become. The essays became chapters and have been rewritten several times under his careful tutelage. Finally I would like to thank my family, Leif and Maggy, for their patience and support.

# Introduction

In November of 1992, the Church of England
approved (by only a two-vote margin) the
ordination of women priests. Two months
earlier the Anglican church of South Africa
had voted to ordain women. As recently as
1976, the Episcopal church in the United
States voted to recognize the ordination of
women priests. The first woman rabbi in the
United States was ordained in 1972. Although
the African Methodist churches have a long
tradition of women clergy, only in the 1950s
did white Methodists allow women to be

ordained. Presbyterians first began ordaining women in the 1950s and Lutherans began in the 1970s.

Although these have been presented as the first ordinations of women priests, more and more historians are now demonstrating, with increasing persuasiveness, that women provided religious leadership in Jewish and Christian communities over long stretches of their histories. Using funerary epitaphs and dedicatory inscriptions, Bernadette Brooten and Ross Kraemer have shown that women in Jewish communities held a range of religious offices, such as ruler of the synagogue, mother of the synagogue, elder, and priest, from the first century B.C.E. to the sixth century C.E. Giorgio Otranto, an Italian professor of church history, has shown through papal letters and inscriptions that women participated in the Catholic priesthood for the first thousand years of the church's history. The last thirty years of American scholarship have produced an amazing range of evidence for women's roles as deacons, priests, presbyters, and even bishops in Christian churches from the first through the thirteenth century.

The controversy over women's ordination in the last half of the twentieth century has occasioned interesting questions having to do with women's roles, female character, sexuality, and the gender of God. The formal processes by which contemporary women have been accepted as religious leaders have been fraught with social and religious controversy; the voting has been close and the debates bitter. Intense conflicts over women's roles, femininity, and sexuality have divided conventions, councils, and congregations so deeply that schisms have sometimes seemed inevitable. The crisis precipitated by the ordination of women has religious and social ramifications. The Church of England's decision to ordain women quashed the hopes of those who wished to see the Anglican and Catholic churches reunited. The Catholic hierarchy, still insisting that the ordination of women would change the very nature of the priesthood, nevertheless cannot ignore the priestly functions its laywomen are performing—reading Scripture, distributing the consecrated bread and wine to the congregation, counseling, teaching, and administration. Now comfortable with their presence at the altar, over 75 percent of American Catholics favor women priests.

The contemporary ordination of women also touches on the volatile issue of sexuality. When Barbara Harris was ordained as the first female bishop of the Episcopal church in 1989, *Time* magazine commented on her red nail polish. Red nail polish, of course, has little to do with a woman's qualifications for the office of bishop, but the reporter was unconsciously stating that the ordination of a woman as bishop brought female sexuality and divinity into uncomfortable proximity. The Vatican's 1976 *Declaration on the Question of Admitting Women to the Priesthood* justifies its exclusion of women from the priesthood on the grounds that the female body does not resemble the male body of Christ. It is therefore impossible for a woman to perform the sacramental functions of a priest. Here again, sexuality enters the picture. A woman, unlike a man, is perceived to be inseparable from her sexual nature, and as a priest she would bring sexuality into the realm of the sacred.

For many denominations the ordination of women clergy raises troubling questions about the gender of God. If women clergy represent God before their congregations, does the perception of God change? Whether a society perceives its deity (or deities) as male or female has everything to do with the way that society thinks about masculinity and femininity. If God is thought of as male, people tend to equate power with maleness. Thus, if females were to represent God, then femaleness would be equated with power.

Each of these issues raised by the ordination of women—women's roles, woman's nature, sexuality, and the gender of God—has a long and complex history. The theological argument used until 1976 to exclude women from the Catholic priesthood, for example, was taken from Thomas Aquinas, a thirteenth-century theologian who argued that women were inferior by nature and therefore incapable of assuming a position of preeminence or leadership (*Quest.* 91). Aquinas borrowed his theological argument, however, from the Greek philosopher Aristotle, who wrote in Athens in the fourth century B.C.E. Ancient Greek and Roman beliefs about gender have been given a Christian baptism and assimilated into Christian doctrine. Thus the issue of women's religious leadership is embedded in a larger context—that of cultural beliefs about gender, those of contemporary American society and those of ancient Greco-Roman cultures.

The complexity of the issue of women clergy, given its larger context of gender, can best be treated by first analyzing the connections among women's roles, female character, and sexuality in the culture of Christ's day. Women's leadership in Christianity is a dramatic and complex story, one in which the radical preaching of Jesus and deeply held beliefs about gender sometimes melded and sometimes clashed. Jesus challenged the social conventions of his day: He addressed women as equals, gave honor and recognition to children, championed the poor and the outcast, ate and mingled with people across all class and gender lines, and with bold rhetoric attacked the social bonds that held together the patriarchal family. When Jesus gathered disciples around him to carry his message to the world, women were prominent in the group. Mary Magdalene, Mary of Bethany, and Mary his mother are women whose names survived the retelling of the Christian story in the language and literary conventions of Roman patriarchal society. Paul's letters reflect an early Christian world in which women were well-known evangelists, apostles, leaders of congregations, and bearers of prophetic authority.

Because Christians distanced themselves from the polytheism of Greek and Roman religions, they avoided using the pagan term "priest" (*hieros*) for their clergy. Instead they used a variety of terms taken from secular life: *diakonos* (minister), *apostolos* (missionary), *presbyteros* (elder), *episcopos* (overseer), prophet, and teacher. Eventually the titles of bishop (*episcopos*), priest (*presbyteros*), and deacon (*diakonos*) came to be identified with the principal offices of the Christian church. Throughout this period of development, women held each of these offices. The Christian title presbyter (elder), meaning an older person entitled to respect, was borrowed from the Jewish synagogue, which was governed by a group of presbyters. After the emergence of the office of bishop as the head of the congregation, the presbyters governed under his or her guidance. Catholic historians translate *presbyter* as "priest." Protestant scholars simply retain the word *presbyter*. In either case, a fully ordained clergyperson is meant. When a woman's name is associated with a title, both Catholic and Protestant translators tend to minimize the office. Instead of translating *diakonos* as "minister" as they do for male office holders, they translate it as "deaconess."

During the first and second centuries, when Christian congregations met in homes, women were prominent as leaders. In early Christian communities women came to clerical offices by the same routes that brought their secular counterparts to public offices in Roman and Greek society. Preliminary training was provided by their assigned social roles as household managers. Women's authority in this domain was well established. Their administrative, economic, and disciplinary tasks in that role were excellent preparation for church (and public) office. In addition, women with relatively more wealth or higher status assumed the role of patron of a group. These patrons were often elected to public office, sometimes as a way of honoring them, and sometimes as a strategy for ensuring the patrons' continued generosity.

By the third century the processes of institutionalization gradually transformed the house churches, with their diversity of leadership functions, into a political body presided over by a monarchical bishop. Over the next two centuries, the legitimacy of women's leadership roles was fiercely contested. In the polemical writings of this period we encounter for the first time the arguments that Jesus appointed only male disciples and therefore women cannot be ordained; that Paul instructed women to keep silent during public discussions and thus women cannot teach; that if Jesus had wanted women to baptize, he would have been baptized by his mother, Mary. Although these arguments were rather weak in themselves, they were buttressed by the Greco-Roman world's beliefs about gender.

Opponents of women clergy appealed to a gender ideology that divided society into two domains, the *polis* (city), a male domain, and the *oikos* (household), a female domain. This system gave a great deal of power to women in the household while attempting to segregate them from public, political life. Christian polemicists insisted that public offices and public honors were a masculine affair and that women exercising such authority in the churches were usurping male prerogatives. During the first three centuries these voices represented a minority of the church's intellectuals, but as the church became increasingly institutionalized during the third and fourth centuries, these arguments carried greater weight.

The public-versus-private convention was in turn supported by a system of cultural values that associated men with honor and women with shame. The quest for honor and precedence associated with public office was viewed as an exclusively masculine enterprise. In contrast, a woman's honor was her shame, that is, her reputation for chastity. A woman exercising public authority could be accused of projecting a masculine personality; but, even worse, she could be called unchaste.

Although these notions about female shame and women's sexuality have their roots in the social order of ancient Greece, they have had a profound effect on Christian understandings of women, sexuality, and sin throughout the history of the church; they are foundational to the Western doctrine of sin, the church's theology of sexuality, and the Christian concepts of the self and even of God.

Understanding why and how women, once leaders in the Jesus movement and in the early church, were marginalized and scapegoated as Christianity became the state religion is crucial if women are to reclaim their rightful, equal place in the church today. Jesus' message and practice were radically egalitarian in their day and constituted a social revolution that likely provoked his crucifixion. It is high time that the church, which claims to embody his good news to the world, stop betraying its own essential heritage of absolute equality.

A veiled woman prays with her hands upraised.
This Orante figure is from a fresco painted in
the mid-third century. Cubiculum of Velatia,
Priscilla Catacomb, Rome.
(Courtesy of Benedictine Sisters.)

# I

# Preachers, Pastors, Prophets, and Patrons

■ ■ ■ ■

## THE EVIDENCE FOR WOMEN'S LEADERSHIP

Under a high arch in a Roman basilica
dedicated to two women saints, Prudentiana
and Praxedis, is a mosaic portraying four
female figures: the two saints, Mary, and a
fourth woman whose hair is veiled and
whose head is surrounded by a square
halo—an artistic technique indicating that the
person was still living at the time the mosaic
was made. The four faces gaze out serenely
from a glistening gold background. The
faces of Mary and the two saints are easily
recognizable. But the identity of the fourth

is less apparent. A carefully lettered inscription identifies the face on the far left as Theodora Episcopa, which means Bishop Theodora.[1] The masculine form for bishop in Latin is *episcopus;* the feminine form is *episcopa.* The mosaic's visual evidence and the inscription's grammatical evidence point out unmistakably that Bishop Theodora was a woman. But the *a* on Theodora has been partially effaced by scratches across the glass tiles of the mosaic, leading to the disturbing conclusion that attempts were made to deface the feminine ending, perhaps even in antiquity.

At a burial site on the Greek island Thera there is an epitaph for an Epiktas named as priest or presbyter (*presbytis*).[2] Epiktas is a woman's name; she was a woman priest sometime in the third or fourth century.

In the opening scene of the *Gospel of Mary,* a second-century gnostic Gospel, Mary Magdalene rallies the despondent disciples after the ascension of their Lord. By exhortation, encouragement, and finally a rousing sermon on the teachings of Jesus, she revives their flagging spirits and sends them off on their mission. Because of her strong leadership role, she appears in some texts with the title Apostle to the Apostles.[3]

Historical evidence like this, from art, inscriptions, and literature, belongs to the hidden history of women's leadership, a history that has been suppressed by the selective memory of succeeding generations of male historians.

In his book *The Ministry of Women in the Early Church,* Roger Gryson exemplifies this consensus of his and preceding generations of scholars:

> From the beginnings of Christianity, women assumed an important role and enjoyed a place of choice in the Christian community.

Paul praised several women who assisted him in his apostolic works. Women also possessed the charism of prophecy. There is no evidence, however, that they exercised leadership roles in the community. Even though several women followed Jesus from the onset of his ministry in Galilee and figured among the privileged witnesses of his resurrection, no women appeared among the Twelve or even among the other apostles. As Epiphanius of Salamis pointed out, there have never been women presbyters.[4]

Most Christians today, including clergy and scholars, presume that women played little or no role in the Jesus movement or in the early church as it spread throughout the Mediterranean. But women did in fact play crucial roles in the Jesus movement and were prominent leaders along with men in a wide variety of roles in the early church. The Christian church, of course, did not spring up suddenly into a well-defined organization with buildings, officials, and large congregations. In its earliest stages it is best understood as a social movement like any other. It was informal, often counter-cultural in tone, and was marked by a fluidity and flexibility that allowed women, slaves, and artisans to assume leadership roles.

Why, then, are we so unaware of the prominence of women in the birth of Christianity? Why does this powerful misperception continue to marginalize women in even the more enlightened branches of contemporary Christianity? The answers to these questions are complex, but they begin and end in cultural views about gender.

The societies to which early Christians belonged (like our society) held definite ideas about male and female roles. According to the gender stereotypes of the ancient Mediterranean, public speaking and public places were the sole prerogatives of males; private spaces, like the household, were the proper sphere for women's activities. Furthermore, society insisted that a respectable woman be concerned about her reputation for chastity and her seclusion in the household; modesty and reticence were accepted as testimony to her sexual restraint. Public activities and public roles seemed incompatible with modesty.

But the real women of that time led lives that were not as circumscribed as we might think. As householders they directed the men and women who lived and worked under their authority and supervised the production and distribution of the wealth. As businesswomen they traveled, bought, sold, and negotiated contracts. Women with sufficient wealth and social status acted as patrons of individuals and groups of lower social standing by providing financial assistance, recommendations to officials, and political protection.

In order to understand the role of women in the early church, it is necessary to understand what functions secular leaders performed and what kind of people they were. We know that leaders arbitrated disputes between members of communities, collected and distributed money, represented the interests of their community to city and imperial governments, financed communal feasts, made gifts of places of worship, taught, and arranged marriages. We also know that social status was the most important factor in the makeup of potential leaders.

For its part the church took its cue from society's leadership models. Mindful of their precarious status in Roman society, Christian communities looked to members with social status and wealth to be patrons and to function as their protectors. On a smaller scale, heads of households, who were accustomed to wielding authority and who had the stores of the household at their disposal, often became leaders of house churches.

In the ancient world, both men and women were patrons and householders. The social authority, economic power, and political influence associated with these roles were not restricted by gender. Even religious authority in Greek and Roman worship was not limited by gender. Women as well as men functioned as prophets and priests. Each of these social positions in Roman society—patron, householder, prophet, and priest—provided an individual with the kind of status, authority, and experience that could be translated into similar leadership roles in the Christian community.

Among ancient mosaics, paintings, statuary, dedicatory inscriptions, and funerary epitaphs, scholars have found numerous pieces of evidence for women's leadership. In literary sources such as the writings of the New Testament, letters, sermons, and the theological treatises of the early church, women's leadership is also well attested. In the literary sources, however, we can see shadows cast by the conflict over women's leadership and the prevailing social conventions about gender roles. The New Testament writers generally mentioned women leaders only as a passing fact while hurrying on to address more pressing concerns. When they paused for a longer discussion of women's leadership, as Paul did in his first letter to the Corinthian church, one catches tones of ambivalence and anxiety. In New Testament passages where women leaders played prominent roles, the male authors muted their contributions by the way they wrote their stories.

By briefly surveying the Christian communities in three cities of the ancient Mediterranean—Philippi, Corinth, and Rome—we can learn something significant about the nature of women's leadership in the early church.

The ancient road to Philippi leads inland from the coast. Shortly before reaching the city it crosses the river Gangites, then it passes through the walled portion of the city at the Krenides Gate and exits on the other side through the Neapolis Gate. Built in the fourth century B.C.E., the ancient walls of Philippi once provided security for the enclosed city, but by the first century C.E. the unplanned growth of four centuries had spilled over these city walls and clustered like barnacles along the main thoroughfares.[5] The story of Paul and Lydia recounted by Luke in Acts took place in Philippi. According to Luke, when Paul arrived in Philippi he asked, as he had in every city, where the Jewish synagogue was. He learned that the Jews met for worship somewhere outside the city walls, in the newer portions of the city. It was probably a house synagogue. On the Sabbath, Paul followed the road out past the old city walls to find what Luke called a *proseuchēs,* a place of prayer.[6] In his accounts of meetings in other cities, however, Luke used the term *synagogue. Proseuchēs* describes a service of traditional Jewish prayers and readings held on the Sabbath day. Why did Luke prefer that term in this instance? Perhaps because those who attended, read, and prayed were primarily women (Acts 16:13). According to New Testament scholar Bernadette Brooten, Luke's reluctance to use the word *synagogue* may signal his ambivalence about the primary role of women in synagogue worship in the light of his attitudes toward female gender roles.[7]

In Luke's story, Paul engaged these women on questions of the interpretation of Scripture and spoke to them of the Messiah (Acts 16:11–15). The first woman to respond to his message was Lydia, a householder and a merchant. Although she was one of the women participating in the reading and prayers, she was not a Jewish convert but a so-called God-fearer—someone who worshiped with the Jewish community but had not taken on the full observance of the Law. Paul's teaching about a Jewish-Christian piety that reverenced Scripture but did not require an exact observance of the Law found in Lydia a ready convert.

As a businesswomen who traveled in connection with her enterprises, Lydia had a wide network of associates. She was financially independent and the ruler of her household. When she converted to Christianity, her household was baptized together with her—another indication of her authority. Lydia's household would have included not only family members but also domestic slaves and slaves involved in the production of purple fabric. Lydia's influence extended as well over a network of clients and friends. Her prosperity put her in a position to invite Paul to accept hospitality in her home, where he lodged for some time. It was there that he carried out his ministry of teaching and preaching as newly converted Christians gathered there to hear and discuss the new doctrines (Acts 16:40).

The position of head of household also qualified an individual for leadership roles. Because household management involved administrative, financial, and disciplinary responsibilities, it prepared an individual to assume corresponding responsibilities in the community. Greek political theorists held that the skills required for political leadership were first developed through the administration of a household. In an oration dedicated to a young Nicocles, who was about to assume the responsibilities of household leadership and citizenship, Isocrates explained: "If kings are to rule well, they must try to preserve harmony, not only in the states over which they hold dominion, but also in their own households, and in their places of abode; for all these things are the work of temperance and justice."[8] This household order was seen as foundational for the right ordering of society as a whole. The harmony and good order of both household and state rested on the virtues of justice (*dikaia*) and self-control (*sophrosynē*). A man who could exercise mastery over himself (*sophrosynē*) was one who would be capable of exercising mastery over others. The ability to impose justice on a household guaranteed that a man would be capable of administering justice in the city-state. (The full range of responsibilities connected with household management is outlined in chapter 2.)

The church at Philippi was not only founded by a woman, but its leadership continued in the hands of women. In Paul's letter to the Philippian church he addressed three women leaders. He exhorted Euodia and Syntyche to reconcile their differences in order to provide more effective leadership for the church. For the third woman he used the affectionate term *syzugē*, which means "mate" or "partner"; he encouraged her to support Euodia and Syntyche, his co-workers, women who "labored with me in the gospel" (Phil. 4:1–3).[9]

## Synagogue Leadership

A sketch of the continuity between the house synagogue and the house church, between Jewish worship and Christian worship, can highlight dimensions of leadership that might otherwise be missed. The urban synagogues of the Hellenistic cities functioned as community centers, schools, places of worship, and political lobbies. To be part of the Jewish community was to be part of a *politeuma*, a "commonwealth"; it meant to be part of a nation. This sense of identity was expressed in a distinctive way of life, a moral code, a set of laws, and a unique form of worship.

The early Christian community understood itself similarly as a people and a nation. The Christian *politeuma*, however, made less sense to the Romans than the Jewish one did, because the Romans could respect the ethnicity of the Jewish people and their faithfulness to ancestral customs. The Christians, by contrast, were a hodgepodge of converts from various ethnic groups. Romans spoke disparagingly of them as a "third race."

From the perspective of the Roman government, the synagogue looked like a *synodos* (assembly), a private association or religious club. The synagogue, like a club, enjoyed the benefactions of patrons, it appointed officers, and it met for both religious and social purposes. The leaders of the synagogue at Sardis successfully lobbied for the rights to have such an association, to be governed by their own laws, and to have a place where they could settle disputes with one another.[10] The influential Alexandrian Jews were successful in their appeal to the emperor Claudius for the restoration of special privileges, particularly the right to govern themselves according to their ancestral laws, but they were unsuccessful in their attempt to gain for Jews the rights of citizenship.[11]

The synagogue was incorporated like a semiautonomous political body that had its own rulers, *archai*, who also represented and lobbied for the interests of their groups with both city and imperial governments. Leaders of Jewish communities acted in the traditional role of political patrons in their relations with governmental authorities. On behalf of their clients, patrons would obtain certain privileges from governmental authorities, such as representation and legal protection in the case of lawsuits, and would secure certain immunities, such as a tax-exempt status and freedom from the obligation to hold public office.

In Roman society, individuals in a position to exercise patronage could also be drawn into leadership roles on the basis of their donations. Members of a city's aristocracy often made financial gifts to the city by undertaking building projects, by underwriting the costs of repairs for water systems, or by donating expensive ornamentations, such as statues or mosaics, for public places. Such benefactors were honored with dedicatory inscriptions, chiseled in marble or stone, that identified the gift and the benefactor. For the church historian, these inscriptions reveal a dimension of leadership not always conveyed in theological histories. (Chapter 3 elaborates the diversity of these forms of patronage.)

In Dura Europas, a remote Roman military colony on the edge of the Persian frontier, a certain Samuel commissioned a series of splendid paintings to adorn the high walls of the assembly room of a second-century synagogue.[12] His titles "priest" and "elder" show both that he was honored for his benefactions and that he exercised leadership. In Myndos a prominent woman, Theopempte, financed a decorated marble post (and probably also the carved marble chancel screen that went with it) for the synagogue. The fourth-fifth–century inscription announces that she was the ruler, *arche*, of the synagogue.[13] In the late third century Klaudios Tiberius Polycharmos donated the lower floors of his house in Stobi, Macedonia, for use as a synagogue and lived with his family in the upper rooms. The grateful community honored him with the office and title "father of the synagogue."[14]

Leadership positions in the synagogue also involved governance of the community. In Jerusalem the council of elders (*presbyteroi*) exercised legal and judicial functions for the Jewish community. They were interpreters of the Law and adjudicated civil disputes between members of the community. Synagogue leaders also collected taxes and made provisions for their distribution. The Jewish appropriation of the Greek term *archōn* (ruler) for synagogue leadership expressed the character of this authority.

## Women's Leadership in the Synagogue

The predominance of women in the leadership of the Christian community at Philippi may have been a natural carryover from their apparent predominance at the Sabbath worship outside the city gates. Women's leadership in synagogue services was nothing extraordinary. It is well attested by inscriptions. Bernadette Brooten's study of nineteen Jewish inscriptions shows that women held the offices of "ruler of the synagogue," elder, priest, and "mother of the synagogue." An inscription from Smyrna reads: "Rufina, a Jewess, head of the synagogue, built this tomb for her freed slaves and the slaves raised in her house. No one else has the right to bury anyone [here.]"[15] Another from Crete reads: "Sophia of Gortyn, elder and head of the synagogue of Kisamos [lies] here. The memory of the righteous one for ever. Amen."[16] An inscription for a Jewish woman bearing the title of priest reads: "O Marin, priest, good and a friend to all, causing pain to no one and friendly to your neighbors, farewell!"[17]

Where Christian communities adopted the Jewish model of governance by elders, women continued to be chosen for this office. Inscriptional evidence shows that Christian women also held the office of elder in their communities. A Christian inscription, dating from second- or third-century Egypt, reads: "Artemidoras, daughter of Mikkalos, fell asleep in the Lord, her mother Paniskianes being an elder [*presbytera,* feminine form]." The Bishop Diogenes in the third century set up a memorial for Ammion the elder (*presbytera,* feminine form), and a fourth- or fifth-century epitaph in Sicily refers to Kale the elder (*presbytis,* also feminine).[18]

The axis of synagogue worship was the reading of the Torah scrolls, which were often housed in a niche that dominated the simple architectural features of the synagogue. During synagogue worship any member might read from the scrolls of the Law and then teach the assembly by interpreting the passages just read. Of equal importance to the reading of the Law was its application to the daily life of the community. This was the work of interpretation, and all members of the synagogue participated. For the educated members of the community, who were literate and could afford books, the work of study and interpretation continued in private as well.

Priscilla, a well-educated woman who had been a member of a synagogue in Rome, was quite skilled in the interpretation of the Law. This acumen in fact provided the foundation for her leadership in the early Christian movement. She was exercising her authority as an interpreter of the Law when she went to Apollos, a silver-tongued rhetorician and new arrival in Corinth, to instruct him more fully in the Christian interpretations of the prophets. Educated Jewish women were also members of a Jewish philosophical school in Alexandria. Days were devoted to a communal scholarship in which men and women studied, discussed, and debated together. In the evenings the community worshiped together with antiphonal singing in which male and female voices answered each other.[19]

Christianity arrived early in the bustling city of Corinth, along with the goods that traveled noisily in carts between the city and its two harbors at Lechaion and Cenchreae. The city stretched up the slopes toward the towering peak called the Acrocorinth. The theater rode upward along the same curve of the slope until it crested at a small plateau, which was crowned with the marble temple of Apollo.

Just inside the old city walls was the temple of Asclepius, where the ill and injured waited for the gift of healing from the god. Near this temple lay a colonnaded court that gave access to three dining rooms with stone couches for dining in a reclined position (cushions were supplied) and tables for food.[20] Here cultic banquets were held in honor of the god. A traveler might also follow the road north from Corinth to Delphi, the famous shrine to Apollo, to seek counsel from the Pythia, a priestess with the title prophetess. She sat on a tripod resembling Apollo's throne and delivered help and advice in the form of oracles from the god.[21] The priestess sat quietly in a trancelike state waiting for the divine inspiration; when it came, words flowed quickly in short, elegant streams of speech called oracles. The rhythmic meter and the imperious tone of these oracles is captured in Aeulius Aristides's memoirs, which records an oracle that he received at the temple of Apollo at Colophon early in the second century:

> Asclepius will cure and heal your disease
> in honor of the famous city of Telephus
> not far from the streams of the Caicus.[22]

The new converts to the Christian movement gathered in private homes, in interior rooms, hidden from the crowded streets. But the ritual activities of the adherents of this new sect would not have seemed strange to the festive throngs who joined the processions taking flowers, grains, wines, and sacrificial animals as gifts to Apollo. In their worship, Christians sang, chanted, and ecstatically prophesied. The Christians also shared a cultic banquet that honored a dying and rising god known simply as *Christos,* the anointed one. Oracles were also a familiar part of Christian worship, especially in Corinth. In writing to the Corinthian community, Paul himself conveyed an oracle that he had received when he prayed for healing from a physical affliction:

"My grace is sufficient for you,
my power is made perfect in weakness." (2 Cor. 12:9)[23]

The oracle Paul received provided comfort, if not healing.

Inside the homes where the Christians met in Corinth, women prophets responded to the Spirit. First one would rise and speak a blessing, a commendation, a revelation, or a word of wisdom. Before her oracle ended, another would arise with a word of encouragement or hope or exhortation. Mingled among these voices were ecstatic exclamations of grace, thanks, or praise.[24] For these new Christians, the presence of the Spirit dramatized the fulfillment of prophecy: "I will pour out my Spirit on all flesh, and your sons and your daughters will prophesy. . . . And upon the men who serve me and upon the women who serve me I will pour out my Spirit and they will prophesy" (Acts 2:17–18).

Some aspects of the rituals of the Corinthian Christians would have been more familiar to the intellectuals who attended the philosophical schools. There were readings from the sacred texts followed by interpretations and exhortations much like the readings from the treatises of the Greek philosophers. Those disciples who remembered the pithy sayings and clever retorts of their master rehearsed these anecdotes for the community. Equally important were the moral exhortations, because their observance would lead to virtue and personal happiness.

### Prophetic Leadership

Such prophesying was one of the vital forms of leadership in early Christianity. Apostles, prophets, and teachers constituted the recurring trio of leaders mentioned in Paul's writings. Apostles were the traveling evangelists, whose work took them from city to city spreading the good news (*euangēlion*) of Jesus' life, death, and resurrection. Prophets and teachers acted as local leaders. According to Heinrich Greeven, the leadership of the Corinthian community was actually in the hands of prophets and teachers together, both of whom functioned as mediators of the Holy Spirit.[25] Prophets delivered inspired messages to the assembly, and teachers instructed the community on matters of belief and praxis. These prophets and teachers gained their authority in the community because their roles meant that they were specialists in mediating divine revelation.[26] David Aune identifies at least three types of prophets: groups of prophets who prophesied during Christian worship (the women prophets at Corinth constituted such a group), prophetic schools, where member prophets formed a kind of guild (John the Seer of the Apocalypse belonged to such a school), and traveling prophets, whose ministry was to carry the work of teaching, prophecy, and exhortation to different communities.

Traveling prophets who came "in the name of the Lord" were accorded the hospitality of the Christian communal meal and a ready audience for their teachings. In Acts, Luke retold a miracle story that confirmed Paul's authority as an apostle. While this story is about a dramatic healing miracle, in fact a resurrection from the dead, it is interesting for present purposes because in the course of telling this story Luke created a tableau of a typical community receiving a traveling teacher.

According to Luke's story, the Christians in Troas had come together for a communal meal (the breaking of bread) in a third-floor room whose windows opened onto a courtyard. After an evening meal that included wine, Paul conversed with them. The room was crowded and warm; the burning of the oil lamps brightened even the farthest corner, and Paul's discussion dragged on into the night. The adolescent Eutyches had found a seat in the window, catching the cool night air on his back. As Paul's discourse continued unabated and the hum of questions and answers wove back and forth in the heavy air, Eutyches fell asleep. Suddenly tragedy interrupted the animated flow of the discussion. Eutyches had fallen from the window. Those who reached Eutyches first pronounced him dead, but Paul insisted that there was hope. Once Eutyches was gently laid on a bed, Paul stretched out on top of him (like the prophet Elijah had done, 1 Kings 17:17-24) to restore his life. After assuring them that Eutyches would live, Paul returned again to the third floor and ate with the community, who continued talking with him until the first light of dawn. In general, the traveling teacher was given lodging and meals; in return he or she instructed the community, speaking on God's behalf, and the community responded with questions, comments, and judgments of its own.

A cluster of churches in Asia Minor eventually felt the need to provide guidelines for the reception of traveling prophets and teachers. Their handbook on church leadership, the *Didache,* offered a picture of prophetic ministry similar to the one portrayed by Luke. A traveling prophet was entitled to lodging and meals. When speaking under the inspiration of the Spirit, a prophet could not be interrupted, but after the oracle had been delivered the community could enter into discussion with him, ask questions, and even challenge the message. The leadership functions of prophets were quite diverse, but their authority always rested on their ability to convey divine revelation. Although prophetic authority could be claimed by any individual, that authority also had to be recognized by the community. Normally the legitimacy of prophets would be tested by the correctness of their teachings and by their practice of the Christian life. In the Corinthian community the other prophets were to evaluate and approve the oracles of a prophet once he or she had spoken. The *Didache* developed a rather strict test for determining the legitimacy of a prophet's claim to speak in the name of the Lord:

> Now about the apostles and prophets: Act in line with the gospel precept. Welcome every apostle on arriving, as if he were the Lord. But he must not stay beyond one day. In case of necessity, however, the next day too. If he stays three days, he is a false prophet. On departing, an apostle must not accept anything save sufficient food to carry him till his next lodging. If he asks for money, he is a false prophet.[27]

If prophets, speaking under the influence of the Spirit, asked for food or money for themselves, then the community would know that they were not true prophets. (What would happen if televangelists today were evaluated as authentic Christians in this way?)

Christian communities valued the ministries of prophecy and revelation and recognized the leadership of women and men who were thus gifted. In the churches of Asia Minor, a prophet in residence in the community was accorded the honor of presiding over the eucharistic meal. Such prophets were not required to offer a liturgical prayer of thanksgiving but were free to pray extemporaneously as inspired by the Spirit.[28] This kind of prophetic leadership was considered worthy of the financial support of the community.

## Women Prophets

Prophecy was central to Luke's story of Christianity, for the activity of the Holy Spirit manifest in prophecy demonstrated the continuity between Judaism and Christianity. Luke's Gospel begins with the story of Elizabeth, who was filled with the Holy Spirit and gave a prophetic witness to the specialness of Mary and the uniqueness of the child in her womb. Mary herself prophesied, and her oracle, the Magnificat (Luke 1:47–55), is perhaps the most loved and recited prophecy delivered by a woman prophet. Mary's words— "He has put down the mighty from their thrones, and exalted those of low degree; he has filled the hungry with good things, and the rich he has sent empty away"—resound across the centuries as authoritatively as the oracles of Isaiah, Amos, or Ezekiel, yet Luke does not call her a prophet.

Mark's Gospel contains the story of a woman whose spiritual insight, sense of calling, and determination place her among the prophets. Mark's story is skeletal:

And while he was at Bethany in the house of Simon the leper, as he sat at table, a woman came with an alabaster flask of ointment of pure nard, very costly, and she broke the flask and poured it over his head. But there were some who said to themselves indignantly, "Why was the ointment thus wasted? For this ointment might have been sold for more than three hundred denarii, and given to the poor." And they reproached her. (Mark 14:3–5)

Who was she? What spiritual insight had led to her sudden appearance at the banquet? Did the guests recognize her when she came in? Did they know who she was? Was she intimidated by their censure? What did she intend through her act? How many understood the prophetic message? The disciples and the Gospel writer did not recognize her as a prophet.

She had received an insight into who Jesus was, and she felt compelled to give a public witness to his identity. She did not choose words for her prophetic revelation; she chose a silent but portentous action. Like the prophet Samuel pouring oil over the head of the rough shepherd David, she lifted her vial over the head of the Galilean Jesus and poured her expensive ointment over his hair. As the prophet Samuel had identified David as the king of Israel, her symbolic action proclaimed Jesus publicly as the Son of David, the coming Messiah, Christ, the anointed one (parallel Matt. 26:6–13). We can hear tones of resentment in the accusing voices of the disciples, who expressed alarm at the money frivolously expended in this gesture. Perhaps she was a landowner and her presence there sparked smoldering tensions between the villagers and landholders. In any case, the Gospel clearly highlights that the disciples—unlike this anonymous woman—weren't able to recognize that Jesus was indeed the Messiah, and that they would not throw caution to the winds to proclaim his divine mission.

Luke mentions only in passing the four daughters of Philip who were prophets and does not pause to comment on their important role in the leadership of the Christian community (Acts 21:8–9). But they no doubt functioned as leaders for the church in Caesarea much as the women prophets of the Corinthian church did.

Women prophets in the Christian communities carried into this new religious movement roles that were similar to those played by their sisters who participated in Greek and Roman religions. Prophecy permeated every aspect of Greco-Roman social life. Professional prophets, or diviners, provided guidance for governments in the matter of military expeditions, the founding of colonies, and the timing of festivals and provided counsel for individuals in matters of marriage, travel, and the bearing of children. In all these arenas prophets were interpreters of a divine will, because they spoke under the influence, inspiration, or possession of a divine spirit. A certain Syrian woman accompanied Alexander the Great on his expeditions and provided oracles. Another Syrian woman, Martha, received prophetic oracles that she conveyed to the wife of Marius and that led to her becoming the religious adviser to this imposing political figure.[29] In both cases the women functioned as professional prophets, or diviners, employed by government officials to serve as consultants.

The authority of women prophets to receive and interpret divine revelations was well established in Greek and Roman religions. Plutarch recorded an incident in which women's prophetic intervention saved an important life. Some Roman women carrying out a ritual sacrifice honoring the Roman goddess Bonadeia and the Greek goddess Gynacea saw a sign. "For on the altar where the fire seemed wholly extinguished, a grey and bright flame issued forth from the ashes of the burnt wood." The virgins presiding over the sacrifice quickly interpreted this sign and sent word to Cicero's wife, Tyrentia, that he was in danger from conspirators and that the goddess had sent a great light to ensure his safety and glory.[30]

The late second century witnessed a revival of prophetic authority within Christianity, and again women prophets were prominent. In Phrygia the prophecy movement was named after one of its founders, Montanus, who worked closely with two women prophets, Priscilla and Quintilla. Because their prophecies were received as oracles from God, they were carefully written down and preserved as a second Scripture by the Montanist communities. The Montanist community's reverence for the oracles of their women prophets was chronicled by one of their bitter foes, Hippolytus:

> And being in possession of an infinite number of their books, they are overrun with delusion, and they allege that they have learned something more through these than from law, and prophets and the Gospels. But they magnify these wretched women above the apostles and every gift of Grace, so that some of them presume to assert that there is in them something superior to Christ. . . . They introduce, however, the novelties of fasts, and feasts, and meals of parched food, and repasts of radishes, alleging that they have been instructed by women.[31]

Hippolytus's complaint was that the authority of these women prophets was accepted as equal to that of Scripture by the Montanist community.

From Tertullian, who was favorably impressed with Montanist moral rigor, we learn of the activities of an African Montanist prophet:

> We have now amongst us a sister whose lot it has been to be favored with gifts of revelation, which she experiences in the Spirit by

ecstatic vision amidst the sacred rites of the Lord's Day in the church; she converses with angels, and sometimes even with the Lord; she both sees and hears mysterious communications; some men's hearts she discerns, and she obtains directions for healing for such as need them. Whether it be in the reading of the Scriptures, or in the chanting of psalms, or in the preaching of sermons, or in the offering up of prayers, in all these religious services, matter and opportunity are afforded her of seeing visions.[32]

During prophetic ecstasy this woman prophet received revelations about individuals, discerned their internal states, and provided counsel and guidance for them. What she spoke was written down and received by the community as revelation from the Spirit.

Another second-century manual on church organization, the *Statutes of the Apostles,* instructed churches to ordain two widows precisely for this ministry of praying and receiving revelations: "Let them ordain three widows, two to continue together in prayer for all who are in trials, and to ask for revelations concerning that which they require."[33] Some revelations responded to individual needs for healing or advice; other revelations were messages for the community as a whole. These widows were also prophets.[34]

## THE COMMUNITY AT ROME

Magnificent Rome. By the first century C.E. this city reveled in the luxury of the new wealth brought by trade and tribute from conquered peoples. Like a gleaming magnet, the imperial city drew philosophers, who founded new schools, and religious visionaries, who taught new doctrines. Christian evangelists arrived too, and the Christian community in Rome was well established within a decade of the death of Jesus. Many of the numerous converts to Christianity came from the synagogues in the imperial city. Conflicts arose between these newly converted Jewish Christians and the skeptical Jewish majority. Eventually their bitter rivalries sparked civil unrest, which required the intervention of government authorities. Emperor Claudius dealt with these "rivalries" by expelling the Jews from Rome in 45 C.E. Prisca and Aquila, Jews who had recently converted, followed their network of connections across the Mediterranean to Corinth and established their household there as exiles from the imperial city. By the time Paul wrote his letter to the Romans (ca. 67 C.E.) the Jews had returned to Rome, and the Jewish Christian community flourished once again.

The city's population density made apartment dwellers of urban Romans. Merchants had living quarters above their shops; more prosperous citizens lived in larger apartments; and the wealthy owned villas. In a metropolis the size of Rome the Christian community was too numerous to meet at a single location. Consequently a number of prosperous householders gathered congregations in their homes. When Prisca and Aquila returned to Rome, they organized and supervised such a house church (Rom. 16:5). Many of these house churches survived into the second and third centuries bearing the name of the householders who originally convened the Christians in their homes. They were known as *tituli* churches. According to tradition, the Church of St. Clement, located east of the Colosseum, had once been a house church belonging to Clement. Excavations under the present church uncovered a first-century private house adjoining a warehouse. In another neighborhood, where the Roman aristocracy lived, is the Church of St. Pudentiana. Tradition has it that Pudens, a Roman senator, gave his house to the Christians to be used as a church and that he dedicated this church to his daughter, Pudentiana.[35] In many cases these householders functioned as patrons of the churches that met in their homes by taking care of their financial needs.

## WOMEN PATRONS IN THE GOSPELS AND EPISTLES

Phoebe, the minister (*diakonos*) of the congregation at Cenchreae, carried Paul's letter to the Romans.[36] She was a woman of some wealth and social status and traveled to Rome in connection with her business and social life and the affairs of the Christian church. She had agreed to carry Paul's letter to the Romans, which he hoped would provide him entry into the Roman Christian community on his upcoming visit. In his letter Paul also introduced Phoebe to the Roman Christians, identifying her as his patron (*prostatis*). With this title Paul acknowledged her generosity and her support of him, then he urged the Roman Christians to help her in whatever way she required in repayment of his own debt of gratitude to her.[37]

Joanna, the wife of Chuza, a steward in Herod's household, was a woman in a position to be a patron (Luke 8:1-3). It is intriguing to find her traveling with the group of evangelists that accompanied Jesus from village to village. Certainly her connections to the ruling Herodian family would have eased the way in any conflicts with minor local officials. It seems that she was a member of a group of women—Mary of Magdala and Susanna are also mentioned—whose patronage protected and supported the Jesus movement. Women as well positioned socially and economically as these often established patron-client relationships.[38]

Paul concluded his letter to the Roman Christians with personal greetings to the leaders of the community there; some he knew by reputation, and others he had met in the course of his ministry. Among the leadership of the Roman Christian community were many women. Prisca, Junia, Mary, Tryphaena, Tryphosa, and Persis were women whom Paul addressed as co-workers; they had established the faith of the Christian community through their work of teaching and exhortation. Other prominent women greeted by Paul were Julia, Olympas, the mother of Rufus, who Paul says was a mother to him also, and the sister of Nereus. Of the twenty-eight prominent people whom Paul considered it politic to greet, ten were women.[39]

Among these women leaders of the Roman congregation was a woman apostle, Junia, whom Paul hailed as "foremost among the apostles" (Rom. 16:7).[40] She and her husband, Andronicus, traveled teaching and preaching from city to city. The turmoil and riots occasionally provoked by Christian preaching landed her and her husband in prison, where they encountered Paul. She was a heroine of the fourth-century Christian church, and John Chrysostom's elegant sermons invoked the image of Junia, the apostle, for the Christian women of Constantinople to emulate.[41]

Wherever Christianity spread, women were leaders of house churches. Mary, the mother of John Mark, presided over a house church of Hellenistic Jews in Jerusalem. It was on her door that the astonished Peter knocked to announce to the Christians assembled there that he had been liberated from prison by an angel (Acts 12:12–17). Apphia presided with two others as leaders of a house church in Colossae (Philem. 2). Nympha in Laodicea, Lydia in Thyatira, and Phoebe at Cenchreae supervised the congregations that met in their homes (Col. 4:15; Acts 16:15; Rom. 16:1).

In John's Gospel Mary Magdalene, not Peter, is presented as the model for discipleship. At a time when Peter and the other male disciples had fled, Mary stood loyally at the foot of the cross. She was not only the first witness to the resurrection but was directly commissioned to carry the message that Jesus had risen from the dead. The original version of the Gospel of John ends with the resurrection appearance to Mary Magdalene and her witness to the Twelve in chapter 20. The story of the appearance to "doubting Thomas" at the end of chapter 20 teaches early Christians to believe without seeing. "Now Jesus did many other signs in the presence of the disciples, which are not written in this book; but these are written that you may believe that Jesus is the Christ, the Son of God, and that believing you may have life" (John 20:30–31). A later copyist added another ending to the Book of John, chapter 21. In this chapter Peter was made the key witness of the resurrection when Jesus appeared to Peter and the disciples while they were on a fishing expedition in Galilee and commissioned Peter to be the shepherd of the flock. New Testament scholars have long puzzled about the reasons for this Gospel's two endings, chapter 20 highlighting the role of Mary Magdalene as witness to the resurrection and chapter 21 highlighting Peter. A recent proposal suggests that chapter 21 was appended at a time when the Johannine community was seeking to integrate with the Christian community that saw Peter as its head. Thus chapter 21 was added to bring the Johannine community within the pale of Petrine orthodoxy by emphasizing Peter's leadership.[42]

## AMBIVALENCE AND CONFLICT OVER WOMEN'S LEADERSHIP

When Paul wanted to claim that he too was an apostle because he had seen the risen Lord, he listed the appearances of Jesus: "He was raised on the third day in accordance with the scriptures. . . . He appeared to Cephas [Peter], then to the twelve. Then he appeared to more than five hundred brethren at one time. . . . Last of all . . . he appeared to me" (1 Cor. 15:4–8). Paul omitted the announcement of the resurrected Christ to Mary even though it is attested in all four Gospels. Even some of the Gospel writers themselves betray signs of ambivalence over women's leadership. Matthew and Mark recount the women's witness to the resurrection, but the women's witness plays no role in the the faith of the rest of the disciples. Luke reports that the women delivered their message to the rest of the disciples, "but these words seemed to them an idle tale, and they did not believe them" (Luke 24:12).

Women's leadership was a widespread phenomenon in the early Christian churches. Tensions were nevertheless generated by the disparity between the socially established fact of women's leadership and the strict Greco-Roman demarcation of gender roles. The mixed messages about Mary Magdalene's significance reflects the ambivalence about women's leadership as the Gospels were taking their final canonical form.

The second-century *Gospel of Mary*, discovered in 1945 among a collection of manuscripts at Nag Hammadi in upper Egypt, reveals a lost tradition about the leadership of Mary Magdalene and portrays Peter as her opponent. The scene described in the fragments of this Gospel took place on the Mount of Ascension after Jesus had departed into heaven. The disciples were disconsolate, depressed, and afraid until Mary stood up and addressed them all. She exhorted them to stop grieving, assured them that the grace of the Savior would be with them, and urged them to prepare for the work of preaching to which they had been called. Finally the disciples took heart and began to discuss the teachings of the Savior. After a while, at Peter's prompting, Mary began a long teaching discourse. When she had finished, she was quiet. Andrew was the first disciple to break the silence. He said, "'Say what you [wish to] say about what she has said. I at least do not believe that the Savior said this. For certainly these teachings are strange ideas.'" Peter then broke in with a resentful challenge: "'Did he really speak with a woman without our knowledge (and) not openly? Are we to turn about and all listen to her? Did he prefer her to us?'" Mary, hurt, turned to Peter and said, "'My brother Peter, what do you think? Do you think I thought this up myself in my heart or that I am lying about the Savior?'" Finally Levi rebuked Peter:

"Peter, you have always been hot-tempered. Now I see you are contending against the women like the adversaries. But if the Savior made her worthy, who are you indeed to reject her? Surely the Savior knows her very well. That is why he loved her more than us. Rather let us be ashamed and put on the perfect man and acquire him for ourselves as he commanded us, and preach the gospel, not laying down any other rule or other law beyond what the Savior said."[43]

When Levi finished his speech, the disciples set out on their teaching mission.

The ambivalence about women's role, implied in Peter's comment "Did he prefer her [a *woman*] to us?" indicates tensions between the existing fact of women's leadership in Christian communities and traditional Greco-Roman views about gender roles. The discomfort of the writer/editor of John with Mary Magdalene's prominence as a witness to the resurrection, and the other Gospels' similar ambivalence about the importance of the women at the empty tomb, betray the deep conflict over women's place that developed as Christianity was becoming established and the canon was being set.

There seems to be no doubt that women figured prominently in Jesus' life and ministry, both during his lifetime and after his resurrection when the first communities were formed and his message began to spread. If these accounts of women's important participation hadn't been grounded in intractable fact, they would not have survived in such a male-dominated culture. But because such independence and prominence on the part of women conflicted directly with the view of women's roles that pervaded Greco-Roman society, these traditions were ignored and submerged as much as possible in order to conform Christian teaching and practice to social convention.

Yet up until the mid-third century, only occasional sparks were generated by this clash between the social strictures on women's roles and the freedom women found in Christianity. For more than two hundred years Christianity was essentially a religion of the private sphere, practiced in the private space of the household rather than the public space of a temple. Its concerns were the domestic life of its community rather than the political life of the city. But during the third century Christianity began evolving toward its eventual form as a public religion. The burgeoning numbers of adherents and the new formality and dignity of the Christian liturgies meant that Christian participation was increasingly a public event. By the fourth century Christians were worshiping in their own public temples, called basilicas. During this period the friction between the social conventions about women's place and women's actual long-standing roles as house church leaders, prophets, evangelists, and even bishops precipitated virulent controversies. As Christianity entered the public sphere, male leaders began to demand the same subjugation of women in the churches as prevailed in Greco-Roman society at large. Their detractors reproached women leaders, often in strident rhetoric, for operating outside the domestic sphere and thus violating their nature and society's vital moral codes. How could they remain virtuous women, the critics demanded, while being active in public life?

With their survival instincts honed, Christian communities had gradually begun to assimilate themselves into Hellenistic culture. Jewish communities had done the same. In their increasing desire for credibility and legitimacy, the church leaders no longer resisted the tide of culture. Gradually they adopted Greco-Roman conventions regarding women's proper place and behavior. Both Jewish and Christian writers, like their pagan counterparts, argued that it was inappropriate for women to hold positions of authority in the public sphere. For both Jewish and Christian theologians, as for pagan philosophers, the good woman was a chaste woman. In their view, female sexual promiscuity posed the greatest threat to women's character. Every aspect of female deportment should evince a concern for shame, expressed through reticence, deference toward men, and sexual restraint.

## WOMEN'S LEADERSHIP CHALLENGED

In the Mishnah, a compilation (ca. 200 C.E.) of the theoretical discussions of the rabbis, there are passages that reveal the attitudes toward women that the rabbis held in common with the larger Hellenistic culture. In the course of their discussion in a tractate entitled *Sotah* (On the Suspected Adulteress), the rabbis debated whether a woman should study the Torah. This case rests in part on the assumption that the wife is the sexual property of her husband. In fact it is for the sake of his suspicion of her sexual infidelity that a wife was required to undergo the ordeal of drinking bitter water. If her body did not respond to the supposedly toxic waters then her innocence was proven. The provisions of the tractate read:

Hardly has she finished drinking before her face turns yellow and her eyes bulge and her veins swell and they say, "Take her away! take her away! That the Temple Court be not unclean!" But if she had any merit this holds her punishment in suspense. Certain merits may hold punishment in suspense for one year, others for two years, and others for three years; hence Ben Azzai says: "A man ought to give his daughter a knowledge of the Law so that if she must drink [the bitter water] she may know that the merit [that she had acquired] will hold her punishment in suspense." Rabbi Eliezer says: "If a man gives his daughter a knowledge of the Law, it is as though he taught her lechery." Rabbi Joshua says: "A woman has more pleasure in one measure with lechery than in nine measures with modesty."[44]

Rabbi Eliezer's surprising assertion equating the teaching of the Torah to a daughter with the teaching of sexual license reflects the Greco-Roman notions of male honor and female shame. A woman who studied the Torah was regarded as acting out of a desire for honor, precedence over men, and personal initiative. Such a woman would no longer be manifesting the requisite concern for the purity of reputation, modesty, sexual restraint, and passivity. It was only by maintaining those qualities associated with shame that a woman could demonstrate her virtue. Because a woman was viewed as sexual property, any sexual independence she might manifest was considered threatening. It was this anxiety about a woman's sexual independence that was expressed by Rabbi Joshua's concern for women's dangerous attraction to the seductive pleasure of lechery.

Jewish women, as was shown earlier in this chapter, did participate in and lead synagogue worship. A passage from the Talmud reveals that women were also called on to read the Torah, but that women could perform this function only in private space. "All are qualified to be among the seven [who read the Torah in the synagogue on Sabbath morning] even a minor and a woman, but a woman should not be allowed to come forward and read the law in public."[45]

Likewise Greco-Roman society, as we have seen, defined proper roles for men and women according to whether they were household (and thus private) functions or public functions. This system gave a great deal of power to women in the household but segregated them from public political life, since public space was male space. The role of teacher, for instance, was not restricted to one gender, but the social space in which teaching occurred was. A woman could teach in the privacy of her household but not in public. Here we may appropriately ask whether the rabbis viewed the synagogue as private space.

The traveling evangelist Paul expressed a similar concern for the boundaries between public and private space in his comment on women's public speech in 1 Corinthians 14:34–35: "The women should keep silence in the churches. For they are not permitted to speak, but should be subordinate, as even the law says. If there is anything they desire to know, let them ask their husbands at home. For it is shameful for a woman to speak in church." Here we may ask the same question of Paul: Did he view the Christian assembly, the *ekklēsia*, as public space and thus forbid women's speech in this setting?[46]

There is considerable disagreement among scholars about which kind of speaking Paul meant. Was it the prophetic, ecstatic speaking of the women prophets, whose authority Paul had acknowledged in 1 Corinthians 11? Or was it the kind of speaking involved in interpreting Scripture and handing on the tradition? His use of the term *lalein* for "to speak" was used in Greek society for free-ranging discussion rather than formal teachings. For Paul the proper place for women's speech was in the household not in the assembly. Paul thought that women's speech in the household would always reflect women's subordination to her man (father, husband, or master). It worried him when women spoke in the public context of the assembly because there women's subordination to men was not clear. Paul also thought that a woman's speaking in public contained the seeds of sexual scandal. *Aischron,* the Greek term that Paul used to insist that it was a disgrace or a scandal for women to speak in public, referred to sexual indiscretion when it was applied to women, and it was most often applied to women.

Nor did women's prophetic leadership in Corinth go unchallenged. Although the prominence of women in leadership may not have been problematic for the Corinthian community in the beginning, it was soon troubling to others. After a time, the church there received a perplexing letter from that traveling evangelist Paul in which he insisted that women prophets must wear veils when giving public instruction (1 Cor. 11:1-16). It was not that Paul directly opposed women functioning in the role of prophets, but if a woman was to prophesy in the assembly then Paul insisted she ought to have her head covered. For Paul the veil carried several symbolic meanings. It meant that a woman was concerned for propriety, specifically sexual modesty, since it preserved the sight of her hair for only her husband and family. The wearing of the veil also meant that a woman publicly acknowledged her subordination to men.[47] It was a way for a woman to remain "private" even in public. Paul was ambivalent about, but not opposed to, women prophets. He acknowledged the authority and leadership that came with prophetic gifts, but his acceptance of the social restrictions on women made his acceptance of women prophets conflicted and problematic. If only the women prophets would wear veils when they were prophesying, then it would be clear that the early Christian movement did not intend to undermine society. (There is no evidence, however, that the Corinthian prophets ever did don veils.) This concern for propriety is more fully explained in chapter 5, where the values of male honor and female shame are elaborated.

The social conventions about women's character also generated tensions relating to women presiding at the eucharistic meal. We catch echoes of such a controversy in an enigmatic passage from the *Statutes of the Apostles,* a second-century manual on church organization. Here stereotypes about women's character are invoked:

John spoke, "Have you forgotten, brothers, that our Master, when He has asked for the bread and wine, blessed them and said, 'This is My body and My blood,' He did not permit the women to be around us?" Martha said, "It is because of Mary, because He saw her laugh." Mary said, "That was not the reason I laughed. He said to us before when He taught that the one who is weak will be saved by the one who is strong."[48]

In this controversy, women defended their right to participate in the eucharistic ministry by arguing that women normally participated in the Passover meal and would have been present at the Last Supper. To counter the women's defense of their right to preside over the Eucharist, the writer of the *Statutes of the Apostles* created a speech for Martha in order to put in a woman's voice the legitimation for excluding women from the Eucharistic ministry: Women, said this Martha, were sent from the room for laughing.

The assertions that women were more frivolous than men and that the weaker sex should be ministered to by the stronger were based on prevailing social views. Roman law held women by nature to be both the weaker sex (*infirmitas sexus*) and mentally frivolous (*levitas animi*), that is, lacking in seriousness. This concept of female nature justified the legal authority of a father over a daughter (*patria potestas*) and the authority of a husband over a wife (*manus*). In both cases the woman, regardless of her age, was effectively a minor and needed a male to represent her in legal transactions.[49]

## WOMEN'S LEADERSHIP DEFENDED

It would be interesting to know how women prophets defended their right to speak publicly in the community, but unfortunately their writings and their treatises were ignored by the generations of scribes who copied valuable books. Male polemicists against women's leadership sometimes repeated—in order to denounce—the arguments by which women defended their public authority, thereby retrieving for us at least elements of their testimony. Epiphanius, a notorious fourth-century critic, recast the multiple forms of Christian spiritual experience as so many forms of deviance from his fourth-century orthodoxy. For him the Montanist movement was a heresy and its women prophets illegitimate:

They bring with them many useless testimonies, attributing a special grace to Eve because she first ate of the tree of knowledge. They acknowledge the sister of Moses as a prophetess as support for their practice of appointing women to the clergy. Also, they say, Philip had four daughters who prophesied. Often in their assembly seven virgins dressed in white enter carrying lamps, having come in to prophesy to the people. They deceive the people present by giving the appearance of ecstasy; they pretend to weep as if showing the grief of repentance by shedding tears and by their appearance of lamenting human life.[50]

We can glean from this at least that the women prophets of the Montanists appealed to Eve and Miriam in the Old Testament and to the daughters of Philip in the New Testament writings, and that the authenticity of their prophecy was underlined by the familiar signs of prophetic ecstasy. Epiphanius claimed that this prophetic ecstasy was just for show.

In the end Epiphanius denounced women prophets not for heretical beliefs or practices but because their active leadership roles in public assemblies contravened his ingrained assumptions about women's place in society. By the fourth century, polemicists against women's leadership called on the authority of Scripture to support their insistence on women's subordination. Epiphanius did not hesitate to base his own objections on arguments from Scripture:

Women among them are bishops, presbyters, and the rest, as if there were no difference of nature. "For in Christ there is neither male nor female." . . . Even if women among them are ordained to the episcopacy and presbyterate because of Eve, they hear the Lord saying: "Your orientation will be toward your husband and he will rule over you." The apostolic saying escaped their notice, namely that: "I do not allow a woman to speak or have authority over a man.'" And again: "Man is not from woman but woman from man"; and "Adam was not deceived, but Eve was first deceived into transgression." Oh, the multifaceted error of this world![51]

Here we see the exegetical battle lines for the fourth-century debate over women's leadership. Defenders of women's right to leadership roles argued from Gal. 3:28, "In Christ there is no male or female," that women were entitled to hold public office in the church because women and men possessed the same nature. The opponents of women's leadership, on the other hand, argued that men and women had different natures and that Scripture (Gen. 1–3) showed that women possessed an inferior nature. Epiphanius interpreted the curse pronounced on Eve, "Your desire will be for your husband and he shall rule over you" (Gen. 3:16), to mean that woman had an inferior nature, because it was her fate to be ruled rather than to rule. By the fourth century, Paul's first letter to the Corinthians had become part of the canon and was given equal weight with the Old Testament. Epiphanius used Paul's argument that woman was created from man to bolster the conviction that women had an inferior nature and so were not fit to rule. Women's inferior nature was further demonstrated by a statement in 1 Timothy: "Let a woman learn in silence with all submissiveness. I permit no woman to teach or to have authority over men; she is to keep silent. For Adam was formed first, then Eve; and Adam was not deceived, but the woman was deceived and became a transgressor" (1 Tim. 2:11–14). By this time the prevailing system of female marginalization had been given a thoroughly Christian baptism.

It was the perceived vulnerability of female sexuality that required the safeguard of male protection. Protection implied subordination, and as subject to fathers and husbands, women became subordinate to all men in general—their subordinate role reinforced by an assumed inferiority of woman's nature. Women's natural inferiority was the declared basis of Paul's insistence in 1 Corinthians 11 that women wear a veil, for it functioned as a public symbol of women's subordination. The writer of the *Statutes of the Apostles* invoked the same view of women's nature when he argued that women were weak and intellectually frivolous and therefore should be excluded from presiding at the Eucharist. Epiphanius appealed to the same understanding of woman's nature for his interpretation of Genesis 1-3 and 1 Corinthians 11. These two critical aspects of Greco-Roman gender beliefs—the distinction between public and private space and the notions about male and female nature—functioned as powerful social forces against women's leadership.

## NOTES

1. Dorothy Irvin, "The Ministry of Women in the Early Church: The Archaeological Evidence," *Duke Divinity School Review* no. 2 (1980): 76–86. See also Joan Morris, *The Lady Was a Bishop: The Hidden History of Women with Clerical Ordination and the Jurisdiction of Bishops* (New York: Macmillan, 1973).

2. *Bulletin de Correspondence Hellenique* no. 101 (1977): 210, 212.

3. Elisabeth Schüssler Fiorenza, "Mary Magdalene: Apostle to the Apostles," *UTS Journal* (April 1975): 22ff.

4. Roger Gryson, *The Ministry of Women in the Early Church*, trans. Jean La Porte and Mary Louise Hall (Collegeville, MN: Liturgical Press, 1976), 109.

5. Philip II captured the ancient city Krenides in 356 B.C.E., settled it with Greek colonists, and renamed it after himself. It was at this time that the city wall was built. Anthony and Octavian conquered the city in 42 B.C.E. and settled it with Roman colonists. Given that there were several long periods of growth and development in the first five centuries between the building of the city walls and first-century

Philippi, it would be natural to assume that the reference to a place outside the city wall is a reference to a newer quarter of the city. (The perimeter of the old walled city at Philippi [two miles] was quite modest compared with the walls at Corinth [six miles] and Ephesus [five miles].) The excavations at Ostia demonstrate this kind of growth. See J. B. Ward-Perkins, *Cities of Ancient Greece and Italy: Planning in Classical Antiquity* (New York: George Braziller, 1974), plates 48–51.

6. Unlike Greek worship, which involved sacrifices offered in open areas before the temples where the presence of the god or goddess resided, Jewish worship, focused as it was on the reading and exposition of the Torah, took place indoors. We have no evidence for Jewish religious gatherings of this kind conducted out of doors. In the light of this, it is strange that many commentators assert that the women were participating in an open-air prayer meeting by the banks of the river.

7. Bernadette Brooten, *Women Leaders of the Ancient Synagogue* (Chico, CA: Scholars Press, 1982), 139–40.

8. Isocrates, *Nicocles,* 36; cited by Michel Foucault, *The Use of Pleasure* (New York: Pantheon, 1985), 171–72. See also 166–84.

9. Clement of Alexandria argued, a century later, that Paul's partner was actually Paul's wife, who elected not to travel with him. Clement believed Paul was referring to his wife when he remonstrated, "Have we not a right to take about with us a wife that is a sister like the other apostles?" (1 Cor. 9:5). Clement assumed that apostolic couples traveled together as a preaching team. Women apostles, he theorized, would have had access to the women's quarters in households (Clement, "On Marriage," *Strommateis* 3).

10. Wayne Meeks, *The First Urban Christians* (New Haven: Yale Univ. Press, 1983), 34.

11. Meeks, *The First Urban Christians,* 38.

12. Hagith S. Sivan, *The Painting of the Dura-Europas Synagogue: A Guidebook to the Exhibition* (1978), 11.

13. Brooten, *Women Leaders*, 13–14.

14. Thomas Kraabel, "Social Systems of Six Diaspora Synagogues," in *Ancient Synagogues, The State of Research*, ed. Joseph Gutman (Chico, CA: Scholars Press, 1981), 84. See Brooten, *Women Leaders*, for discussion of these offices/titles: ruler, 37; elder, 46; priest, 77; mother/father, 64.

15. Brooten, *Women Leaders*, 5.

16. Brooten, *Women Leaders*, 11. Ross Kraemer has added to this collection six other epitaphs about women who were elders: Sara Ura, Beronike, Mannine, Faustina, Rebeka, and Makaria. *Maenads, Martyrs, Matrons, Monastics* (Minneapolis: Fortress Press, 1988), 219.

17. Brooten, *Women Leaders*, 73.

18. Paniskianes, *Cahiers de recherches de l'Institut de Papyrologie et d'Egyptologie de Lille* 5 (1974): 264, no. 1115; Ammio, *Greek, Roman and Byzantine Studies* 16 (1975): 437–38; Kale, *L'Anee epigraphique* (1754): 454.

19. Philo *On the Contemplative Life*, 83.

20. Jack Finegan, *Archaeology of the New Testament* (Boulder: Westview Press, 1981), 143–52.

21. David Aune, *Prophecy in Early Christianity and the Ancient Mediterranean World* (Grand Rapids, MI: Eerdmans, 1983), 23, 28.

22. Aune, *Prophecy*, 60.

23. Aune, *Prophecy*, 149.

24. Antoinette Wire, *The Corinthian Women Prophets* (Minneapolis: Fortress Press, 1990), 135–58.

25. Heinrich Greeven, "Propheten, Lehrer und Vorsteher bei Paulus: Zur Frage der Ämter im Urchristentum," *ZNW* (Zeitschrift für Neutestamentliche Wissenschaft) 1–2 (1952): 1–43.

26. Aune, *Prophecy*, 201, 202.

27. *Didache* 11, trans. Cyril Richardson, *The Early Christian Fathers* (New York: Macmillan, 1970), 176.

28. *Didache* 10.

29. Aune, *Prophecy,* 41.

30. Plutarch *Life of Cicero,* 20.1–2, trans. M. Lefkowitz and M. Fant, *Women's Life in Greece and Rome* (Baltimore: Johns Hopkins Univ. Press, 1977), 253.

31. Hippolytus *Refutation of All Heresies* VIII.12, trans. Kraemer, *Maenads,* 255. See Ronald Heime, *The Montanist Oracles and Testimonia,* North American Patristic Society, Patristic Monograph Series, no. 14 (Macon, GA: Mercer Univ. Press, 1989), 2–9, for a collection of the surviving oracles delivered by these women prophets. All that is left is what has been preserved by their detractors.

32. Tertullian *On the Soul* 9, trans. Kraemer, *Maenads,* 224.

33. *Statutes of the Apostles* 21, Sahidic text, trans. G. Horner, *The Statutes of the Apostles or Canones Eccleseastici* (London, 1904), 304.

34. A third-century manual on church organization, the *Didascalia,* reveals that widows were powerful leaders in the communities for which this manual was written. H. Achelis, in his analysis of the widows who functioned as leaders in the *Didascalia,* states that "the widows the author has in view are not weak little women but spirit-empowered prophetesses." Achelis's assumption that the widows in the *Didascalia* were prophets was based on the practices enjoined by the apostolic canons that the church was to ordain two widows to receive revelations. Hans Achelis and Johs. Flemming, "Die Syrische Didascalia," *Texte und Untersuchungen,* Bd 25,2: 275. See also chap. 5 below.

35. Finegan, *Archaeology,* 233–34.

36. See Elisabeth Schüssler Fiorenza, *In Memory of Her: A Feminist Reconstruction of Christian Origins* (New York: Crossroad, 1983), 170–71.

37. Phoebe's title *prostatis* means "leader" or "president." In New Testament writings the term is used for persons with authority in the community. This would certainly describe Phoebe's relationship to the congregation at Cenchreae. But Paul says of her in Rom. 16:2 that she is his *prostatis* and that of many others. In this context *prostatis* would be better translated as "patron." Fiorenza, *In Memory of Her,* 181.

38. L. Wm. Countryman, "Patrons and Officers in Club and Church," *SBL Seminar Papers,* no. 11 (Missoula, MT: Scholars Press, 1977), 135–43.

39. See also Fiorenza, *In Memory of Her,* 169ff.

40. The RSV reads, "Greet Andronicus and Junias, my kinsmen and my fellow prisoners; they are men of note among the apostles" (Rom: 16:7). Junias is in fact a woman, but the bias of male translators has suppressed this fact.

41. Bernadette Brooten, "Junia, Outstanding Among the Apostles," and Elisabeth Schüssler Fiorenza, "The Apostleship of Women in Early Christianity," in *Women Priests,* ed. L. and A. Swidlers (New York: Paulist Press, 1977), 135–40.

42. G. Franklin Shirbroun, "Mary Magdalene and the Editing of the Fourth Gospel," unpublished paper delivered at the Pacific Coast Regional Meeting of the Society of Biblical Literature, April 1989.

43. *Gospel of Mary,* 17, trans. Karen L. King, George W. MacRae, R. McL. Wilson, and Douglas M. Parrott, *The Nag Hammadi Library,* James Robinson, gen. ed. (San Francisco: Harper & Row, 1988), 526–27.

44. Soṭa iv.3, trans. Herbert Danby, *The Mishnah* (London: Oxford Univ. Press, 1933), 296.

45. Tosephta *Megilla,* iv.II.226. See also *Nedarim* iv.3.

46. Although many New Testament scholars read 1 Cor. 14:34–35 as a later interpolation into Paul's letter, Antoinette Wire has presented a convincing argument based on the manuscript tradition that this passage is vintage Paul. See Wire, *Corinthian Women Prophets,* 149–52.

47. Wire, *Corinthian Women Prophets,* 116–34.

48. *Statutes of the Apostles,* 25–26, trans. Horner, *Statutes,* 305.

49. Sarah Pomeroy, *Goddesses, Whores, Wives, and Slaves: Women in Classical Antiquity* (New York: Schocken Books, 1975), 150.

50. Epiphanius *Medicine Box,* 49, trans. Kraemer, *Maenads,* 226.

51. Kraemer, *Maenads,* 227.

A woman breaks bread at an early Christian eucharist. The clothing and hairstyles worn by the participants suggest that most of them are women. Early third-century fresco. Greek Chapel, Priscilla Catacomb, Rome. (Courtesy of Benedictine Sisters.)

# Household Management and Women's Authority

## *(with Virginia Burrus)*

■■■■

The villa of Cornelius the Italian centurion commanded a fine view of the Mediterranean and the new harbor of Caesarea in Palestine. A throng had gathered around a large pool, the centerpiece of his elegant garden. A knot of sturdy soldiers surrounded Cornelius's personal attendant, plying him with questions about his recent mission to escort a certain Peter back to Caesarea. Peter and the other Jews who accompanied him from Joppa clustered awkwardly together, uncomfortable at finding themselves in the home of a man who was both a Gentile and a commander of occupying troops. Slaves who served the household were arrayed behind the Jews. Cornelius himself stood near his wife, flanked on the right and left by several close friends. On this day Cornelius had called together all the members of his household, his kinfolk, and his close friends to hear the message of Peter, the religious teacher commended to him in a vision while he was at prayer. Once Peter was finished preaching, the large group assembled in Cornelius's garden would be initiated in the Christian rite of baptism. Cornelius's family, slaves, and close associates were collectively changing their religion out of deference to Cornelius and in keeping with the Roman custom that all members of the household should worship the gods honored by the head of the household.

In the bustling Roman colony of Philippi in Macedonia a group was assembled in Lydia's apartment in the center of town. Her shop, on the floor below, was filled with strange smells from vats of purple dye brewing in the back. A ladder led from the shop to the living quarters upstairs. Lydia's personal slaves came and went continuously, bearing steaming bowls of food and taking away empty dishes. The few slaves who worked in the shop waited discreetly in a corner. Several business associates were present, along with some women friends, a client, and the freedwoman who was Lydia's apprentice. According to Lydia's orders, all the members of her household had been baptized with her into this new religion. But within days of their baptism, Paul and Silas, the teachers of the new religion, had been arrested for creating an uproar in town. They had been beaten, and now they were in prison. The assembled group was discussing what might happen to them now.

Suddenly a breathless messenger was admitted into the apartment. There had been an earthquake, he reported, and the chains holding Paul and Silas had been miraculously torn from the walls! Paul and Silas were free! Under the circumstances, it was unlikely that new arrests would follow. When Paul and Silas returned to Lydia's home, they gave final exhortations to the new converts in her household before continuing on their travels.

These two stories, woven from the text of Acts (10:1-9, 19-24, 44-48; 16:11-15, 19-40), illustrate both the household context of earliest Christianity and the authority typically exercised by the heads of Christian households. The religious authority of householders was not unique to Christian circles but drew on social precedents deeply rooted in the Greco-Roman world. When the father of a traditional Roman family (the *paterfamilias*) returned home after an absence, he ceremonially greeted the chief household deity (*lar familiaris*).[1] On the three sacred days of each month and on other festival days, his wife (the *materfamilias*) draped the hearth with garlands of flowers and prayed to the *lar familiaris*.[2] Offerings of food and wine were placed in the shrine of the household gods (*lares* and *penates*) as a sign of both honor and symbolic inclusion in the family meal.[3] Such reverent rituals guaranteed the continued favor and patronage of the domestic and familial gods, and it was the responsibility of the heads of the household to see that they were carried out properly.

Since the legal and philosophical texts of antiquity portray households as ruled by men, we expect to read Christian parallels of the time like the story of paterfamilias Cornelius. But most of us are initially surprised by the example of Lydia. We may think of her as an exception. In fact, however, ancient women did exercise authority alongside men in most areas of household life, as is clearly revealed by sources less familiar and more mundane—scraps of letters, contracts, or administrative records preserved in the dry sands of the Egyptian desert. Such documentary sources record, for example, that Appollonia became the sole head of her household at the death of her husband, Dryton, in 126 B.C.E. and inherited four slaves, a vineyard with wells of baked brick, a wagon with harnesses, a dove cote, and other equipment, such as a grain mill, an oil press, and stands for water jars.[4] Other female heads of households bought and leased land, orchards, vineyards, and olive groves, which they worked themselves. These women landowners paid taxes, had legal liability, and administered their own properties. In addition to supervising agricultural work, female heads of household oversaw a variety of cottage industries, with spinning, weaving, and the manufacture of clothing being principal among these. Just as Lydia was involved in the dyer's trade, other women were involved in such businesses as brewing beer and the weaving of garlands for festival days.[5]

The familiar figure of head of household, male and female, pervaded both the daily lives and the imaginations of ancient people. When Christian writers reached for a metaphor that would express the authority of the one who oversees and cares for people's welfare, they frequently seized upon the householder. Matthew's rendering of a parable of Jesus begins, "For the kingdom of heaven is like a householder who went out into the early morning to hire laborers for his vineyards." The Gospel writer went on to describe how the enterprising householder made five expeditions to the marketplace during the same day to hire needy migrant workers. When he paid each of them the same wage regardless of the number of hours worked, he reminded them that they had all contracted their labor for that same wage. The parable based its central message on the familiar authority of the householder, who asked in conclusion, "Am I not allowed to do what I choose with what belongs to me, or do you begrudge my generosity? So the last will be first and the first will be last" (Matt. 20:1–16). In a similar if more mythical vein, the *Secret Book of John,* from the second century, implicitly casts its central savior figure Pronoia in the role of a householder who demonstrates the authority, care, and managerial skills of the materfamilias. Pronoia's mission is to recover the souls who are imprisoned in the material world and return them to her treasury in the spiritual realm of light; collecting the payments due to her, she is the protector of her dependents and the guardian of the resources of her heavenly household.[6]

Closer to home were the comparisons drawn between heads of households and those men and women whose leadership was acknowledged by the Christian community. Matthew notes that "every scribe who has been trained for the kingdom of heaven is like a householder who brings out of his treasure what is new and what is old" (13:52). And the role of the "overseer" or "bishop" (*episcopos* [masculine] or *episcope* [feminine]) was consistently modeled on household leadership. "For if someone does not know how to manage a household, how can that one care for God's church?" is the rhetorical question posed by the writer of I Timothy (3:4). Since the early Christian movement took shape largely within the setting of households, like those of Cornelius and Lydia, it is hardly surprising that not only theological conceptions but also early Christian models of leadership were based on the traditional authority of the head of the household.

As we take a closer look at the household-based model for leadership in the early church, and at its precedents for women's leadership, we confront certain perplexing inconsistencies in the ancient sources, already hinted at in the disjunctions between the legal and philosophical depictions of household leadership and the documentary evidence. Ancient perspectives on the household and the role of women often varied depending on the context. On the one hand, when the household was considered in relation to the polis, the juridical authority of the male was underlined and women were portrayed as strictly subordinate members of the household. On the other hand, ancient writers also attempted to contrast male and female gender roles by aligning them with the state and the household, respectively, resulting in a portrayal of women as the sole rulers of the household. In texts that focus primarily on the household, still a third view frequently emerges: an idealized complementarity of male management of the outdoor portion of the household and female management of the indoor.

What all of these seemingly contradictory claims have in common is that they are assertions about *how things ought to be.* They express cultural assumptions and stereotypes—ideologies, if you will—that *influence* social reality but do not adequately *describe* that reality. The first challenge, then, is to sort out social reality from ideological distortions of household roles. In so doing, we shall discover that there was in fact a high degree of role interchangeability between the women and men who functioned as heads of households; in many practical respects, the household was a sphere of action that defied rigid categories for the sexes.

The next task is to determine how these household models, "ideological" as well as "real," influenced social roles and attitudes toward women's leadership within the Christian church. Here both the everyday experience of women exercising authority as heads of households and the stereotype of the woman as sole ruler of the household prove to be significant for understanding the prominence of women leaders in the early Christian movement.

## HOUSEHOLD MANAGEMENT: THE POLITICAL PERSPECTIVE

Two of the most prominent and most distorted views of women's household roles are heavily influenced by an ancient form of political discourse that distinguishes sharply between the private sphere of the household (*oikos*) and the public sphere of the state (*polis*).[7] This public-versus-private ideology pervaded the thoughts of antiquity's politicians, philosophers, and rhetoricians as well as of the common men who conversed casually in the marketplaces of Athens or Rome. All of these men, and probably many women as well, would have agreed not only in emphasizing the distinction between the oikos and the polis but also in linking that primary dualism with others—male and female, outdoor and indoor, mobile and stationary, civilized and natural, superior and inferior.

| Public State (*Polis*) | Private Household (*Oikos*) |
| --- | --- |
| male | female |
| outdoor | indoor |
| mobile | stationary |
| civilized | natural |
| superior | inferior |

In the terms of the ancient public-private social theory, the public sphere of the state was inherently superior to the private sphere of the household; it constituted the only arena of freedom and civilized culture; and it was the primary locus of male identity.

Out of this public-versus-private ideology arose, first, the juridical view of women's household roles. In the juridical view, the figure of the male householder stood at the center of the spotlight. He was the representative of his household in the eyes of his fellow citizens. At the same time, he was the agent of the household's subordination to the loftier goals of the state, providing the crucial link between the public and private spheres. The centrality of the male householder in the juridical view led to a corresponding marginalization of the role of his wife; clearly the subordinate, the female householder tends to fade into insignificance in the texts that reflect this perspective.

The Greek philosopher Aristotle offered the classic statement of the juridical authority of the male head of household over his wife and children.

Of household management we have seen that there are three parts—one is the rule of the master over slaves, which has been discussed already, another of a father, and the third of a husband. A husband and father, we saw, rules over wife and children, both free, but the rule differs, the rule over his children being a royal, over his wife a constitutional rule. For although there may be exceptions to the order of nature, the male is by nature fitter for command than the female, just as the elder and full-grown is superior to the younger and more immature.[8]

To point out that Aristotle's perspective is male-centered is to state the obvious. In a work of political philosophy, it did not occur to Aristotle to define the nature of the authority of female head of household. His analysis of the household takes place within the context of a discussion of the political state, which Aristotle described as the "end" of all social life and "by nature clearly prior to the family and the individual."[9] It is only because the state is made up of households that he must speak of household management at all, Aristotle explains.[10] Since women were not participating citizens of the state, their authority in the household was of no interest to Aristotle. And since the household was inferior and subordinate to the state, the noncitizen members of the household were clearly subordinate to the citizen male head of household.

This politically defined principle of women's subordination was codified in the legal systems of both Greece and Rome. According to Roman law, a woman traditionally remained either under the "power" (*potestas*) of her father or under the "hand" (*manus*) of her husband. The second-century jurist Gaius highlighted the sexual asymmetry of the early Roman legal system: "While both males and females are found in *potestas,* only females can come under *manus.*"[11] Gaius went on to explain that when a woman came under a husband's *manus,* she ranked as a daughter in his family.[12] This represents a degree of legal subordination of married women still more extreme than that articulated by Aristotle, who distinguished between a father's more absolute "royalty" over his children and a husband's "constitutional" authority over his wife. Yet in Gaius's own day, marriage with *manus* had long ceased to be the common practice, and this change increased the independence of married women, in spite of the fact that technically they remained under the authority of their fathers or their fathers' male relatives. By the first and second centuries of the common era, a woman could escape both the father's *potestas* and the husband's *manus* by placing herself under the guardianship of a nonfamilial "tutor," whom she might even choose herself. Gone were the days when a husband could expel a wife for drinking or execute his daughter for having an affair.[13]

While some women pursued their lives virtually unencumbered by the legal authority of their nominal tutors, others were emancipated from the legal authority of males altogether. The special provisions of the laws of the Emperor Augustus, for example, offered the status of legal independence (*sui juris*) to freeborn women who bore three children and freed slave women who bore four children. Most women, however, still required the representation of a man, whether father, husband, or guardian, if they wanted to enter into a contractual agreement or pursue a lawsuit. The legal principle of woman's subordination was partially eroded but never altogether abolished in antiquity.[14]

The juridical view of women as subordinate members of the household stands in dramatic contrast to a second view that is likewise closely linked to public-versus-private ideology: women as domestic matriarchs. As we have seen, the public sphere was considered the intrinsically superior locus of male activities, and the private sphere, the intrinsically inferior domain of female activities. It followed that men's private activities and associations were frequently deemphasized or even denied. The ideal man was a "political animal"[15] and had to be free to devote himself to the higher life of the public sphere; he therefore left the leadership of the household to his wife. In Xenophon's classical Greek dialogue on household management, the protagonist, Isomachus, is anxious to persuade his companion Socrates that he pursues such an ideal male life: "I certainly do not pass my time indoors; for, your know, my wife is quite capable of looking after the house by herself."[16] Columella, a first-century Roman writer on estate management, confidently reasserted this tradition that household management was women's work, and public, political life, a male affair:

> Both amongst the Greeks and afterwards amongst the Romans down to the time which our fathers can remember domestic labor was practically the sphere of the married woman, the fathers of families betaking themselves to the family fireside, all care laid aside, only to rest from their public activities.[17]

We hear the same ideal echoed in the words of Philo, a first-century Alexandrian Jew:

> For the nature of communities is twofold, the greater and the smaller, the greater we call cities and the smaller households. As to the management of both forms, men have obtained that of the greater, which bears the name of statesmanship, whereas women have obtained that of the smaller, which goes under the name of household management.[18]

The male denial of household responsibility resulted in a neat theoretical division of authority between men and women. A treatise produced within a second- and third-century B.C.E. Italian community of Neopythagoreans put it succinctly: "Men should be generals and city officials and politicians, and women should guard the house and stay inside and receive and take care of their husbands."[19] Even later, John Chrysostom, court preacher in fourth-century Constantinople, still expressed the same conviction that the household was not the proper province of men:

> [A woman] provides complete security for her husband and frees him from all such household concerns, concerns about money, woolworking, the preparation of food and

decent clothing. She takes care of all other matters of this sort, that are neither fitting for her husband's concern nor would they be satisfactorily accomplished should he ever lay his hand to them—even if he struggled valiantly![20]

This theoretical division of public male and private female spheres of authority lent itself to frequently drawn analogies between political and household leadership. Xenophon waxed eloquent on woman's role as household regent. He likened the female head of household to a general leading an army; the admiral of a warship; the guardian of the state overseeing the carrying out of its laws; the commander of a garrison inspecting his guards; the Athenian council scrutinizing the calvary; and, finally, a queen punishing and rewarding her subjects.[21] One of Xenophon's favorite epithets for the female householder was "queen bee"—in Greek literally "commander of the bees" (*he ton melitton hegemon*).[22]

Such a depiction of women as quasi-political rulers within the household contrasts dramatically with the juridical emphasis on woman's subordination. It is a contrast, however, with which Greek and Roman writers seem comfortable:

A good wife should be the mistress of her home, having under her care all that is within it. . . . This then is the province over which a woman should be minded to bear an orderly rule; for it seems not fitting that a man should know all that passes within the house. But in all other matters, let it be her aim to obey her husband. . . . Nay, it is fitting that a woman of well-ordered life should consider that her husband's uses are as laws appointed for her own life by divine will, along with the marriage state and the fortune she shares. If she can endure them with patience and gentleness, she will rule her home with ease; otherwise not so easily.[23]

Some writers attempted to define leadership roles of men and women within the household more precisely. One ancient source suggested, for example, that while the male head of household possessed the power of decision (*arbitrium*) in the household, the female was the one actually concerned with the household's administration (*ministerium*).[24] A scene from the twenty-first book of Homer's *Odyssey* may flesh out the significance of such a distinction in terms. Here the inexperienced teenager Telemachus addresses his mother, Penelope, in the presence of banqueting male guests: "Go to your quarters and busy yourself with your own tasks, with loom and spindle, and direct your slaves at their work." He concludes these admonitions with the proud proclamation, "I am the ruler of the household." Upon hearing her son's words, the mature and capable Penelope, who has managed her household successfully during the long and difficult years of her wandering husband's absence, quite appropriately "gazes in wonder."[25]

## HOUSEHOLD MANAGEMENT: THE ECONOMIC PERSPECTIVE

While the treatises on household management (*oikonomia*) bear the clear imprint of political perspectives, they also have a more distinctly "economic" way of describing the household roles of men and women, and that is as partners in the administration and leadership of the household. The complementarity of male and female natures and roles was frequently idealized in the assertions of this model of partnership. Nevertheless the economic depiction of male and female heads of household stands much closer to social reality than do the political depictions of women as either completely subject or completely dominant within the household.

Plutarch's first-century *Advice to Bride and Groom* offers an eloquent, if somewhat romanticized, expression of the model of male and female partnership:

> It is a lovely thing for the wife to sympathize with her husband's concerns and the husband with the wife's, so that, as ropes, by being intertwined, get strength from each other, thus, by the due contribution of goodwill in corresponding measure by each member, the copartnership may be preserved through the joint action of both.[26]

A sample Egyptian marriage contract provides a more concrete perspective on the social and economic partnership on which a marriage was based. In the marriage of Heraclides of Temnos and Demetria, the equal social status of the two parties was announced first: "He is free; she is free." The economic resources that Demetria brought to the household were then specified: "marriage clothing and ornaments valued at 1,000 drachmas." Next, carefully parallel language delineated the mutual obligations of Heraclides and Demetria to protect their partner's honor and their mutual right to dissolve the union should the terms of the partnership be violated.

> If Demetria is caught in fraudulent machination to the dishonor of her husband Heraclides, she shall forfeit all that she has brought with her. But Heraclides shall prove whatever he charges against Demetria before three men whom they both approve. It shall not be lawful for Heraclides to bring home another woman for himself in such a way as to inflict contumely on Demetria, nor to beget children by another woman, nor to indulge in fraudulent machination against Demetria on any pretext. If Heraclides is caught doing any of these things, and Demetria proves it before three men whom they both approve, let Heraclides return

to Demetria the dowry of 1,000 drachmas which she brought, and forfeit 1,000 drachmas of the silver coinage of Alexander.[27]

The duties of the partners who ran ancient households were complex, because households were both social units for the preservation of a family's lineage and status and economic units for the preservation of a family's material wealth. Both parents actively participated in arranging marriages for their children, and both of them reviewed the field of eligible candidates with an eye to the social status, political prospects, and economic resources of potential spouses, although it was the father, who moved within the male space of public life, who actually negotiated the contracts. Consider, for example, the case of the distinguished Roman Appius Claudius and his wife, Antisia. Appius Claudius returned from a dinner party bursting with news: He had drawn the promising Tiberius Gracchus aside and offered him his daughter's hand, and Tiberius had instantly accepted. "Antisia, I have betrothed our Claudia," he cried. Before he could tell her the name of the young man, Antisia impatiently interrupted his excited report: "Why so eager, or why so fast? If you had only found Tiberius Gracchus for betrothal to her!" Both parents were involved in this crucial decision, and father and mother had come up with the same candidate in their calculations as to who would best preserve the family lineage.[28]

Greek and Roman families wished their children to marry well, but marrying well was not enough: They must also produce heirs. The future generations of the family were a part of the household, and the sons and daughters of the household felt keenly their responsibility to preserve and maintain their family's line. A first-century poem of Martial, sent to Pudens and his wife, Claudia, on the birth of their third child, celebrates the continuance of the family line: "May the gods bless her in that she, a fertile wife, has borne children to her constant spouse, in that she hopes, though youthful still, for sons—and daughters—in-law."[29]

The vital role of educating the children to preserve and enhance the family's prestige and honor was assigned to the materfamilias, and Roman society greatly admired the matron who performed this duty well. According to Tacitus, Rome's ancient greatness could be traced to the mothers of her aristocrats:

> With scrupulous piety and modesty she regulated not only the boy's studies and occupations, but even his recreations and games. Thus it was, as tradition says, that the mothers of the Gracchi, of Caesar, of Augustus, Cornelia, Aurelia, Atia directed their children's education and reared the greatest of sons.[30]

Not only future but also past family members counted as part of the household, and the virtues and public honor of the deceased created a kind of social capital on which living members of the household could draw. Religious observances celebrated by the living maintained good relations with the ancestral figures, who exercised a kind of patronage on the family's behalf. Women as well as men, it should be recalled, were involved in the rituals of domestic religion.

Good marriages, multiple births, and reverence for ancestors preserved the household as a social unit, but only good management could preserve it as an economic unit. Unlike the contemporary household, which is a unit of consumption, the ancient household was a unit of both production and consumption. It manufactured its own food and clothing and often produced surpluses for marketing. Thus the role of household manager would be closer to the job of manager of a small factory than to the role of the contemporary housewife.

Xenophon's classical economic treatise divided the duties of household management into the oversight of what goes on outdoors (agriculture and husbandry) and what goes on indoors (the production of food and clothing and the storage and distribution of equipment and supplies). This division was meant to underline the separate and complementary roles of men and women within the economic sphere.

> The gods with great discernment have coupled together male and female, as they are called, chiefly in order that they may form a perfect partnership in mutual service. . . . For he made the man's body and mind more capable of enduring cold and heat, and journeys and campaigns; and therefore imposed on him the outdoor tasks. To the woman, since he has made her body less capable of such endurance, I take it that God has assigned the indoor tasks.[31]

Xenophon went on to explain that the innate virtues of men and women likewise suited them to their tasks: Men had more courage to aid them in their outdoor pursuits, while women had more timidity and caution to make them better guardians of the household stores. Both had memory, attention, and self-control in equal portions, since these virtues were required for the management functions of both men and women.[32]

Xenophon specified that the male household manager have charge of such matters as the planting of crops, the cultivation of vines, the tending of olive groves and fruit trees, and the grazing of livestock.[33] The female manager was to receive what was procured in these open-air occupations—grain, wine, oil, wool—and store it in a safe place: "the dry covered rooms for the corn, the cool for the wine."[34] The complexities of storage on a large estate were brought out by both Xenophon and his Latin successor Columella.

Having prepared suitable storerooms we proceeded to distribute the utensils and furniture; and first of all, we set aside the objects which we are in the habit of using for the worship of the gods, after that the women's apparel, which is provided for festal days, and the men's apparel for war and also their dress for solemn occasions, and likewise footwear for both sexes. Next arms and weapons were stored apart, and in another place implements used for manufacturing wool. After this a place was found for vessels which are generally used for keeping food, and then those connected with washing and the toilet and with ordinary meals and with banquets were set out.[35]

The female manager was responsible not only for the proper storage of goods but also for their effective distribution. Xenophon specified that she was to see that the goods were apportioned justly and wisely and that "the sum laid by for a year is not spent in a month."[36] It becomes clear why the virtues of memory, attention, and self-control were essential. Both Xenophon and Columella stressed that the female steward of an estate be carefully examined to determine that she was free from those particular vices that would undermine the efficiency of a household manager: "It is of the first importance to observe whether she is far from being addicted to wine, greediness, superstition, sleepiness and the society of men, and whether she readily grasps what she ought to remember and what she ought to provide for the future."[37]

Xenophon dealt with the householder's management of slaves as well as of material resources. While the male manager oversaw the actual work of the outdoor slaves, the female manager was responsible for sending the outdoor slaves to the fields, as well as for directing and supervising the indoor slaves.[38] Xenophon's text suggests that the duties of the indoor slaves encompassed cleaning and the production of food and clothing.[39] Documentary evidence from Egypt shows more specifically that female slaves who worked inside the house cleaned with reed brooms, carried water, looked after babies and dogs, spun wool, and helped their mistress to wash and dress.[40] Xenophon encouraged even a wealthy woman to work alongside her slaves, since the activity would have a positive effect on her health, and her direct involvement would enable her to oversee the work more effectively.[41]

Xenophon described the mistress of the household as the guardian of its laws, whose task it was to reward and praise, as well as to rebuke and punish.[42] In a rather different genre, the Greek poet Herodas, in a lively parody of the relationship between mistress and slave, captured something of the ethos of the management of household personnel. Here a middle-class female head of household, Koritto, alternately addresses her friend Metro and her slave:

KORITTO: Metro, sit down (to her slave). Get up and give the lady your chair—I have to *tell* her to do everything—you couldn't do anything on your own, could you? Bah, she's a stone, sitting in the house, not a slave. But when I measure out the barley ration you count the crumbs, and if even a little bit falls off the top you complain for the entire day—the walls fall in with your shouting. Oh, now you're polishing and making it shine, you pirate, just when we need it. Offer a prayer to my friend, since without her here you'd have had a taste of my hands.[43]

It is clear even from this humorous account that authority over slaves often rested on the threats of bodily violence or starvation.

An anonymous Greek economic treatise reduced the problem of the management of slaves to a stark and simple formula:

> We may apportion to our slaves (1) work, (2) chastisement, and (3) food. If men are given food, but no chastisement nor any work, they become insolent. If they are made to work, and are chastised, but stinted of their food, such treatment is oppressive, and saps their strength. The remaining alternative, therefore, is to give them work, and a sufficiency of food; unless we pay men, we cannot control them; and food is a slave's pay.[44]

The author of this treatise also likens the proper distribution of work, chastisement, and food to the physician's administration of appropriate medicines.[45]

Both women and men supervised the labor of slaves, and both meted out the conventional forms of discipline, whether reward or, more frequently, punishment. Indeed Chrysostom, the fourth-century bishop of Constantinople, urged Christian widows not to remarry by arguing that they themselves were perfectly capable of disciplining their slaves without recourse to a husband.[46] While a statement such as this, on the one hand, offers some rare male appreciation for female capabilities and authority, it, on the other hand, underlines the unfortunate acceptance of slavery in Greco-Roman society. Here the institutional church once again unquestioningly adopted, as it soon did with women's roles, a social convention that did not necessarily reflect the liberating message of its founder.

Managers of households also trained and educated their slaves. An enthusiastic Xenophon declared, "It is delightful to teach spinning to a maid who had no knowledge of it when you received her, and double her worth to you: to take in hand a girl who is ignorant of housekeeping and service, and after teaching her and making her trustworthy and serviceable to find her worth any amount."[47]

As valuable as productive skills were in a slave, even more valuable was the cultivation of loyalty. The obedience of slaves who worked the fields could be commanded by threats of violence, but the obedience of household slaves and slaves with administrative responsibilities had to be more carefully nurtured: Loyalty, not fear, was the basis for their service. One writer explained that there were two kinds of slaves, "those in positions of trust and the laborers." He noted that the training for those in positions of trust was particularly important: "Since it is a matter of experience that the character of the young can be molded by training, when we are required to charge slaves with tasks befitting the free, we have not only to procure the slaves, but to bring them up for the trust."[48] Xenophon's character Isomachus explained how he and his wife trained a female steward: "We also taught her to be loyal to us by making her a partner in all our joys and calling on her to share our troubles. Moreover, we trained her to be eager for the improvement of our estate, by making her familiar with it and by allowing her to share in our successes."[49] Cultivating loyalty in a steward involved instilling not only understanding and motivation but also morality. Isomachus continued: "And further, we put justice in her, by giving more honor to the just than to the unjust, and by showing her that the just live in greater wealth and freedom than the unjust; and we placed her in that position of superiority."[50]

In spite of Xenophon's opening emphasis on the separate and complementary nature of male and female roles in household management, the very intensity of the interest of his male protagonist, Isomachus, in those aspects of management that he labels "female" belies his own purported separation from the indoor portions of household management. The second-century African Christian writer Tertullian was familiar with men like Xenophon's Isomachus, who falsely professed male ineptitude in the management of the private sphere. Tertullian exclaimed sarcastically, "Of course the houses of none but married men fare well! The families of celibates, the estates of eunuchs, the fortunes of military men, or of such as travel without wives, have gone to rack and ruin!"[51] In Tertullian's view, men were clearly capable of overseeing the management of a household, indoors as well as outdoors.

Women were likewise capable of managing both the outdoor and indoor portions of a household. The public duties of many Greek and Roman men required their wives to manage the entire household in their absence. The first-century writer Plutarch referred to the circumstance of male absence as if it was commonplace: "Why is it that, when men who have wives at home are returning either from the country or from abroad, they send ahead to tell their wives that they are coming? . . . Is it because during their husbands' absence the wives have more household duties and occupations?"[52]

Many household matters—indoor and out—were run by widows who preferred not to remarry. Indeed, classical society frequently exalted the ideal of the wife who remained faithful to one husband—the *univira*. The widow Cornelia, mother of the eminent Gracchi brothers, both Roman statesmen, was praised for not remarrying: "Cornelia took charge of the children and the estate."[53] In other cases, wealthy women living with husbands simply preferred to manage their own property: Varro's treatise *On Agriculture,* from the second century B.C.E., is addressed to his wife, to whom he offered advice on making her newly acquired property more profitable.[54]

Columella hints that there was a great deal of overlap between the indoor and outdoor functions of men and women not only in the upper levels of management represented by wealthy landowners but also in the day-to-day running of an estate supervised by male and female stewards. Although he initially appears to endorse Xenophon's idealized indoor-outdoor division of labor, Columella subsequently instructs the female steward to do woolwork only when, due to inclement weather, "a woman cannot be busy with field work under the open sky."[55] "Hers is not a sedentary task," remarks Columella, noting that the female manager must supervise not only those who are working at the loom and in the kitchen but also those who clean the cowsheds and milk and shear the sheep.[56]

The documentary evidence points even more clearly than these literary sources toward the basic interchangeability of male and female roles in household leadership. The following letter addressed by an Egyptian woman named Ptolema to her brother Antas describes her management of the family fields and livestock.

All the fields are in good condition. The southern basin of the seventeen arurae has been sold for the use of cattle. Your cattle have eaten one arura and have gone off to Pansoue. All the land there has been given over to the cattle. The rest of the vegetable plot has been given over for grass cutting. We have sold the grass in the cleruchies excepting the six eastern basins for 112 drachmas. Grass is exceedingly cheap.[57]

Neither innate female characteristics nor social convention barred Ptolema from tending to any of the affairs of her household. Although the law clearly subordinated a woman to her husband as her legal guardian, she nevertheless maintained a significant measure of autonomy within the domestic sphere as household manager. Not only did she administer the resources of the household—

its agricultural and domestic productivity—she also retained control over the resources she brought to the marriage in the form of a dowry. In her capacity as householder she was free to buy and sell, contract day laborers, and conduct household—hence "private"—business in the "public" sphere.

## HOUSE CHURCH LEADERSHIP:
## MANAGERS OF THE HOUSEHOLD OF GOD

Women and men as heads of households possessed important resources for the early Christian communities. First, they owned homes. These were presumably large enough for the communal gatherings, which probably took place in the dining room, or triclinium. Prayers, preaching, and exhortation were carried out in the context of a communal meal, and the meal itself was provided out of the resources of the household's store of food—grain, olive oil, cheese, and fruit. Such gifts of food and hospitality, an ancient form of benefaction commonly provided to clubs or to the poor, gave a host or hostess the status of a patron. The male and female householders who served as patrons of the early churches may not have always been the titular leaders of those churches. Nevertheless the similarities between the duties of householder and those of early bishops and presbyters are striking. These similarities suggest that the role of household manager served as a significant model for these early Christian leadership roles.

What does church leadership look like when we view it from the perspective of household management? Where do the tasks and responsibilities of church leaders parallel those of household managers? A first major area is in the management of goods. Like household managers, church leaders received, inventoried, and distributed the common goods of the community. One early conflict in the church revolved around the question of who would carry out the "table ministry," a duty that included the purchase of food, the preparation of the meal, and the distribution of food.[58] In the following centuries leaders continued to preside over the distribution of food at the eucharastic meal, which was at the center of Christian worship; those same leaders were responsible for the distribution of food to the widows and to the sick of the community. The *Didache,* an early church manual, instructs members of the community to take the firstfruits of the harvest and the slaughter to their leaders; similarly, whenever they baked bread or opened a jar of wine or oil, they were to contribute firstfruits.[59] Roughly a century later, the so-called *Apostolic Tradition* provides for liturgical prayers to be spoken over gifts of bread, wine, oil, cheese, and olives brought to the church.[60] As the wealth of communities grew, so did the value of the material resources that were guarded by the church leaders.

Just as writers on household management stressed that managers should not be greedy or addicted to wine, so the *Didache* instructed Christians to "choose for yourselves bishops and deacons who are worthy of the Lord, individuals who are humble and not eager for money but sincere and approved."[61] The New Testament letter to Timothy also urged that a bishop be neither a drunkard nor a lover of money (1 Tim. 3:4–5). Such considerations were immediately relevant, given the responsibilities of church leaders in guarding the community's food, wine, and other material resources.

Church leadership, like household management, required experience in the management of people as well as of goods. The household of God was made up of men and women, old and young, married and widowed, free and slave. Regimenting the behavior and interrelations of these various groups was a primary concern of church leaders as of households. The virtues that I Timothy required in a bishop are familiar from the the treatises on household management:

> A bishop [*episkopos,* lit. overseer] must be above reproach, the husband of one wife, temperate [*sophrosune*], sensible [*kosmion*], dignified [*epeikei*], hospitable, an apt teacher, no drunkard, not violent but gentle, not quarrelsome, and no lover of money. He must manage his own household well, keeping children submissive and respectful in every way; for if a man does not know how to manage his household, how can he care for God's church?" (I Tim. 3:2–5)[62]

First of all the bishop should be *sophrosynē,* one who exercises self-control. *Kosmion,* a person's sense of order, implied that he or she could govern a household, or even a larger community, well. A sense of appropriateness (*epeikei*) assured that a person knew what was called for in a particular situation or at a particular time.

It was important that a bishop maintain authority (*proistein*) over his or her household by keeping children and slaves in subordinate roles. At the same time this exercise of power could not be abusive; it could not rely on beatings. The overseer, who in a Christian community would also be the financial administrator of church affairs, was not to be "greedy for gain" (*aphilargumon*). Hospitality (generosity with gifts of meals and lodging), teaching, and imparting valuable skills to slaves and children were household duties that readily translated into responsibilities of church leaders. The logical conclusion for the writer of I Timothy is that if people did not know how to preside over their own households, they would hardly be able to manage the churches or assemblies of

God. The letter goes on to provide instructions on how cross-generational relationships should be conducted, how widows should behave and how they should be treated by the rest of the congregation, when women should and should not remarry, and how slaves should behave toward their masters (1 Tim. 5:1–2, 3–13, 14; 6:1–2).

Roughly contemporary with the First Letter to Timothy is a letter written by Ignatius, bishop in Syrian Antioch, in which he advised his colleague Polycarp, bishop in Smyrna in Asia Minor, on the fine points of church leadership. Ignatius instructed Polycarp to see that the widows were not neglected; he was to view himself as their protector, providing financial support if necessary.[63] Next Ignatius advised Polycarp that slaves in the congregation should neither be treated contemptuously nor allowed to be insolent; such advice closely parallels the language of a treatise on household management: "In our intercourse with slaves we must neither suffer them to be insolent nor treat them with cruelty."[64] The bishop should furthermore use great discretion in determining which slaves should be given church monies for the purchase of their freedom, noted Ignatius (Ign. *Pol.* 4.3). Finally, with respect to the supervision of husbands and wives, Ignatius instructed Polycarp to tell wives to be content with their husbands, and husbands to love their wives (Ign. *Pol.* 4.1). Marriages should be approved by the bishop, although they were contracted between families (Ign. *Pol.* 4.2).

Like the writers of economic treatises, Ignatius used education and medicine as metaphors when discussing the disciplinary functions of church leaders. "It is no credit if you are fond of good pupils," he admonished. "Rather by your gentleness subdue those who are annoying." "Not every wound is healed by the same plaster," he continued, concluding with the advice, "In all circumstances be as wise as a serpent and harmless as a dove" (Ign. *Pol.* 2.1–2). Like the householder, the leader of a Christian community could not always enforce obedience through firm discipline but was to campaign actively for loyalty and support. Ignatius offered Polycarp shrewd and concrete counsel on how to win the goodwill of his congregation:

Lend everybody a hand, as the Lord does you. Out of love be patient with everyone, as indeed you are. (1.2)

Take a personal interest in those you talk to, just as God does. "Bear the diseases" of everyone, like an athlete in good form. The greater the toil, the greater the gain. (1.3)

Hold services frequently and call everyone by their names. (4.2)

The primary functions of church and household are clearly distinct—economic productivity versus spiritual salvation. Yet this brief review of early Christian texts suggests striking points of correlation between the two social institutions and their models of leadership. Both household managers and bishops were responsible for receiving, storing, and distributing goods. Both were responsible for supervising, educating, disciplining, and nurturing the members of the community in their various roles and relationships as free persons and slaves, men and women, married and single, elders and young people. And both household managers and bishops derived their authority not only from their formal positions but also from their personal abilities to persuade and win respect through constant presence and involvement in the community.

## FROM HOUSEHOLD TO HOUSE CHURCH: THE LEADERSHIP OF WOMEN

We have seen from ancient texts that husbands and wives functioned together as well as individually as heads or managers of households. Although a certain complementarity of male and female roles was idealized and perhaps sometimes realized, the various administrative tasks in household management were not fundamentally restricted to one gender alone. Neither was household authority.

Alongside this day-to-day functioning of household social roles there existed literary depictions of those roles that were shaped by the gendered ideology of the political sphere. These emphasized the juridical authority of the male as ruler of the household, while simultaneously insisting on the disengagement of men from the inferior "female" private sphere. Such ideological representations do not directly reflect social reality, but they did have their own power in influencing that reality. The tendency of men to devalue private life often left women to their own devices in managing the private sphere, while the theory of women's separation and subordination was successfully invoked to restrict and control women's behavior within their own households.

As we shift our focus to the sphere of the Christian house church, we are likewise confronted with sources that offer conflicting representations of women's roles. In them we can hear the voice of public ideology about gender roles. The theme of women's subordination, for example, is familiar to readers of the New Testament. "Wives, be subject to your husbands, as to the Lord. For the husband is the head of the wife as Christ is the head of the church, his body, and is himself its Savior. As the church is subject to Christ, so let wives also be subject in everything to their husbands" (Eph. 5:22–24). Yet sources also implicitly corroborate the pivotal part women and their authority played in Christian communities. One second-century detractor of Christianity attacked and dismissed the religion as a woman's movement. Consider the following disdainful remarks from the pen of the pagan Celsus:

[When] in private houses workers in wool and leather, and fullers, and persons of the most uninstructed and rustic character . . . get hold of the children privately, and certain women as ignorant as themselves, they pour forth wonderful statements. . . . [They tell the children] that they must . . . go with the women and their playfellows to the women's apartments or to the leather shop, or to the fuller's shop, that they may attain perfection.[65]

Society's stereotype of the woman as ruler of the household may have contributed to the legitimacy of women's leadership within Christianity. But in the earliest Christian communities, which—inspired by Jesus' radical teaching and example—were much more egalitarian than the society at large, such ideological perspectives remained muted and their influence on social roles limited. By and large, the ungendered roles and functions of household leadership were transferred with quiet and unconscious ease to the sphere of the house church. Lydia led her Christian household with the same natural and unquestioned authority as Cornelius.

So long as church leadership continued to model itself on the familiar role of household manager, there was no cultural barrier to women assuming leadership roles. First- and second-century Christians, familiar with the authority and leadership role of the female head of household, would have perceived women's leadership within the church as not only acceptable but natural. The early church's specific leadership functions posed no barriers to women, whose skills and experiences as managers amply prepared them to assume the duties of teaching, disciplining, nurturing, and administrating material resources. This would have been the case as long as Christian communities remained closley identified with the social structures of the private sphere.

1. Cato *On Agriculture* 2.

2. Cato *On Agriculture* 143; here the duties of the female steward or *vilica* can be taken to reflect those of the absent materfamilias.

3. See David G. Orr, "Roman Domestic Religion: The Evidence of the Household Shrines," *Aufstieg und Niedergang der römischen Welt* II.16 (Berlin: Walter de Gruyter, 1978), 1557–91.

4. Sarah B. Pomeroy, *Women in Hellenistic Egypt* (New York: Schocken Books, 1984), 105.

5. Pomeroy, *Women in Hellenistic Egypt,* 148–73; see also Jane F. Gardner, *Women in Roman Law and Society* (Bloomington: Indiana Univ. Press, 1986), 233–56.

6. *The Nag Hammadi Library,* ed. J. M. Robinson (San Francisco: Harper & Row, 1988), 122. We owe to Karen King this comparison of Pronoia to householder.

7. Anthropologist Michelle Zimbalist Rosaldo ("Woman, Culture, and Society: A Theoretical Overview," in *Woman, Culture and Society,* ed. Rosaldo and Lamphere [Stanford, CA: Stanford Univ. Press, 1974], 17–42 has suggested that the public-versus-private distinction is a universal—though "nonnecessary"—aspect of culture and society. Rosaldo has proposed three ways women can exercise power within the constraints of the public-versus-private structure: 1. by taking on male roles, 2. by creating a secondary "public" sphere within the private sphere, and 3. where the home is the center of social life for men and women, by using the domestic role as a vehicle for power.

8. Aristotle *Politics* 1.12.1259a-b, trans. Richard McKeon, *The Basic Works of Aristotle* (New York: Random House, 1941), 1143.

9. Aristotle *Politics* 1.2.1253a-b, McKeon, *Basic Works,* 1130.

10. Aristotle *Politics* 1.3.1253a, McKeon, *Basic Works,* 1130.

11. Gaius *Institutes* 1.97–117, trans. M. R. Lefkowitz and M. B. Fant, *Women's Life in Greece and Rome* (Baltimore: Johns Hopkins Univ. Press, 1982), 190.

12. Gaius *Institutes* 1.97–117, Lefkowitz and Fant, *Women's Life,* 190.

13. The Laws of the Kings from the eighth century B.C.E. and the Twelve Tables of the fifth century B.C.E. attest to the absolute authority of the ancient *paterfamilias.*

14. An overview of the position of women in Roman law is found in Sarah B. Pomeroy, *Goddesses, Whores, Wives, and Slaves: Women in Classical Antiquity* (New York: Schocken Books, 1975), 150, 163; or the more recent and detailed treatment of Gardner, *Women in Roman Law and Society,* 5–29.

15. Aristotle *Politics* 1.2.1253a, trans. McKeon, *Basic Works,* 1129.

16. Xenophon *Economics* 7.3, trans. E. C. Merchant, *Xenophon, Memorabilis and Oeconomicus* (Cambridge, MA: Harvard Univ. Press, 1953), 415.

17. Columella *On Agriculture* 12, pref. 7, trans. E. S. Forster and E. H. Heffner in *Columella, On Agriculture and Trees* (London: William Heinemann, 1955), 3:179.

18. Philo *The Special Laws* 3.170, trans. David Wilson, *Philo of Alexandria* (New York: Paulist Press, 1981), 280.

19. Trans. Lefkowitz and Fant, *Women's Life,* 104.

20. John Chrysostom *The Kind of Women Who Ought to Be Taken as Wives* 4, trans. Elizabeth A. Clark, *Women in the Early Church* (Wilmington, DE: Michael Glazier, 1983), 37.

21. Xenophon *Economics* 8.4–8, 9.14–15.

22. Xenophon *Economics* 7.17, 32–34.

23. Pseudo-Aristotle *Economics* 3.1, trans. G. C. Armstrong, *Aristotle, Oeconomica and Magna Moralia* (Cambridge, MA: Harvard Univ. Press, 1935), 18:401–3.

24. *Laudatio Turiae,* in G. H. R. Horsley, *New Documents Illustrating Early Christianity* (Australia: Macquarie Univ., The Ancient History Documentary Research Centre, 1983), 33–35.

25. Homer *Odyssey* 21.350–54.

26. Plutarch *Advice to Bride and Groom* 20, trans. F. C. Babbitt in *Plutarch's Moralia* (Cambridge, MA: Harvard Univ. Press, 1928), 2:313.

27. Pomeroy, *Women in Hellenistic Egypt*, 86.

28. Plutarch *Life of Tiberius Gracchus* 4.1–2, trans. B. Perrin, *Plutarch's Lives* (London: William Heinemann, 1921), 10:151–53. See also Pierre Grimal, *Love in Ancient Rome* (Norman: Univ. of Oklahoma Press, 1981), 73.

29. Martial *Epigrams* 11.53.

30. Tacitus *Dialogue* 28, trans. Church and Brodribb in Lefkowitz and Fant, *Women's Life*, 141–42.

31. Xenophon *Economics* 7.18, 23, trans. Marchant, *Xenophon*, 419–21.

32. Xenophon *Economics* 7.25–27.

33. Xenophon *Economics* 16–21.

34. Xenophon *Economics* 9.3, trans. Marchant, *Xenophon*, 439–41.

35. Columella *On Agriculture* 12.3.1–2, trans. Forster and Heffner, *Columella*, 3:187–89. Cf. Xenophon *Economics* 9.6–10.

36. Xenophon *Economics* 7.33, 36, trans. Marchant, *Xenophon*, 425.

37. Columella *On Agriculture* 12.1.2–3, trans. Forster and Heffner, *Columella*, 3:181. Cf. Xenophon *Economics* 9.11.

38. Xenophon *Economics* 7.35.

39. Xenophon *Economics* 7.36, 10.10–11.

40. Pomeroy, *Women in Hellenistic Egypt*, 132.

41. Xenophon *Economics* 10.10–11.

42. Xenophon *Economics* 9.15.

43. Herodas *Mime* 6, trans. Lefkowitz and Fant, *Women's Life*, 107.

44. Pseudo-Aristotle *Economics* 1.5.3, trans. Armstrong, *Aristotle*, 18:337.

45. Pseudo-Aristotle *Economics* 1.5.4.

46. John Chrysostom *Against Remarriage*, 4, trans. Sally Rieger Shore, *Studies on Women in Religion*, vol. 9 (New York: Edwin Mellen Press, 1983).

47. Xenophon *Economics* 7.41, trans. Marchant, *Xenophon,* 427.

48. Pseudo-Aristotle *Economics* 1.5.3, trans. Armstrong, *Aristotle,* 18:335.

49. Xenophon *Economics* 9.12, trans. Marchant, *Xenophon,* 443.

50. Xenophon *Economics* 9.13, trans. Marchant, *Xenophon,* 443.

51. Tertullian *On Chastity* 12, trans. S. Thelwall, *The Ante-Nicene Fathers* 4, reprint (Grand Rapids, MI: Eerdmans, 1982), 56.

52. Plutarch *Roman Questions* 9, trans. Babbitt, *Plutarch's Moralia,* 4:21.

53. Plutarch *Tiberius Gracchus* 1.4, trans. Perrin, *Plutarch's Lives,* 10:147.

54. Varro *On Agriculture* 1.1.1–4.

55. Columella *On Agriculture* 12.3.6, trans. Forster and Heffner, *Columella,* 3:191.

56. Columella *On Agriculture* 12.3–8, trans. Forster and Heffner, *Columella,* 3:193.

57. Second-century Egyptian papyrus, trans. A. S. Hunt and G. C. Edgar in *Women's Life in Greece and Rome,* ed. Mary R. Lefkowitz and Maureen B. Fant (Baltimore: Johns Hopkins Univ. Press, 1982), 236.

58. Acts 6:16. See also Elisabeth Schüssler Fiorenza, *In Memory of Her: A Feminist Reconstruction of Christian Origins* (New York: Crossroad, 1983), 162–68.

59. *Didache* 13.

60. *Apostolic Tradition* 5–6.

61. *Didache* 15.

62. The writer's implication that all bishops were men is part of his general campaign against women's leadership roles—women should not teach, consecrated widows should limit their ministries to prayer, and women should seek salvation through having children. See Dennis MacDonald, *The Legend and the Apostle: The Battle for Paul in Story and in Canon* (Philadelphia: Westminster Press, 1983).

63. Ignatius *Letter to Polycarp* 4.1 (hereafter, in text, Ign. *Pol.*), trans. Cyril Richardson, *Early Christian Fathers,* vol. 1 (New York: Macmillan, 1970). In the context of this discussion of the widows, Ignatius urged, "Let nothing be done without your knowledge." In later church orders, these same words were used to indicate that bishops should control the flow of money between wealthier and poorer Christians; here too they probably indicate financial support of some widows.

64. Pseudo-Aristotle *Economics* 1.5.2, trans. Armstrong, *Aristotle,* 18:335.

65. Origen *Against Celsus* 3.5, trans. F. Crombie, *The Ante-Nicene Fathers* 4, reprint (Grand Rapids, MI: Eerdmans, 1982), 486.

*Livia, wife of Augustus.* Livia's patronage made
her one of the most powerful political figures in
first-century Rome. Found at Pompeii. Museo
Nazionale, Naples. (Alinari/Art Resource, NY.)

# 3
# Patronage and Women's Power

■■■■

Early in the fourth century the African church was in crisis. The edicts of Diocletian fell on the church like a series of hammer blows. Soldiers pounded on church doors and demanded that bishops surrender the Christian Scriptures to the Roman government. The imperial edicts ordered the confiscation of church properties and liturgical equipment. Christians who had been arrested were confined in dank and foul-smelling prisons. Their only food was what friends and family carried in from the outside (Roman prisons provided room but not board). They might wait in chains for weeks before going to trial. If they confessed that they were Christians, death would surely follow. Yet that death would be a martyr's death, a powerful witness to the truth of the Christian faith.

In this climate of persecution, suffering, and martyrdom a new spirituality was born. Through this spirituality the trauma of martyrdom—the frightening arrest, the public trial, and the gruesome execution of faithful Christians—was glorified into the honor and riches of sainthood, establishing the saint as a powerful spiritual patron who could grace petitioners with wondrous benefits.

Lucilla, a Spanish noblewoman residing in Carthage, typified this spirituality. She kept in her possession a martyr's bone, which she would honor with a kiss.[1] Touching the physical remains connected her to the powerful spiritual presence of this saint. The act of reverencing those who had died the martyr's death guaranteed that suffering for the faith would be recognized as noble and significant.

Lucilla made her household a center for this martyr spirituality. Several clergy of the Carthaginian church rallied to the cause of the martyrs championed by her leadership. Marjorinus the lector was a client of hers, as was Donatus of Casaenigerae, a Numidian bishop in exile. Lucilla had secured the support of a number of other Numidian bishops as well.

Some members of the Carthaginian clergy firmly opposed this martyr spirituality. Mensurius, bishop of Carthage, along with his archdeacon, Caecilian, moved to dampen the fervor of martyrdom by draconian measures. He issued orders restraining his clergy from taking food to imprisoned Christians, in principle leaving them to die of starvation. In a high-handed manner Caecilian forbade the cult of the saints and insulted Lucilla publicly during a eucharistic celebration by censuring her for kissing the saint's bone.

When Caecilian, the antimartyr archdeacon, was elected to the episcopacy on Mensurius's death, Lucilla used her considerable political power to remedy this new disaster. At the head of the Carthaginian and Numidian clergy, she challenged the election of Caecilian on the grounds of an irregularity (that the Numidian patriarch, the "superintendent" of the Numidian clergy, had not been present at Caecilian's ordination as had been the custom for Carthaginian episcopal nominations). She then appealed to the Numidian patriarch, notifying him of the protest against the election of Caecilian. The patriarch gathered a number of Numidian bishops and arrived in Carthage in 312, where they convened a synod and deposed Caecilian.[2]

Lucilla exercised control over this synod by establishing relationships of patronage with a number of bishops by means of financial gifts and by securing the election of Marjorinus, her client, to the office of bishop. In this movement a new African church was born that traced its history back to Marjorinus. After Marjorinus died, Donatus was elected bishop, and this branch of the African church was named the Donatist church; thus Lucilla's role was obscured. Yet this Spanish noblewoman was in effect the founder of this African church, which called itself the church of the martyrs and continued to be a vital expression of African Christianity up through the seventh century.[3]

Lucilla's political power and her leadership in the African church, like that of her male counterparts, derived from the patronage system. As a member of the aristocracy Lucilla enjoyed a higher social status than the clergy of the Carthaginian church. Caecilian's public rebuke of this woman of high social rank was a grievous social offense. Lucilla's patronage of some of the Carthaginian clergy and the Numidian bishops involved financial gifts and political protection through her connections to the ruling class. Her relationships to the clergy were ongoing personal ones, and these men were frequently guests in her home. They subscribed to her political goals for the African church and assisted her in achieving them. For Marjorinus, being a client to this powerful patron meant his elevation from the position of deacon to the office of bishop. Appointment to a political office in the Roman Empire was often achieved through the influence of a patron, and church politics operated the same way.

Patronage was a way of weaving the fabric of social life; it defined reciprocal roles and responsibilities for both patron and client. The complex network of patronage relationships, a web of social relations, provided a way of consolidating and deploying political power. Only men and women with certain wealth and social standing were in a position to exercise patronage. It was the preeminent way that members of the ruling classes consolidated political power, pursued political strategies, and exercised leadership.

## TYPES OF PATRONAGE

The social status of women of the ruling classes enabled them to exercise this form of political power and leadership. Apart from brief summaries in dedicatory inscriptions and funerary epitaphs, which list the honors a woman received and offices she held, the only place where it is possible to glimpse some details of women's political activity and political power is in the ancient historians' accounts of Roman imperial families. There are no surviving political memoirs of the women of these families, detailing their political objectives and their strategies for achieving them. We only have their cameo appearances in the lives and politics of Roman men. But from these fleeting appearances we can discern the outlines of women's practice of patronage and the ways in which it translated into political power. We can also discern the conflicts women's political power caused as it challenged the social ban on women's leadership roles in public.

The patron–client relationship depended on differentials in status and social class. Roman citizens were ranked according to five social classes based on wealth. The senatorial and equestrian classes were the two highest, and thus the ruling, classes. In Roman society there were three kinds of patron-client relations that involved political functions and therefore political power: (1) the relationship between a member of the senatorial or equestrian class and a person of lower social standing, including even the common people, or plebs; (2) the relationship between a member of the senatorial or equestrian class and foreign communities who sought autonomy and protection from exploitation through this relationship; and (3) the relationship characterized by *amicitia* (friendship), in which the difference between the social status of patron and client was not so great. These last were cultivated as a way of fending off political attacks, which were often conducted through the criminal courts and could result in exile or death, and as a means of procuring administrative offices.[4]

The patronage of cities and the cultivation of *clientes* could endow the patron with considerable political power. Clients were bound to patrons in lifelong bonds of loyalty; they provided information, offered gifts, and refused to testify against the patron.

A client was "obligated to enhance the prestige, reputation, and honor of his patron in public and private life." Their chief function was to endow their patrons with social honor through "public attestation, and memorials of his patron's benefactions, generosity and virtue."[5] Additionally patrons drew clients into their circle of influence as links to other persons of power, and as loyal associates who would protect and enhance their public reputation and as valuable sources of information.

## WOMEN AS PATRONS

Historians have been reluctant to see in Lucilla an example of patronage. Typical portraits of Lucilla show her as an uppity woman with an eccentric piety, who dabbled in church politics and bribed weak-willed bishops.[6] Livia, a woman of the Julio-Claudian dynasty, wife of the emperor Augustus, and mother of the emperor Tiberius, has received more positive treatment from historians, but they also have been reluctant to see her role as that of a patron. Yet, like Lucilla, whose practice of patronage translated into significant power in church politics, Livia's patronage made her one of the most powerful political figures in first-century Rome.[7]

Livia exercised that form of patronage which linked members of the senatorial classes with persons of lower social standing. For example, she worked to secure citizenship for a client from Gaul. Citizenship would guarantee her client important political immunities and access to good appointments.[8] On several occasions she played the role of patron to the plebeian class when she provided relief for the victims of fires that periodically swept through portions of the city.[9] By providing dowries for the daughters of numerous families, Livia gained their loyalty.[10] A dowry guaranteed a woman financial security; she retained control over her dowry during marriage, and she took it with her if she divorced. It was her portion of her family's inheritance and absolutely essential for contracting a good marriage. With Livia's financial help these families were able to contract good marriages for their daughters who were able to enjoy a measure of status and independence; at the same time Livia greatly expanded her network of clients.

These relationships of patronage provided Livia with a distinct kind of status and political power, since it was the responsibility of her clients of lower social standing to enhance her reputation and honor. Clients made morning visitations to the residences of their patrons; they formed a retinue when the patron appeared in public, and they made public attestations of their loyalty. It was easy to identify important people moving through the city of Rome by the retinue following in their wake.

Livia also exercised the second form of patronage, whereby a foreign community sought protection and autonomy through client relations with a member of the ruling class. Livia was a patron of the residents of Samos. She petitioned the senate on their behalf for freedom and for immunity from taxes, which came with the status of free ally.[11] These were much-sought-after privileges, and it was a fortunate group indeed who could boast of a patron within the imperial family. The Jewish community in Jerusalem also enjoyed Livia's patronage. Philo recorded that she sent gifts of golden vials and libation bowls and a variety of other expensive gifts to the Jewish temple in Jerusalem.[12] The system of patronage also linked Livia with the Herodian family ruling in Jerusalem. Herod himself was a client of Livia's and in that capacity he left five hundred talents of silver to her on his death.

Patron-client relations could also involve the exchange of cities and territories over which a patron or client would have the right to rule. Herod the Great, appointed by Rome to rule over the Jews, was a client of both Caesar Augustus and Livia, his wife. Salome, Herod's sister, inherited client status to Livia and Augustus from Herod. The emperor Augustus gave Salome the city of Archelais, whereby she became its ruler, and a royal residence in the city of Askelon as well.[13] In her will Salome consigned the city of Archelais to Livia as a gift to her patron.[14]

But Livia probably derived her greatest political power from her patronage of members of Rome's ruling aristocracy—the *amicitia* form of patronage. Among Livia's clients were many men and women in the senatorial class who owed their lives to her. She created relationships of patronage by protecting those accused of the dangerous political crime of treason. The life of Plancina, a wealthy Roman noblewoman and an important political figure in her own right, was in jeopardy because of the criminal condemnation of her husband—engineered, as usual, for political reasons. Piso, Plancina's husband, was accused of murder, and Plancina's enemy Agrippina accused her of complicity in this crime. Livia's intervention as patron secured Plancina's pardon; her husband was condemned and committed suicide.[15]

When the emperor Augustus had finally secured the arrest and conviction of his political enemies, Livia urged leniency and clemency as the policy that would secure the loyalty of the patricians who had so violently opposed his imposition of a monarchy on the older democratic form of rule by the senate. Her policy was well advised; Augustus did secure the loyalty of those who had been his enemies.[16] According to the philosopher Seneca's version, when Lucius Cinna was arrested for treason, Livia counseled her husband, "Will you take a woman's advice? Follow the practice of the physicians who, when the usual remedies do not work, try just the opposite. So far you have accomplished nothing by severity. Try now how mercy will work. Pardon Lucius Cinna; he has been arrested, now he cannot do you harm, but he can help your reputation." Seneca continued, "Happy to have found a superior, he thanked his wife" and gave the necessary orders.[17]

A certain Cornelius, along with many others, was charged with plotting the death of Augustus and condemned to death. Through Livia's intervention his pardon was secured, and he was even appointed a consul. Dio Cassius, a Roman politician and historian, reported that "as a result of this course he [Augustus] so conciliated both him and the other persons so treated that neither they, nor any of the rest thereafter, either actually plotted against him or were suspected of doing so."[18] Livia's intervention on their behalf placed these grateful citizens in client roles, which both increased her political power and enhanced her public honor.

For clients the *amicitia* form of patronage was also a means of obtaining political office, and Livia was a powerful patron in this respect as well. Rufius, who eventually became consul (the highest military and civilian office), owed his political career to Livia's patronage. She was also a patron of Galba, who developed such a wide sphere of influence through her that he eventually succeeded in becoming emperor. As one of her principal clients he was named in her will to receive fifty million sesterces.[19]

Since one of the reciprocal obligations of clients was the duty of calling upon their patrons, Livia received visits from a significant number of senators. These respectful calls would have provided her with information and would have been the means for her to realize her own political objectives in the senate. Livia's lobbying was a recognized part of the Roman political system—the visits of senators to her home were duly recorded in the public records. The letters of Tiberius carried her name as well as his, and communications were addressed to both of them.[20]

Livia thus used patronage to create her own network of clients, who included senators, emperors, and foreign kings. It provided her a real and legitimate power base through which she was able to secure political offices for some clients, help others gain citizenship, and effect the passage of legislation favorable to her clients. For foreign communities she was able to provide tax-exempt status and autonomy.

From the third century we catch a glimpse of another powerful female patron. The Syrians of Palmyra spoke with pride about their queen, Zenobia. Her successful empire building had extended her rule from Syria to Egypt. In marketplace stalls and in government offices Syrians rehearsed stories of her beauty and virtue. The queen was also an intellectual, and the royal city of Samosata drew her to its vibrant intellectual community. Once she became a member of this community she established relationships of patronage with the well-known philosopher Longinus and with the Christian theologian Paul of Samosata.[21] According to one tradition, when the office of bishop in Samosata became vacant, she chose her client Paul to fill it. According to a similar tradition, she secured for him the office of *procurator ducenarius*—an administrative post close to the queen, which came with a substantial salary (*ducenarius* indicated an annual salary of two hundred thousand sesterces).[22]

Paul's critics accused him of flaunting his wealth and of claiming honors inappropriate for a bishop. When a synod of bishops met in Antioch in 269 and deposed Paul from his episcopal office for heretical beliefs about the person of Christ, it looked as if his career were over. They even went so far as to appoint a new bishop to his now-vacant episcopal see. Zenobia was able to protect her client Paul, and he remained in the episcopal residence and continued in the office of bishop. Zenobia had nullified the action of the synod. (Paul was dislodged from his episcopal office only after the military defeat of Zenobia by the emperor Aurelian.)

Cyprian of Carthage, also of the third century, provides a useful case study of another way in which patronage played a major role in the election of a bishop. The enclosed gardens of one of his larger estates were considered the most beautiful in the city. This wealthy landowner and aristocrat was converted to Christianity by a diligent presbyter. Shortly after Cyprian's conversion he liquidated part of his estate and distributed it in the form of benefactions to the Christian community. According to the *Vita Cypriani*, "No widow returned with an empty lap, no blind man was unguided by him as a companion, none faltering in step was unsupported by him for a staff, no one stripped of help by the hand of the mighty was not protected by him as a defender."[23] During a plague that afflicted Carthage, Cyprian provided relief to members of the Christian community and residents of the city.[24]

As a member of the aristocracy experienced in city politics, a benefactor, and a protector, Cyprian appeared an attractive candidate for the office of bishop. When the office became vacant, however, Cyprian was still in the catechumenate, a period of training in Christian doctrine and morality that often lasted as long as three years. As a catechumen Cyprian was not able to participate in the Eucharist; that would happen only after he was baptized at the end of his catechumenate. Cyprian was nevertheless elected to the episcopacy by acclamation of the people, and some alleged that it was the extravagance of Cyprian's benefactions that led to his precipitous elevation.[25]

In Alexandria, at the beginning of the third century, an unidentified woman of wealth, probably also an intellectual, like Zenobia, became a patron of a promising young scholar. She was a church leader in her own right, the head of a community of gnostic Christians in Alexandria who held their worship services in her home.[26] She was the patron of this community through providing the hospitality of her household, which probably meant that she was the head of that house church.

When persecution under the emperor Maximinus propelled the young man's father into martyrdom and the governor confiscated the family's property, this "remarkable woman," as the church historian Eusebius called her, financed the rest of the young man's education and provided him further financial support as he launched his career teaching rhetoric and lecturing at the catechetical school in Alexandria.[27] Her judgment was astute, for this young man, Origen of Alexandria, became one of the first and foremost theologians of the Greek-speaking churches.

Melania the Elder, a member of an illustrious family of the Roman senatorial class, was a patron of Rufinus, the famous scholar who translated Origen's writings into Latin. Rufinus accompanied her to Jerusalem where she founded a double monastery on the Mt. of Olives.[28] In Constantinople, the new capital of the eastern empire, Olympias, a wealthy member of the aristocracy, became the patron of two bishops, Nectarius and the famous Christian orator, John Chrysostom. Her patronage of Chrysostom during a bitter struggle over his episcopacy cost her dearly: She was exiled following his removal from office.[29] Perhaps the most extravagant patron of the fifth century was Melania the Younger (granddaughter of Melania the Elder) who liquidated her vast fortune in her travels from Thagaste, North Africa, to Egypt to the holy land, establishing monasteries in Africa and, like her grandmother, on the Mt. of Olives.[30]

## PATRONAGE AND HONOR

While patronage was an important means of acquiring and exercising political power, power itself was not the ultimate objective of patronage in its Roman context; rather social honor was. A typical litany of virtues invoked to praise a patron or benefactor indicates the sort of honor that a patron might hope to achieve: noble, generous, lover of honor, just, faithful, and civic-minded.[31] The awards a city council or senate might bestow on a benefactor or patron included statues erected in their honor, tax-exempt status, citizenship, inviolability of person and/or property, public support, and in the case of some emperors divine status.[32]

The city council of Syros voted the following honors for the priestess Berenice:

> The resolution of the *prytaneis,* approved by the council and the people: Whereas Berenice, daughter of Nichomachus, wife of Aristocles, son of Isidorus, has conducted herself well and appropriately on all occasions, and after she was made a magistrate, unsparingly celebrated rites at her own expense for gods and men on behalf of her native city, and after she was made priestess of the heavenly gods and the holy goddess Demeter and Kore and celebrated their rites in a holy and worthy manner, has given up her life—meanwhile she had also raised her own children. [The *prytaneis* has] voted to commend the span of this

woman's lifetime, to crown her with the gold wreath which in our father-land is customarily used to crown good women. Let the man who proposed this resolution announce at her burial: "The people of Syros crown Berenice, daughter of Nichomachus, with a gold crown in recognition of her virtue and her good will towards them."[33]

Livia received many of the public honors that are the reward for patronage and the salutary exercise of political power. Augustus erected a statue in her honor and granted her the right of administering her affairs without a guardian and the same diplomatic immunity that tribunes enjoyed.[34] Livia was given the office of priestess in the newly established cult of Augustus, as the senate had voted him divine honors on his death. She was given the right to employ a lictor, an official escort provided by the senate, when she carried out her duties.[35] On Livia's death the senate decreed that an arch be erected in her honor.[36] There was also a move in the senate to bestow on her the title of Parent of the Country or Mother of Country and a motion to extend to her divine honors as well.[37]

The exercise of political power through the patronage system allowed women to acquire many of the institutionalized forms of honor that men received. An inscription dedicated to Euxenia for her benefactions to the city of Megalopolis praises Euxenia for financing the construction of a wall for the temple of Aphrodite and for constructing an adjoining house for public guests. The inscription reads, "that a woman trades her wealth for a good reputation is not surprising, since ancestral virtue remains in one's children."[38] Achieving a "good reputation" amounted to the acquiring of social honor through her acts of patronage; ancestral virtue meant the status of the family into which she was born, attained by distinguishing itself in serving the common good over several generations. In

Bythinia, Plancia Magna was honored because she built at her expense the large gate complex and adjoining buildings that provided the magnificent entrance into the southern portion of the city.[39] The patron Archippae, who financed the construction of the assembly hall for the council, was honored by her city also.[40]

It was an honor to be appointed to a public office. Men and women listed on their gravestones each of the public offices they had held. Holding public office was an expensive honor, however. Often the newly elected officeholder had to finance a municipal office. For example, the *gymnasiarchos* was responsible for providing the costly olive oil athletes used in the gymnasium during workouts and competitive games. To ease the burden, the term was sometimes set at one month; thus in a year a city might elect twelve *gymnasiarchoi*. Menadora, a patron of Sillyon in the second century, distributed wheat to her city and donated three hundred thousand denarii to provide food for the city's children. In acknowledgment of these and many other benefactions, she was elected to the offices *gymnasiarch, decaprotos* (tax collector), priestess of Demeter, and *ktistria* (builder and restorer).[41]

## PATRONAGE AND GENDER IDEOLOGY

Although both women and men patrons competed for honor and political power in the same ways, women's exercise of patronage collided with the endemic prejudice against women's public power. Sexist social attitudes apportioned to men and women different sets of activities, different roles, and different standards for excellence. The domain of political activity dedicated to the welfare of the polis belonged to men. The domain of household business was assigned to women.

What happened, then, when women took an active part in public life? Dio Cassius conveys the extent of Livia's political power by explaining "that she undertook to manage everything as if she were sole ruler," except, he says, for the fact "that she never ventured to enter the Senate chamber, or the camps, or the public assemblies."[42] This comment reveals two interesting details: (1) Livia functioned effectively as ruler of the empire, and (2) she did so within the boundaries set by the public-versus-private gender system. The senate chamber (*synedrion*), the military camps (*stratopeda*), and the public assemblies (*ekklesias etolmese*) constituted the exclusively male space of the public political domain into which Livia did not venture.

Livia used her position as wife of the emperor Augustus to gain access to other powerful figures in the ruling class. Livia's son Tiberius, however, was jealous of her political power and attempted to mute it whenever possible. Suetonius wrote: "Vexed at his mother Livia, alleging that she claimed an equal share in the rule, he shunned frequent meetings with her and long and confidential conversations, to avoid the appearance of being guided by her advice; though in point of fact he was wont every now and then to need and to follow it." In one of their quarrels, during which Livia urged him to appoint a man recently made a citizen to the office of juror, Tiberius conceded petulantly, declaring "that he would do it only on the condition that she would allow an entry to be made in the official lists that it was forced upon him by his mother."[43]

Tiberius invoked the prejudice against women in public roles to justify his refusal to allow the senate to name Livia as Parent of her Country, insisting that it was not proper for a woman to receive conspicuous public honors. Tiberius also invoked the public-versus-private gender ideology to accuse Livia of unfeminine behavior when she took command over a group of soldiers after a fire broke out in the temple of Vesta. Public speaking and the exercise of military authority were considered exclusively male activities in the polis. It is interesting that Suetonius himself does not criticize Livia for this. Different interpretations existed about where the boundaries between public and private domains actually ran. Nevertheless a woman's political power was always assailable, since people could always credibly object that it was improper for women to exercise such power.

Philo, the Jewish philosopher and theologian, struggled to reconcile the social reality of Livia's political power with the sexual code that excluded women from public life. She was an important patron of the Jewish community, and Philo wanted to persuade the emperor Gaius to follow her policy. He drew on the theological tradition that reason, or the rational nature, was the image of the divine in man. Reason was that mental faculty that through abstraction could begin with things in the visible world, perceived by sense, and arrive at unchanging principles and concepts. Philo, like his contemporaries, believed that this capability belonged to men alone and that it was this capability to reason that formed the basis for sound political judgments. Philo's dilemma was that he wished to appeal to Livia's sound political judgment in protecting Jewish institutions in her role as patron of the Jewish people. Because she had the intrinsically domestic nature of a woman, the value of her judgment might have been dubious. Hence to attribute sound judgment to her he had to say that she possessed a virile mind, a masculine mind that she acquired through her aristocratic training. Therefore her political judgments were as valid as the judgments of any male.

Here is how he puzzled out Livia's political acumen:

What made her to do this, as there was no image [of God = rational nature] there? For the judgements of women as a rule are weaker and do not apprehend any mental conception apart from what their senses perceive. But she excelled all her sex in this as in everything else, for the purity of the training that she received, supplementing nature and practice, gave virility to her reasoning power, which gained such clearness of vision that it apprehended the things of mind better than the things of sense and held the latter to be shadows of the former.[44]

Thus Livia—and presumably any woman who exhibited astute political judgment—succeeded by transcending her female nature. Regarding a woman who functioned well in the political sphere as a man was a way of resolving the tensions between the experience of women's actual power and the conviction that women had no aptitude for or role in public life. Nearly two thousand years later, some people continue to have trouble reconciling themselves to female competence: "Some of our best men are women" says one ad slogan.

NOTES

1. Optatus 1.16. Partaking of the eucharistic elements was closely associated with the communion of the saints. Lucilla's reverence for this martyr's bone was part of the convergence of the eucharist and the cult of the saints. A eucharistic meal was often celebrated at the grave of the martyrs, and eventually the bones of the saints were placed under the altar on which the eucharistic meal was set.

2. W. H. C. Frend, *Martyrdom and Persecution in the Early Church* (Oxford: Basil Blackwell, 1965), 499–505.

3. Nearly all the surviving sources for the history of the Donatist church were written by its opponents. One of the few sources by a Donatist refers to Lucilla as *"clarissima femina,"* illustrious woman, which indicated both her social standing and her character. She is credited with convening the African bishops and making Marjorinus bishop. Through these events the schism was created and the Donatist church was formed. See Augustine, *Contra Crescens* III.32–33.

4. S. N. Eisenstadt and L. Roniger, *Patrons, Clients, and Friends* (Cambridge, U.K.: Cambridge Univ. Press, 1984), 52–53.

5. John H. Elliott, "Patronage and Clientism in Early Christian Society," *Forum* 3,4 (December 1987): 40–41.

6. This is as true of the ancient historians of Donatism as it is of contemporary scholars. Optatus calls her *factiosa* (powerful or power-hungry), Augustine calls her *factiosissima* and *pecuniosissima* (terribly ambitious and terribly rich). *The Dictionary of Christian Biography* and the *Encyclopedia of Early Christianity* present the same portrait of Lucilla.

7. Erich Gruen called attention to the importance of the Julio-Claudian women for women's history at the 1984 meeting of the American Classics Society in Washington, DC.

8. Suetonius *Lives of the Caesars* II.40.

9. Dio *Roman History* LVII.

10. Dio *Roman History* LVIII.2.

11. Joyce Reynolds, "Aphrodisias and Rome," *Journal of Roman Studies Monographs*, no. 1 (1982): 105–6.

12. Philo *Embassy to Gaius*, 319.

13. Josephus *Jewish Wars* 2:167; 2:98; K. C. Hanson in "Mediterranean Kinship: The Herodians, Part 3: Economics," *Biblical Theology Bulletin* 20 (1990): 10–21, notes that the standard textbooks delete Salome from the list of rulers who succeeded Herod (Koester, 394–95; Perrin and Duling, 19; and Kee, 40). Josephus *Jewish Antiquities* 17:321; 18:31.

Salome II also inherited from Herod territories over which she subsequently ruled. The *toparchia* that she governed consisted of the cities of Jamnia, Azotes, and Phasaelis. She bore the title *despotes* (ruler).

14. Josephus *Jewish Antiquities* 17:190; 18:31.

15. Tacitus *Annals* III.15.

16. Dio *Roman History* LV.21.

17. Seneca *On Mercy* 1.9.6.

18. Dio *Roman History* LV.22. Archelaus, king of Cappadocia, mistakenly trusted the patronage and protection of Livia and answered a dangerous summons to Rome by the emperor Tiberius, whom he rightly judged to be a political enemy. Livia did not (or was not able to) provide protection; he was arrested, charged, and in the course of these events committed suicide.

19. Suetonius *Lives of the Caesars* II.7.5.

20. Dio *Roman History* LVII.12.

21. Athanasius calls her a *proeste* of Paul, a patron. *History of the Arians,* 71. Both Athanasius and Theodoret note that Zenobia was Jewish. See Eusebius, *Ecclesiastical History,* VII.27-31, for an indignant account of Paul's teaching and way of life.

22. See Fergus Millar, "Paul of Samosata, Zenobia and Aurelian: The Church, Local Culture and Political Allegiance in Third Century Syria," *Journal of Roman Studies* 61 (1971): 1-51, for a discussion of this appointment. Bishops throughout the Mediterranean benefited from this kind of patronage and many held the office of procurator simultaneously with their office of bishop. See Theodor Klauser, *Jahrbuch fuer Antike und Christentum* 14 (1971), 140-49.

23. *Vita Cypriani* XCV.14-17; this description of Cyprian's patronage is taken from Job 29:12-16.

24. *Vita Cypriani* X.23, 21.

25. *Vita Cypriani* X.XCV.7-12.

26. Eusebius *Church History* VI.2.14.

27. Eusebius *Church History* VI.2.14.

28. F. X. Murphy, "Melania the Elder: A Biographical Note," *Traditio* 5 (1947): 59–77.

29. Elizabeth Clark, *Jerome, Chrysostom and Friends* (New York: Edwin Mellen Press, 1979), 107–57.

30. Elizabeth Clark, *The Life of Melania the Younger* (New York: Edwin Mellen Press, 1984).

31. Frederick W. Danker, *Benefactor: Epigraphic Study of a Graeco-Roman and New Testament Semantic Field* (St. Louis: Clayton Publishing House, 1982), 317–66; A. R. Hands, *Charities and Social Aid in Greece and Rome* (London: Thames and Hudson, 1968), 49–61.

32. Danker, *Benefactor*, 436–86.

33. Ross Kraemer, *Maenads, Martyrs, Matrons, and Mystics* (Minneapolis: Fortress Press, 1988), 217.

34. Dio XLIX.38.

35. Dio LVI.46.

36. Dio LVII.12.

37. Tacitus *Annals* I.14.

38. Riet van Bremen, "Women and Wealth," in *Images of Women in Antiquity,* ed. Averil Cameron and Amlie Kuhrt (Detroit: Wayne State Univ. Press, 1983), 223.

39. Van Bremen, 223.

40. Van Bremen, 235.

41. Van Bremen, 223.

42. Dio LVII.12.

43. Suetonius *Lives of the Caesars* III.50–51.

44. Philo *Embassy to Gaius* 320, trans. F. N. Colson. Loeb ed. vol. 10 (Cambridge: Harvard Univ. Press, 1962).

*Empress Theodora and her Ladies in Waiting.*
Theodora, in an official pose and royal costume,
bears a golden chalice in her role as benefactor
for the church of San Vitale. Mosaic detail.
San Vitale, Ravenna. (Alinari/Art Resource, NY.)

# 4
# Public Women, Private Virtues

Christian writers who attacked women's authority evoked the frightening image of the female leader as a disreputable woman who was probably also promiscuous. John the Seer wrote to the church in Thyatira in opposition to one of their woman leaders:

> Yet I have this against you: you tolerate that Jezebel, the woman who claims to be a prophetess, who by her teaching lures my servants into fornication and into eating food sacrificed to idols. I have given her time to repent, but she refuses to repent of her

fornication. So I will throw her on a bed of pain, and her lovers into terrible suffering, unless they forswear what she is doing; and her children I will strike dead. (Rev. 2:20–23, NEB)

The heresy fighter Epiphanius reduced his theological controversy with some gnostic Christians to a seduction scene:

I happened on this heresy myself, beloved, and was actually taught these things in person, out of the mouths of practising gnostics. Not only did women under this delusion offer me this line of talk, and divulge this sort of thing to me. With impudent boldness, moreover, they tried to seduce me themselves . . . because they wanted me in my youth.[1]

During a theological controversy in Alexandria, Bishop Alexander protested that his opponents "bring lawsuits through the accusations of disorderly little women whom they have deceived and disparage Christianity when the younger women among them run around dishonorably in every public place."[2] He neglected to mention that these dishonorable women were in fact consecrated virgins who were publicly supporting his theological opponent.

Ancient writers were able to conjure up this image by invoking a set of ethical standards that distinguished between good women and bad women: Good women were chaste and private, while bad women were unchaste and public. The first-century Jewish philosopher Philo, after explaining that household management was the domain of women, continued:

A woman, then, should not be a busybody, meddling with matters outside her household concerns, but should seek a life of seclusion. She should not show herself off like a vagrant in the streets before the eyes of other men, except when she has to go to the temple, and even then she should take pains to go, not when the market is full, but when most people have gone home, and so like a freeborn lady worthy of the name, with everything quiet around her, make her oblations and offer her prayers to avert the evil and gain the good.[3]

The tone of these speeches is biting. These rhetoricians are trained to strike the right emotional chords: fear, outrage, indignity, shame. Highly colored comments like these signal a major social conflict, a conflict over values, mores, and the fundamental ordering of society itself. A woman whose social standing, resources, skills, and abilities enabled her to assume a leadership role could always be attacked for abandoning women's social space, the household, and for forsaking the womanly virtue of chastity, which meant keeping her sexual presence far from the public eye. The ancient Roman gender code—public roles were for men and the domestic sphere was for women—granted legitimacy for this strident rhetoric.

Many Christian intellectuals embraced this public-versus-private gender ideology. In the late 300s John Chrysostom explained:

Our life is customarily organized into two spheres: public affairs and private matters. . . . To woman is assigned the presidency of the household; to man, all the business of the state, the marketplace, the administration of justice, government, the military, and all other such enterprises. . . . [A woman] cannot express her opinion in a legislative assembly, but she can express it at home.[4]

Origen of Alexandria, who ironically, as noted in chapter 3, would never have become a theologian without the sponsorship of a woman patron, appealed to this gender system in his polemic against the

Montanist woman prophets. He commented on 1 Cor. 14:34-35,

In short let a woman learn from the man who is her own, taking "man" in its generic sense, as the counterpart of woman. For it is improper for a woman to speak in an assembly, no matter what she says, even if she says admirable things or even saintly things; that is of little consequence since they come from the mouth of a woman. A woman speaking in an assembly—clearly this abuse is denounced as improper, an abuse for which the entire assembly is responsible.[5]

The Christian apologist Tertullian (died ca. 220) insisted with some strindency, "It is not permitted for a woman to speak in church, but neither is it permitted her to teach, nor to baptize, nor to offer, nor to claim for herself any manly function, least of all a public office."[6]

Modern church scholars have invariably assumed that the condemnation of women's leadership by these ancient Christian writers was based on theological arguments. When Tertullian and his ilk bar women from teaching and baptizing, scholars have tended to see divine, and therefore unassailable, justification behind it. But such interpretations are guilty of a serious oversight: They fail to take into account the enormous extent to which the Christian church allowed Greco-Roman social dogma to pervade its teachings—in this case, the secular circumscriptions on women's activities. They have also somehow missed an important implication in these ancient denunciations: that women actually held significant positions of leadership in the churches. Otherwise, there would have been no need for these fulminations, which convey the unmistakable tone of threatened authority.

As we have seen already, there is considerable evidence, literary and epigraphic, for women's leadership in this period, in both the *polis* and the church. Pliny, the Roman governor of Bythinia (ca. 110), mentions two slave women (*ancillae*) who were ministers (*ministrae*) of a Christian community in Bythinia.[7] Cyprian (third century) mentions a woman presbyter in Cappadocia.[8] A fourth-century Egyptian papyrus refers to a Christian woman, named Kyria, as a teacher (*didaskalos*).[9] The era and its institutions were virtually saturated by contradictions between the codes that purported to limit women's roles and the obvious fact of women's influence in every sector, including the public.

## GENDERED VIRTUES

Parallel to the notion of the separate spheres was the Greco-Roman system of gendered virtues. Men were assigned the virtues of courage, justice, and self-mastery. These were public virtues, essential for participation in the life of the community. Women were assigned the virtues of chastity, silence, and obedience.

The correlation between male virtues and the male gender role can be seen by tracing the historical development from the noble warrior of archaic Greece to the citizen of the Greek polis. The polis was not the original setting for the Greek notion of *aretē*, "virtue." *Aretē* meant excellence, although the nature of this excellence could vary. The term developed its first set of meanings among the warrior aristocracy of the archaic period.[10] During this period the principle meanings of *aretē* were strength, skill, and valor in war. Arete was manifest in heroic deeds and victory in battle and was rewarded with honor and praise. Such arete secured that imperishable fame so coveted by Greek warriors. This arete, then, was indissolubly linked with the male gender and the aristocratic social class.[11]

In the democratic polis the heroic ideals of ambition for honor clashed with the need to limit the individualism and self-assertion of warrior arete within the city-state. *Sophrosynē*, which means control of the appetites and passions, self-knowledge, and self-restraint, thus came to be the principal form of arete associated with the city-state.[12] The transformation of *sophrosynē* into a political virtue was complete by the fourth century B.C.E., where we read that the *sophron* (the man with a balanced disposition) was a good citizen who hated oligarchy and was essentially generous with his wealth in the form of "liturgies" (financial services to the city).[13] The virtue of *andreia*, "courage" (which referred to physical bravery in its early Greek context), was also adapted to the context of the polis and came to mean simply "manliness" (strength, endurance).

Justice was also a form of arete, or virtue, associated specifically with the city-state. The Sophists describe it as a political arete. Plato recounted the story of how the gift of the virtue of justice was distributed in his retelling of the Prometheus myth. When the human race was on the verge of extinction due to terrible internecine strife, Zeus sent Hermes to the human race with the gift of virtue. Unlike the gifts of the crafts, which were not given to everyone in equal proportion, the gift of justice was to be given to all men. The myth makes it clear that the social function of the virtue of justice is the harmonious life of the polis. If all men possess the virtue of justice, harmony will reign in the polis.[14]

Male virtues, then, had both a social function and a personal function. Courage, justice, and temperance were defined as civic virtues because they enhanced civic life.[15] This was their social function. At the same time these virtues were the measure by which a man attained personal excellence within the polis. As the early arete of the warrior nobility of Homeric times was the basis for the praise that guaranteed imperishable fame, so also the civic virtues gained a member of the aristocracy public recognition and a place in the collective memory.

The virtues of courage, justice, and temperance lay at the intersection of the public life and the quest for honor. The public political sphere of the male citizen was the stage on which he competed for honor. If his claim to honor was to be acknowledged, then the citizens would have to acclaim his public virtues of courage, justice, and self-control.

Both Greeks and Romans believed that the passion for honor was rooted in a natural desire for precedence associated with male nature. The quest for precedence in a hierarchically arranged society involves both status and authority. Status was acquired through competition for honor, through the public recognition of one's virtue. Authority was exercised in household relations to wife, slaves, and children.

Women, by contrast, gained honor by guarding their sexual purity. While honor, that is, competition for precedence, was an appropriate expression of male nature, shame, that is, discretion and timidity, were the appropriate and natural expressions of female nature. Political authority and public life were associated with men's exercise of sexual freedom; female dependence and vulnerability implied that her sexuality had to be protected and guarded. Thus the restriction of woman's space to the household was a mechanism for protecting her sexuality and preserving her shame.

It is interesting to note that the social function of the female virtues of chastity, silence, and obedience conflicted with the authority implied by women's economic and managerial functions within the household.

## WOMEN'S VIRTUES: CHASTITY, SILENCE, AND OBEDIENCE

Just as the male virtues of courage, justice, and self-control are expressions of male honor, the female virtues of silence, chastity, and obedience are the signs by which society holds a woman accountable for preserving female shame.

Because Greek intellectuals and moralists were anxious to underscore the universality of the virtues, they applied the Greek terms for the virtues of courage, justice, and temperance to men and women alike. Nevertheless the difference in gender roles and the asymmetry between male and female virtues made this an awkward fit, requiring some exegetical tricks to keep the same words and get them to mean different things when applied to men or women. The writer of a treatise on the female virtue of chastity explained:

Now some people think that it is not appropriate for a woman to be a philosopher, just as a woman should not be a cavalry officer or a politician. I agree that *men* should be generals and city officials and politicians and *women* should keep house and stay inside and receive and take care of their husbands. But I believe that courage, justice and intelligence are qualities that men and women have in common. Courage and intelligence are more appropriately male qualities because of the strength of men's bodies and the power of their minds. Chastity is more appropriately female.[16]

The Greeks used the same word, *sophrosynē* (self-control), for the female virtue of chastity and the male virtue of temperance.

Male *sophrosynē* was a discipline of the mind; female *sophrosynē* was a way of life.

Chastity was first of all a matter of sexual fidelity. Many epitaphs extolling the virtue of wives praise them for their chastity.[17] The sentiment behind the value placed on sexual fidelity is poignantly expressed in an epitaph to Lady Pantheia: "Lady Pantheia, hail from your husband. My grief for your sorrowful death is everlasting. For never did Hera, Lady of Marriage, look on a wife who was like you for beauty and sober discretion. It was you who bore me children entirely like myself."[18] Lady Pantheia's sexual fidelity is delicately signaled by the phrase "who bore me children entirely like myself." The chastity of a wife guaranteed that her children belonged to her husband.

Chastity had other dimensions as well. It entailed modesty in dress and seclusion in the private sphere. According to a philosophical treatise on chastity, this virtue regulated a woman's movement about the city; if she wished to go out, she could do so only at midday and then only in the company of a single female servant. She could go out during the day to attend a public religious festival, but chastity precluded her from participating in the mystery religions that were celebrated in private homes because these "forms of worship encouraged drunkenness and ecstasy."[19] The virtue of chastity reinforces the value placed on women's seclusion in the private sphere.

Silence was another prominent virtue praised in women. Aristotle, appealing to the wisdom of the poets, insisted that silence was *the* distinctively female virtue. "All classes must be deemed to have special attributes; as the poet says of women, 'Silence is a woman's glory,' but this is not equally the glory of men."[20] An epitaph for a freedwoman, Allia Potestas, praises her with the words

"She spoke little and was never rebuked (for speaking at the wrong time)."[21]

Because significant speech was public speech, and public speech had its place in the polis, public speaking became a male prerogative and a male tool of power. While heroic valor in battle brought status and power to the Greek male in the archaic period, in the classical city-state public speaking was the source of political power. According to Jean Pierre Vernant, "The system of the *polis* implied first of all, the extraordinary prominence of speech over all other instruments of power. Speech became the political tool, par excellence, the key to all authority in the state, the means of commanding and dominating others."[22] Significant speech became a public event and a mode for exercising political power.

The virtue of silence for women created another protective barrier against women's intrusion in the public sphere. Women's speech, because it was private speech, was trivialized and demeaned. The New Testament letter to Timothy considers women's speech in a similar vein. "Besides that they learn to be idlers, gadding about from house to house, not only idlers, but gossips and busybodies, saying what they should not" (1 Tim. 5:12–13). In a misogynist treatise *On the Female Mind,* Semonides characterized types of wives as animals. "Another he made from a bitch, own daughter of her mother, who wants to hear everything and know everything. She peers everywhere and strays everywhere, always yapping, even if she sees no human being."[23] Since silence counted as a virtue for women, women's speech could easily be disparaged and criticized. Paul instructed women to keep silent in the assembly. Origen discredited a woman's public speech even if it conveyed a spiritual truth.

Even when they went by the same name, Greco-Roman virtues were applied to each gender differently. There was one set of virtues for citizen males and another for private females. Aristotle concluded, "It is manifest that all the persons mentioned have a moral virtue of their own and that the temperance of a woman and that of a man are not the same, nor their courage and justice, as Socrates thought, but the one is courage of command, and the other that of obedience and the case is similar with the other virtues."[24]

Obedience as a virtue expressed the value placed on subordination in social relations. As a virtue for women it expressed primarily their subordinate position in relation to their husbands. According to Plutarch, if women subordinate themselves to their husbands, "they are commended, but if they want to have control, they cut a sorrier figure than the subjects of their control. And control ought to be exercised by the man over the woman, not as the owner has control of a piece of property, but as the soul controls the body."[25]

The New Testament letters echo the theme of a wife's obedience found in the Greco-Roman household codes.[26] "Let wives be submissive [*upostasthe*] as is appropriate in the Lord" (Col. 38:18). "Let wives be submissive to their own husbands as to the Lord" (Eph. 5:20). "Likewise, wives be submissive to your own husbands as to the Lord" (1 Pet. 3:1).

## DIFFUSING THE TENSIONS
## OF "PRIVATE" WOMEN IN PUBLIC ROLES

This convergence of the public-versus-private ideology and notions about male and female virtues was rich with rhetorical possibilities. The public woman was a sexual woman. Her public presence meant that her sexuality was no longer under the control of her husband. Greek and Roman males, who projected onto women their anxiety about keeping their libido under control, believed that the "animality" of women would disturb the rational process of the public sphere. Fourth-century Christian polemicists against heresy exploited this notion that the public woman was a sexual woman. Women leaders of movements labeled heretical (the Gnostics, the Montanists, and the Arians) were public women and by implication sexually promiscuous. Epiphanius, as quoted at the beginning of this chapter, triumphantly explained that gnostic women tried to convert him by seducing him.

Although male rhetoricians could use these social codes to discredit individual women or groups of women in public roles, as we shall see in chapter 5, society in general ameliorated the tension created by the clash between these codes and women's actual leadership by firmly wedding the private virtues to the public woman. Whenever a woman's public roles were affirmed, her private virtues were also praised, so that although she held public roles, she excelled as a model of private virtues. An epitaph from 300 C.E. for Aurelia Leite lists her public honors and praises her private virtues:

> To the most renowned and in all respects excellent Aurelia Leite, daughter of Theodotus, wife of the foremost man in the city Marcus Aurelius Faustus, hereditary high priest for life of the cult of Diocletian and his co-ruler, priest of Demeter and gymnasiarch. She was gymnasiarch of the gymnasium which she repaired and renewed when it had been delapidated for many years. The glorious city of the Parians, her native city, in return for her many benefactions, receiving honor rather

than giving it, in accordance with many decrees, has set up a marble statue of her. She loved wisdom, her husband, her children, her native city: this woman with her wisdom, best of mothers, his wife Leite, renowned Faustus glorifies.[27]

Aurelia Leite was a public woman; she held the office of gymnasiarch; her wealth made her a powerful force in city politics. Her public presence in the city was recorded for posterity when the city erected a statue of her in its most public place. A public name remembered by generations to come was a male form of honor and was eagerly sought. Thus the inscription that honors Aurelia as a public person with unselfconscious irony praises her as a private woman, as a wife and mother.

Lalla, who held the public office of priestess, was similarly praised by the city of Arneae:

> The people of Arneae and vicinity, to Lalla daughter of Timarchus, son of Diotimus their fellow citizen, wife of Diotimus son of Vassus; priestess of the Emperor's cult and gymnasiarch out of her own resources, honored five times, chaste, cultivated, devoted to her husband, and a model of all virtues, surpassing in every respect. She has glorified her ancestors' virtues with the example of her own character. [Erected] in recognition of her virtue and goodwill.[28]

Lalla, a public woman, priestess, and gymnasiarch, who five times received public honors, is praised for her chastity and her devotion to her husband.

Judith Hallet attempts to unravel the paradox of Roman women's public roles and private virtues by investigating the roles of elite Roman women within their family systems.[29] The materfamilias (mother of the family) was revered for her wisdom, moral authority, and judgment. She was a key figure in promoting the political career of her son through her own network of connections, that is, her access to senators and her own political influence.

Similarly some sisters were esteemed by their brothers, publicly honored by them, and sought out for their advice. Servilia was the sister of Cato and a close associate of Julius Caesar and Cicero; she headed the family council when political decisions had to be made, and even told the forceful Cicero when he should and should not speak and asserted that she could see a senatorial resolution reversed and the like.

Sylvia was the wife of Claudius and later of Marc Anthony. She was Anthony's advocate in Rome after the assassination of Caesar and kept him from being declared a public enemy. She was Anthony's representative in Italy and when Octavian went to war with Anthony, Anthony's troops were commanded by Sylvia, together with her brother-in-law.[30]

Hallet finds that Roman women's power in public life was related to their being wives, sisters, and daughters of Rome's great families.[31] She concludes that women exercised influence in public affairs insofar as their central position in the family gave them power and influence largely through male family members who were active in public life. Since Roman political power was entrusted only to aristocratic families, women in those select few families could be very active in politics. In the politics of the city of Rome, the public and private domains were enmeshed. The tensions between the reality of women's leadership and the public-versus-private gender ideology were mitigated by the fact that the boundaries themselves were often blurred.

In the Greek cities of the Roman Empire, the same theoretical separation of public and private domains prevailed. Nevertheless

Greek women also held public office and participated in the political life of their cities. Wealthy women financed public works and undertook civic responsibilities that often translated into appointments to public office, and hence into political power. Funerary inscriptions list women's offices, and the many statues of women in public marketplaces testify to public gratitude toward the women who made significant contributions to the polis. In examining the political roles of aristocratic women in the Greek cities, Riet van Bremen speaks of the ambiguity between

> the ideology and mentality regarding women and the prominent public role wealthy women could be seen playing in their cities. . . . In seeming contradiction to the public activities and independent behavior of these women, the most frequent epithets used for women are to be found in exactly the traditional feminine areas of modesty, loving dedication to husband and family, piety, and decency.[32]

She proposes that the tensions between a Greek woman's public roles and her society's preference for private virtues were ameliorated by women's civic philanthropy. In the system of benefactions, moreover, the boundaries between public and private spheres became blended, for the relationship of the female benefactor to the polis was often defined in family terms. Thus women who assumed public office on the basis of their philanthropy could be praised for private virtues.

While male polemicists might exploit the public-versus-private gender ideology and women leaders might circumvent it, the society as a whole was still faced with the dilemma of real women holding public offices and a public-versus-private ideology that made public political life the exclusive domain of men.

Christian communities must also contend with this paradox. There the tension between the public-versus-private gender ideology and women's authority was diffused by the perception that these were institutions of the private sphere. This is not to say that the early Christian house churches are to be equated with households; the membership of a house church included persons not in residence in the household, nor were the relationships within the Christian community initially modeled on the hierarchical relationships of the patriarchal household.[33] The Christian house churches existed—along with the various forms of the Greco-Roman voluntary associations and mystery cults—in that "interstitial space" in which elements of the private and public spheres were mingled. However, the private sphere not only provided the physical location but also shaped many aspects of the social organization and functions of the early Christian house churches.[34]

The earliest Christians conceived of themselves explicitly as an alternative family or household. The Gospels portray the bonds among the followers of Jesus as familial, superseding even biological bonds. The Christian communities of the apostolic period designated themselves a "household church" (*hē kat' oikon ekklēsia*, literally "coming together at home"; 1 Cor. 16:19; Philem. 2; Col. 4:15). Christians addressed one another as brother and sister, although, significantly, the term *father* was reserved for God. They were "slaves" to one another, although, again, only God was "master" or "mistress." The seriousness of this familial self-understanding can be seen in their experiments with communal property, signifying the solidarity of the household. The preservation of property within a bloodline was disavowed, and the creation of a new family structure was affirmed in the practice of holding properties in common and in the collective responsibility assumed for the poor, the sick, and the widowed.

Not only their "familial" relationships but also their forms of worship identified the Christians with the household. After the Roman army's destruction of the Jerusalem temple in 70 C.E. and the expulsion of Jewish Christians from synagogues, Christian worship evolved in part from Jewish family worship. The structure of the Eucharist, with the centrality of the Sabbath meal, points to the origin of Christian worship within the private sphere of the household.[35]

Up until the middle of the third century, early Christian worship took place in the homes of prosperous householders. Architectural evidence suggests that after the middle of the third century Christian communities were able to buy private houses and adapt them for worship through minor remodeling.[36] The wealth and size of the congregation at Rome would suggest that the transition from homes to buildings exclusively used for worship took place sooner in that city.[37] While the earlier "house congregations" were clearly located in the private sphere, these remodeled "house churches" represented a transitional stage on the way to Christian worship taking place in the public sphere. But not until the erection of basilicas in the fourth century did architectural space clearly define Christian worship as public.[38]

The private associations so popular in Greco-Roman society also provided models for leadership roles for the early Christian churches. Private associations were democratically organized clubs with an elected president, scribe, treasurer, and sergeant at arms. Dues were collected to finance the banquet meal around which the club organized its activities. The early Christian churches were like private associations in the centrality of the banquet meal and in the nonpublic, nonpolitical character of the organization.[39] The title of president of these associations was *prostatis;* and we find women leaders in the early Christian church also carrying this title. Phoebe of Cenchreae was called *prostatis.*[40]

Early Christianity's distinctly nonpublic nature was in fact the cause of some concern. Pagan critics "saw in Christianity a privatizing of religion. . . . Critics sensed that Christianity was loosening the ties that bound religion to the social and political world."[41] Neither the populace nor Roman officialdom recognized in Christianity a religion that had as its aim the welfare of the empire. In response, the apologists of the second century argued that Christian rites were indeed devoted to securing the public welfare.

In the end, it was not only Christianity's self-perception as an alternative family but also the capriciousness of popular feeling and the uncertainties of the political climate that conspired to keep Christianity within the private sphere for nearly two centuries. Had Christianity, like Judaism, gained the status of a *religio licita,* it might have emerged sooner into the public sphere. But its lack of a legal status kept Christianity vulnerable to persecution. By remaining in the private sphere and maintaining relative secrecy about membership and meeting places, it was possible to keep the persecutions of the first two centuries from sweeping them away entirely. In this way they also managed to maintain the acceptability of women leaders in the churches.

NOTES

1. Epiphanius *Panarion* 37.2, translations from Virginia Burrus, "Demythologizing the 'Heretical Woman'? An Investigation of Sym-

bolic Language in the Texts of Alexander, Athanasius, Epiphanius and Jerome," unpublished paper.

2. *Ep. Alexander* 1.

3. Philo *The Special Laws* 3.169ff.

4. John Chrysostom *The Kind of Women Who Ought to Be Taken as Wives*, 4, trans. Elizabeth A. Clark, in *Women in the Early Church* (Wilmington: Michael Glazier, 1983).

5. Origen "Fragments on 1 Corinthians 74," *Journal of Theological Studies* 10 (1959): 41–42.

6. Tertullian *On the Veiling of Virgins* 9.1.

7. Pliny *Ep.* 96. The range of meanings for the word *minister* range from associate or assistant in a religious office to a household servant. It is the Latin equivalent to the term New Testament writers use for the leader of a congregation.

8. Cyprian *Epistle* 75.10.5.

9. ZPE 18 (1975), 317–23.

10. *Aretē* could be possessed only by the warrior nobility. The term itself derives from *aristos*, meaning "superior." The collective plural, *aristoi*, designated the nobility as a social class.

11. J. Kautsky, *The Politics of Aristocratic Empires* (Chapel Hill: Univ. of North Carolina Press, 1982), 170–77.

12. Werner Jaeger, *Paideiea, The Ideals of Greek Culture* 2d ed. (Oxford, U.K.: Oxford Univ. Press, 1945), 1:3–14.

13. Helen North, *Sophorosune, Self-Knowledge and Self-Restraint in Greek Literature* (Ithaca, NY: Cornell Univ. Press, 1966), 86–87.

14. North, *Sophrosune*, 32–33; Jean Pierre Vernant, in *The Origins of Greek Thought* (Ithaca, NY: Cornell Univ. Press, 1982), 62–63, locates the origins of the virtue of *sophrosynē* in a military context in the transition from mounted soldiers inspired by the passions of fighting to Hoplites, who must move as a unit and not break rank and were therefore praised for the virtue of *sophrosynē*.

15. Michel Foucault, *The Use of Pleasure* (New York: Random House, 1986), 82–84; Vincent Wimbush, "Self-Restraint in the Exercise of Male Dominance: The Origins of a Type of Ascetic Piety in Greco-Roman Antiquity," paper delivered at Asceticism Seminar, Duxbury, MA, 1987.

16. Neopythagorean "Treatise on Chastity," in M. R. Lefkowitz and M. B. Fant, *Women's Life in Greece and Rome* (Baltimore: John Hopkins Univ. Press, 1982), 104.

17. It is only in epitaphs dedicated to women that we find women praised for their effective household management and for their economic skills in the production of wool, but even here the virtue of chastity predominates.

18. R. Lattimore, *Themes in Greek and Latin Epitaphs* (Urbana: Univ. of Illinois Press, 1962), 276.

19. Neopythagorean "Treatise on Chastity," in Lefkowitz and Fant, *Women's Life,* 104.

20. Aristotle *Politics* 1.13.

21. Lattimore, *Themes in Greek and Latin Epitaphs,* 298.

22. Vernant, *The Origins of Greek Thought,* 49.

23. Lefkowitz and Fant, *Women's Life,* 14.

24. Aristotle *On Politics* 1.13; I.9.8.

25. Plutarch *Advice to Bride and Groom* 33.

26. David Balch, "Let Wives Be Submissive . . . The Origin and Form of the Apologetic Function of the Household Duty Code in I Peter," Yale. diss. 1974.

27. Lefkowitz and Fant, *Women's Life,* 158–59.

28. Lefkowitz and Fant, *Women's Life,* 157.

29. Judy P. Hallet, *Fathers and Daughters in Roman Society* (Princeton: Princeton Univ. Press, 1984), 6.

30. J. P. D. Balsdon, *Roman Women* (New York: Harper & Row, 1962), 49–50.

31. Hallet, *Fathers and Daughters,* 31.

32. See Riet van Bremen, "Women and Wealth," in *Images of Women in Antiquity*, ed. A. Cameron and A. Kuhrt (Detroit: Wayne State Univ. Press, 1983), 234.

33. Elisabeth Schüssler Fiorenza, *In Memory of Her: A Feminist Reconstruction of Christian Origins* (New York: Crossroad, 1983), 175–84, strongly emphasizes the distinction between egalitarian community structures of the early house churches and the hierarchic structures of the patriarchal household; while in basic agreement with her on this point, I would argue that the household functioned in many ways as a model for the house church.

34. The close connection of the early Christian church with the private sphere of the household has been noted by a number of scholars. See especially Floyd V. Filson, "The Significance of the Early House Churches," *Journal of Biblical Literature* 58 (1939): 105–12; Raymond E. Brown, "New Testament Background for the Concept of Local Church," *Catholic Theological Society of America Proceedings* 36 (1981): 1–14; Abraham J. Malherbe, "House Churches and Their Problems," *Social Aspects of Early Christianity*, 2d ed. (Philadelphia: Fortress Press, 1983), 60–91; Hans-Josef Klauck, "Die Hausgemeinde als Lebensform im Urchristentum," *Münchner Theologische Zeitschrift* 32 (1981): 1–15; and Klauck, *Hausgemeinde und Hauskirche im frühen Christentum* (Stuttgart: Katholisches Bibelwerk, 1981); Rafael Aguirre, "La Casa como estructura base del cristianismo primitivo; las iglesias domesticas," *Estudios Eclesiasticos* 59 (1984): 27–51; Ernst Dassmann, "Hausgemeinde und Bischofsamt," in *Vivarium. Festschrift Theodor Klauser zum 90. Geburtstag* (Münster in Westfalen: Aschendorffsche, 1984), 82–97.

35. See J. P. Audet, "Literary Forms and Content of a Normal Eucharistia in the First Century," *Studia Evangelica, Texte und Untersuchungen* 73 (1959): 643–62. Modifications and refinements of his theory of the origins of the eucharistic prayers in Jewish table blessings appear in Thomas J. Talley, "From Berakah to Eucharistia: A Reopening Question," *Worship* 50 (1976): 115–37; and Talley, "The Literary Structure of the Eucharistic Prayer," *Worship* 58 (1984): 404–20.

36. See Carl H. Kraeling, *The Christian Building at Dura-Europas* (Locust Valley, NY: J. J. Augustin, 1967); and Gorbo Virgilio, *The House of St. Peter at Capharnum, Publications of the Studium Franciscanum, Collectio minor, No. 5* (Jerusalem: Franciscan Printing House, 1969).

37. See Klaus Gamber, *Domus ecclesiae* (Regensburg: Friedrich Pustet, 1968).

38. See Sir Thomas Graham Jackson, *Byzantine and Romanesque Architecture* (1920; reprint, New York: Hacker Art Books, 1975), 17ff.; and H. Kahler, *Die Frühkirche, Kult and Kultraum* (Berlin, 1972), 54ff.

39. L. Wm. Countryman, "Patrons and Officers in Club and Church," SBL Seminar Papers, no. 11 (Missoula, MT: Scholars Press, 1977), 135–41.

40. Rom. 16:1. Fiorenza, *In Memory of Her*, 181.

41. Robert L. Wilken, *The Christians as the Romans Saw Them* (New Haven, CT, and London: Yale Univ. Press, 1984), 202.

*Lucretia* was much admired by Latin writers for
defending her reputation for modesty and shame
at the price of her life. Marcantonio Raimondi,
after Raphael. Engraving, 212 x 130 mm. Harvey
D. Parker Collection, courtesy of Museum of
Fine Arts, Boston.

# 5

# A Woman's Honor Is Her Shame

■ ■ ■ ■

When the ire of a Roman man had been aroused by some woman's actions, he would rise to full rhetorical height and declare the actions "dishonorable" and her "shameless." Cicero, the popular lawyer for the Roman aristocracy, used this rhetorical weapon against women with cruel success. Cicero sought to blunt the political influence of a certain Roman matron in order to undermine her role in the prosecution of a case against his client and to pay off a grudge against her brother.

Our whole concern in this case, jurors, is with Clodia, a woman not only noble but also notorious. . . . Woman, what business did you have with Caelius [the defendant], a man scarce out of his teens, a man not your husband? Why were you so friendly with him as to lend him gold? . . . Did you forget that only recently you were the wife of Quintus Metellus, a gentleman of the highest type, a distinguished patriot, who had only to show his face to eclipse almost all other citizens in character, reputation, dignity? Born of a high-ranking family, married into a prominent family, how did it happen that you admitted Caelius to such familiarity? Was he a relative or a friend of your husband? Not at all. What was it then but hot and headstrong passion? If the portraits of us male ancestors meant nothing to you, how could my granddaughter, Quinta Claudia, have failed to inspire you to emulate her domestic virtue and womanly glory? . . . The prosecutors have been lavish with their tales of affairs, amours, adulteries, Baiae [a spa on the bay of Naples], beach picnics, banquets, drinking bouts, songfests, music ensembles, and yachting parties.[1]

A woman's honor was her good reputation, and this had always to be a reputation of chastity.

## HONOR AND SHAME

Honor was equivalent to reputation, "a claim to worth and the social acknowledgement of that worth."[2] Quintus Metellus, Cicero reminded his audience, was a man who possessed honor: He excelled other citizens "in character, reputation, dignity." Shame was concern for reputation, "sensitivity for one's own reputation and sensitivity to the opinion of others."[3] As Cicero painted the life of Clodia, it was her lack of concern for her reputation that made her shameless: "If this person, being widowed, lived loosely, being forward, lived wantonly, being rich, lived extravagantly, being prurient, lived like a harlot, am I to think a man an adulterer if he does not address her exactly like a lady?" In the rhetoric of Cicero, Clodia had lost her honor—the right to be treated as a matron—by her lack of concern for her reputation. Cicero's livid strokes paint a portrait of a shameless woman. As a matter of fact, Clodia's activities were typical for women of her class.

Although both men and women strove to enhance their honor and guard their reputations, they did so according to specific means prescribed for each gender. Maleness itself functioned as a cultural symbol for honor. Male honor was signaled by manliness, courage, authority over family, willingness to defend one's reputation, and refusal to submit to humiliation.[4] A man gained honor through challenging another man's honor successfully or by avenging any loss of honor of his own. A woman, however, demonstrated her honorability by comporting herself with shame, signifying that she understood her sexual vulnerability, and avoiding all appearances of indiscretion. Femaleness functioned as a cultural symbol for shame, and the hymen, the penetrable boundary of the female sexual body, typified women's appropriate sexual exclusiveness. The cultural value of shame prescribed the feminine personality as discreet, shy, restrained, and timid, those qualities deemed necessary to "protect" female sexuality.[5] In this sexual division of moral labor, honor was considered an aspect of male nature expressed in a natural desire for precedence and an aggressive sexuality. Shame, the defining quality of womanhood, was indicated by passivity, subordination, and seclusion in the household.

The value placed on female shame is a common feature of patriarchal societies. When men give women in marriage, or when younger men acquire wives through some form of payment, women's sexuality is treated as a commodity. As a valuable economic good, it must be controlled. Society therefore prescribes virginity for women before marriage and sexual fidelity after marriage, although it leaves male sexuality unregulated in both cases.[6] The social control of women's sexuality produces a "feminine" personality conditioned by dependency.[7] Furthermore for patrilineal inheritance to work, a man had to know that the children his wife bore were his progeny, and only her chastity could guarantee this. Thus male anxiety about paternity led to the identification of shame and chastity as female virtues. In the process of socialization in patriarchal societies, the sexual energies of the libido are "honored" in the raising of little boys, and they are encouraged to develop an active, if not aggressive, sexuality. But these energies must be repressed in little girls, from whom chastity will be required. Their socialization encourages them to develop passive, "feminine" personalities, and their sexuality is surrounded with a sense of shame.[8]

The legend of Lucretia illustrates the complex interplay between male honor and female shame in Mediterranean societies. Lucretia was much admired by Latin writers for defending her reputation for modesty and chastity at the price of her life. Livy begins her story at a drinking party outside Rome. Hotheaded young men were competing with each other for honor, each claiming that his wife was the most virtuous. They agreed to settle the dispute by a visit that would surprise their wives at their evening activities. The unexpected visit discovered the wives of the competitors at a luxurious banquet, "whiling away the time with their young friends." But one, Lucretia, the wife of Collatinus, "though it was late at night, was busily engaged upon her wool." Livy concludes, "The prize of this contest in womanly virtues fell to Lucretia. The victorious husband courteously invited the young princes to his table."[9]

First we note that a woman's chastity—her avoidance of all appearances of sexual indiscretion—gains her a prize in the competition for honor and redounds to her husband's honor as well. Collatinus is designated the victorious husband.

Livy's story continues:

> Sextus Tarquinius was seized with wicked desire to debauch Lucretia by force; not only her beauty, but her proved chastity as well, provoked him. When a few days had gone by, Sextus Tarquinius, without letting Collatinus know, took a single attendant and went to Collatia [a village north of Rome]. Being kindly welcomed, for no one suspected his purpose, he was brought after dinner to a guest-chamber. Burning with passion, he waited until it seemed to him that all about him was secure and everybody fast asleep; then, drawing his sword, he came to the sleeping Lucretia. Holding the woman down with his left hand on her breast, he said "Be still, Lucretia! I am Sextus Tarquinius. My sword is in my hand. Utter a sound, and you die! Then Tarquinius began to declare his love, to plead, to mingle threats with prayers, to bring every resource to bear upon her woman's heart. When he found her obdurate and not to be moved even by fear of death, he went farther and threatened her with disgrace, saying that when she was dead he would kill his slave and leave him naked by her side, that she might be said to have been put to death in adultery with a man of base condition. At this dreadful prospect her resolute modesty was overcome, as if with force, by his victorious lust; and Tarquinius departed, exulting in his conquest of a woman's honor.[10]

Sextus, defeated in his contest of honor with Collatinus, wished to avenge his lost honor by depriving Lucretia of her honor (her chastity) and depriving Collatinus of his (Lucretia's sexual fidelity). Lucretia was ready to sacrifice her life for her honor (her chastity) but was not willing to sacrifice her public honor (her reputation for chastity) for her chastity and so succumbed to Sextus's threat to destroy her reputation. Sextus emerged the victor in this contest for honor because he succeeded in dishonoring both Lucretia and Collatinus.

Lucretia then summoned her father and husband to her and asked them to bring a trusted friend. When they greeted her with the question "Is all well?" she replied, "What can be well with a woman when she has lost her honor?" When she had gained from them a pledge to punish the adulterer, she closed her speech with the words "though I acquit myself of the sin, I do not absolve myself from punishment; not in time to come shall ever unchaste woman live through the example of Lucretia." Then drawing a knife from beneath her robe, she plunged it into her breast.

Lucretia had found a way to redeem her honor and restore her reputation for chastity, but it was at the price of her life.

## CHASTITY AS FEMALE HONOR

In the honor and shame system of values, which persists in cultures around the world today, a woman's publicly demonstrable chastity establishes her social worth. The chastity of female family members also affects the social worth of a kinship group. Thus an entire family is disgraced and suffers dishonor if one female member fails to maintain the value of female chastity.[11] A story from modern Sicily, for instance, tells of a young woman's suicide just before her wedding in order to avoid the local lord's exercise of the "right of the first night" with her. She thereby preserved her family's honor, though at the cost of her life.[12]

The central value of female chastity continues to shape the construction of maleness and femaleness in Mediterranean culture. According to M. Giovannini, in contemporary Sicily "young boys from infancy on were rewarded for aggressive and domineering behavior by laughs, claps and shouts, 'che maschio' (what a man!). In contrast, similar behavior on the part of little girls was ignored or responded to by 'che vergogna' (how shameful!)." While a little girl might be praised for her gentle and obedient behavior, those qualities would elicit ridicule if exhibited by a boy.[13]

In "Seeds of Honor, Fields of Shame," anthropologist Carol Delaney elaborates the connection between femaleness, shame, and sexuality in Mediterranean culture.

> Women, on the contrary, are, by their created nature, already ashamed. The recognition of their constitutional inferiority constitutes the feeling of shame. Shame is an inevitable part of being a female; a woman is honorable if she remains cognizant of this fact and its implications for behavior, and she is shameless if she forgets it. A man's birthright is his honor; he can lose it if he cannot protect the boundaries of his women. At the most reduced level, the boundary of a woman is her hymen. It is reserved for and is the possession of the husband. In breaking it, he possesses the woman. Once [it is] broken, he can come and go as he pleases, as he, but no one else, may enter his fields with ease. If the boundary of what is his has been penetrated or broken by someone else, he is put in the position of a woman and is therefore shamed. Thus male honor is vulnerable through women.[14]

A six-year-old boy in contemporary Sicily expressed these concerns in telling his mother he wanted to have a baby brother because "if we have a sister Carlo [his younger brother] and I will have to make sure that no one calls her *puttana* [whore] or the family will be laughed at. But if the doctor brings us a brother, then we will be able to call everyone else's sister *puttana* when we fight with them."[15]

The whore is an important symbol whose negative stereotype functions to underscore the values associated with female chastity. She represents the woman whose sexuality is uncontrolled. By not belonging to one man, she becomes available to all. Thus her uncontrolled sexuality is perceived as dangerous, corrupting both men and women and threatening the social order itself. Returning to antiquity, we find Philo's scathing denunciation of the whore, the antitype of the woman who preserves her sexual reputation. She is:

the stranger to decency and modesty and temperance and the other virtues. She infects the souls both of men and women with licentiousness. She casts shame upon the undying beauty of the mind and prefers in honor the short-lived comeliness of the body. She flings herself at the disposal of chance comers, and sells her bloom like some ware to be purchased in the market.[16]

The woman who valued her reputation made public demonstration of her concern for modesty. She not only preserved the sanctity of her marriage bed, she also attested to her sexual restraint by her public demeanor. She dressed in white, avoiding the ostentation of color, she eschewed cosmetics—the reddening of the cheeks, the lightening of the complexion, and the accenting of the eyes—and was restrained in the wearing of jewelry. She did not go out in the evening to attend banquets and was always attended by servants when she went to the marketplace during the day.[17]

For women the public-versus-private gender ideology and beliefs about honor and shame converged in the household. The good woman stayed at home. A woman who cared for her reputation, who had a sense of shame, reserved her sexuality for her husband alone. She was discreet, withdrawn from public life, and quiet. The woman who left the boundaries of the household and entered public space was no longer a good woman because she had abandoned female space. A woman who was not retiring, discreet, or silent (the hallmarks of chastity) was naturally regarded as unchaste. The good woman who stayed at home was chaste; the public woman was by definition loose.

## WOMEN'S LEADERSHIP AND THE VIRTUE OF CHASTITY

Women who undertook leadership roles in their communities, like Lydia, Lucilla, and Livia, crossed the boundary into the male domain. In traversing the streets and marketplaces on their errands and in attending communal gatherings outside the household, they were moving about in male space. When they accepted public office, received titles of honor, asserted the status of their birth or family, they were competing for male symbols of honor. This competition was a masculine field.

In those situations where a woman's presence and authority commanded respect, she was manifesting the male virtues of courage, justice, and self-mastery. It was precisely in those moments that she was furthest from demonstrating the female virtues of chastity, silence, and obedience. When a woman spoke in public with public authority, when she contended in a debate, she was exercising male prerogatives. Women's practice of leadership thus came directly into conflict with the entrenched gender ideology of separate domains and distinct male and female virtues. Women who chose to exercise considerable political power, like Hillary Rodham Clinton in our time, consciously adopted the strategy of fusing the public and the private woman. In Rome Livia affirmed her chastity as the pivot of her political power. Dio reports with admiration,

When someone asked how and by what course of action she had obtained such a commanding influence over Augustus, she answered that it was by being scrupulously chaste herself, doing gladly whatever pleased him and not meddling with any of his affairs [the private ones!] and in particular, by pretending neither to hear of nor to notice the favorites that were the objects of his passion.[18]

In this way Livia appealed to her reputation for chastity as a sanction for her public, political role. In another incident she affirmed the power of her chastity in a dramatic and political way. Dio reports that once some naked men (probably athletes) chanced to run into her and were to be put to death as a consequence because they had, in effect, violated her chastity. She saved their lives by saying that to chaste women such men are no whit different than statues.[19]

A similar strategy, this time undertaken by a male, underlies Paul's dispute with the women prophets of Corinth. Their prophetic roles were leadership roles, involving authority, precedence, prestige, and honor. These attributes (associated with maleness) conflicted with women's obligation to symbolize shame, submission to authority, sexual exclusiveness, deference, and passivity. Paul's solution to this tension was to enjoin them to wear head coverings. Paul, early in his diatribe, reveals that the issue is the necessity for women prophets to preserve female shame and avoid shamelessness. He accused women who prophesied without a veil of being shameless (1 Cor. 11:6). Her indiscretion was as shameful as having her head shorn. Paul argued that a woman without a veil had no shame because she was signaling by the absence of the veil that she no longer intended to be sexually exclusive. Paul pressed that point by asserting that women who prophesied without their heads covered were inciting the angels to lust (1 Cor. 11:10; cf. Gen. 6:1).[20]

Furthermore, Paul contended, women prophets would be perceived as refusing their female role of passivity, deference, and submission to authority if they did not wear veils. Wearing veils would make it clear that they recognized the precedence of man over woman and the authority of male over female.

> For a man ought not to cover his head, since he is the image and glory of God; but woman is the glory of man. (For man was not made from woman, but woman from man. Neither was man created for woman, but woman for man.) That is why a woman ought to have a veil on her head, because of the angels. (1 Cor. 11:7–10)

Paul could be comfortable with women's leadership in the Corinthian congregation if the women prophets were willing to signal publicly that they were not breaking with woman's role as the culture's symbol for shame. If Paul were able to "shame" Corinthian prophets into wearing veils, they would then publicly manifest the values of women's subordination to authority, thereby reaffirming the function of femaleness to symbolize shame even though they were exercising authority and precedence.

## WOMEN'S VIRTUES USED AGAINST WOMEN LEADERS

When Christian polemicists began to agitate for the removal of women from leadership roles, they nearly always used the rhetorical strategy of casting these women as transgressors against the private virtues of chastity, silence, and obedience. Women leaders were, in short, without shame.

The *Didascalia,* a third-century manual on church organization, is an especially important document for studying the controversy over women's leadership. The objective of its writer was to consolidate the ministries of disciplining, evangelizing, catechizing, and baptizing in the hands of the bishop. The widely respected ministries of women in the order of widows were an obstacle to that program of centralization.[21]

The widows' involvement in the ministry of church discipline was the first to come under rhetorical attack. A distinctive feature of the Christian community was its moral discipline, and one of the tasks of leadership was to see that it was enforced. By the time of the writing of the *Didascalia,* a set of disciplinary procedures had evolved. A sinner would be corrected in a public confrontation. If the confrontation provoked repentance, the penitent would be assigned a period of fasting and prayer. At the end of this period the penitent was publicly readmitted to the assembly. It was customary for widows to fast and pray with these penitents and then restore them to fellowship with the church.

The pastoral ministry of correction was the most powerful ministry and the most contested in the third century, for implicit in confronting a sinner, assigning a period of fasting, and restoring a sinner to fellowship was the power to decide who was in the church and who was not.

Since the writer of the *Didascalia* wanted to see this ministry brought under the central authority of the bishop, he contended that widows should no longer involve themselves in the ministry of correction. If a disciplinary problem was reported to a widow, he wrote, "let her be as though she didn't see or hear it. For a widow should be concerned with nothing more than to pray for the benefactor and for the whole church" (xv).

This pastoral ministry involved public confrontation, the exercise of authority, and a public act (that of reconciling the individual to the congregation). Women exercising this ministry were not manifesting the appropriate characteristics of femaleness — passivity, shyness, and restraint. This writer therefore caricatured widows in a public ministry as talkative, gossips, scolds, and lovers of controversy. Because they were women, their public speech could be discredited. The writer encouraged widows to emulate the values of the system — to be meek, quiet, and gentle. Then he reframed the ministry of the widow — not to discipline the wayward but to pray for the church. His strategy was to shift the widows from a public to a private ministry.

The writer of the *Didascalia* also warned widows active in the ministry of converting the pagans to keep silence.

> But let her send those who desire to be instructed to the leader. And to those who ask let them [the widows] give answer only about the destruction of idols and about this, that there is only one God. It is not right for the widows to teach nor for a layman. About punishment and reward, and about the kingdom of the name of Christ and about his dispensation, neither a widow nor a layman ought to speak. (xv)

Widows were teaching those doctrines that refuted pagan religion (arguments against idolatry and polytheism) and explaining the Christian faith (the doctrine of rewards and punishments, the sovereignty and rule of Christ, and the power of his name). According to the writer of the *Didascalia*, evangelizing and teaching were exclusive rights of the bishop, and widows were infringing on them. If a woman, he declared with an edge of scorn in his voice, explained the mystery of the incarnation to a pagan, he would laugh and jeer. In failing to come to belief, he would be damned and the preaching widow would bear the guilt of his damnation because her low status as a woman had undermined the power of her message.

These widows who were evangelizing and teaching were also probably baptizing their own converts, for the polemic continues: "About this, however, that a woman should baptize or that one should be baptized by a woman, we do not counsel." The writer claimed that baptism should be the prerogative of the bishop alone. And the problem was not only with the baptizing widows. Apparently some people wished to be baptized by the widows. The writer tells them, "Indeed if it were lawful to be baptized by a woman, our Lord and teacher Himself would have been baptized by Mary His Mother. Now He was baptized by John, like others also of the people. Therefore do not bring danger upon yourselves, brethren and sisters, by acting beyond the law of the Gospel" (xv).

First widows were told that instead of engaging in pastoral ministries they should pray. Then they were told that they were commissioned to pray and not to convert the pagans. Now we see that in the mind of the author, praying and staying at home are indissolubly linked: "But let a widow know that she is the altar of God. And let her constantly sit at home, and let her not wander or run about among the houses of the faithful to receive. The altar of God, indeed, never wanders or runs about anywhere, but is fixed in one place" (xv). The metaphor of the widow as an altar of God makes the widow a passive subject of the church's charity rather than an active agent who ministers the church's benefits to others. The immovable altar, enclosed in the church, receives the gifts the congregation brings to God. The humorous spectacle of the altar wandering about in the streets evokes a fear simultaneously of desecration and loss of control, which the writer has been trying to associate with widows who are active in ministry.

"Good" widows stay at home; "bad" widows (those active in public ministry) are shameless:

> A widow must not therefore wander or run about among the houses. For those who are roving and have no shame cannot stay quiet even in their houses. For they are not widows, but blind and they care for nothing else but making themselves ready to pick up on something. And because they are talkative and chatterers and murmurers, they incite strife and they are bold and they have no shame. (xv)

First we should notice that the widows' ministry of visitation is depicted using the inflammatory terms "wandering and running about," which were applied to women when their chastity was in question. The writer associates boldness and shamelessness with visitation. Widows who were going from home to home to give theological instruction and scriptural interpretation were gossips stirring up controversies. They were, in the writer's perspective, violating the virtues of chastity and silence.

The author's strategy for persuading churches to bar widows from their ministries was to invoke the honor-shame system of values. Since societal norms defined the virtuous woman as chaste, silent, obedient, and content within the domestic sphere, this writer could portray widows active in public ministries as violating the fundamental canon of women's virtues. They are the "bad" widows, because they were exercising their ministries in the public sphere.[22]

1. Cicero *Pro Caelio*, in M. Lefkowitz and M. Fant, *Women's Life in Greece and Rome* (Baltimore: Johns Hopkins Univ. Press, 1982), 147.

2. Bruce Malina, *The New Testament World* (Atlanta: John Knox Press, 1981), 28.

3. Malina, *New Testament World*, 44. See also D. Gilmore, *Honor and Shame and the Unity of the Mediterranean* (Washington, DC: Special Publication of the American Anthropological Association [no. 22], 1987).

4. Malina, *New Testament World*, 42.

5. Malina, *New Testament World*, 28.

6. Gerda Lerner, *The Creation of Patriarchy* (New York: Oxford Univ. Press, 1986), 36–53, 212–30.

7. Gayle Rubin, "The Traffic in Women," in *Toward an Anthropology of Women*, ed. Rayna Reiter (New York: Monthly Review, 1975), 157–87.

8. Rubin, "Traffic in Women," 187–210.

9. Livy I.57–58, trans. B. O. Foster (Cambridge, MA: Harvard Univ. Press, 1988).

10. Livy I.56–57.

11. M. Giovannini, "Female Chastity Codes in the Circum Mediterranean: Comparative Perspectives," in *Honor and Shame and the Unity of the Mediterranean*, ed. D. Gilmore, 61.

12. Giovannini, "Female Chastity Codes," 66.

13. Giovannini, "Female Chastity Codes," 67.

14. Carol Delaney, "Seeds of Honor, Fields of Shame," in *Honor and Shame and the Unity of the Mediterranean*, ed. Gilmore, 35–48.

15. Giovannini, "Female Chastity Codes," 67.

16. Philo *The Special Laws* 3.51.

17. Neopythagorean "Treatise on Chastity," in Lefkowitz and Fant, *Women's Life*, 104.

18. Dio 58.2.

19. Dio 58.2.

20. See also Antoinette Wire, *The Corinthian Women Prophets* (Minneapolis: Fortress Press, 1990), 21.

21. For an English translation, see *The Didascalia Apostolorum in Syriac,* ed. Arthur Vööbus, vol. 408 (C.S.C.O., 1905), 143–55. A structural analysis of chap. xv of the *Didascalia* shows that for its author there were seven problem areas in the church's relationship to the influential women who formed the order of widows. Four of these areas had to do with women's leadership: the exercise of the pastoral ministry of discipline and penance, the evangelistic ministry of teaching pagans, the ministry of instructing the faithful, and the ministry of baptism (which was generally associated with the conversion of pagans). The other three areas concern the way the widows handled their finances, their criticisms of the way the bishop handled his finances when it came to distribution to the widows, and the necessity of the widows' submission to the bishop in the exercise of the ministry of prayer. The overarching objective of the writer with respect to the first four was to disqualify widows from these areas of leadership. His objective with respect to the last three was to bring the remaining activities of the widows firmly under the bishop's control.

The author's approach to these problem areas was guided by a rhetorical strategy that makes his objectives fairly transparent. This rhetorical strategy can be seen in the pattern of six repeating elements in the treatment of each problem area. They are (1) the vices of "bad" widows, (2) the virtues of "good " widows, (3) what widows were doing, (4) what they ought not to do, (5) what they should do instead (stay at home and pray), and (6) the arguments for the specific prohibition. The first two items, vices and virtues often used to introduce a problem area, really function to reinforce (4) and (5). The vices correspond to what widows should stop doing and are negative characterizations of the activities that are neutrally detailed in (3). For example, "bad" widows are talkative and quarrelsome in the sections where widows are instructed to give up teaching. The virtues of the "good" widows underwrite the instructions in item (5) that the proper ministry of widows is to stay home and pray. Generally the longest section by far is that comprised by item (6).

This method of rhetorical analysis of church orders has been pioneered by S. Laeuchli, *Sexuality and Authority: The Synod of Elvira* (Philadelphia: Temple Univ. Press, 1972).

22. Gerda Lerner shows in *The Creation of Patriarchy*, 123–41, that part of the evolution of the patriarchal system involved dividing women into two classes, women whose sexuality was available to one man and women whose sexuality was available to all men. This is the basis here for the distinction between good women and bad women. The distinction between good widows and bad widows follows this same typology.

*The Celestial Banquet.* The participants in this
*agape* feast seem astonished that it is led by a
woman. From the Catacomb of SS Pietro e
Marcellino. (André Held.)

# 6

# When the Church Goes Public

■■■■

## THE CHURCH AS PUBLIC SPACE

Somewhere around the beginning of the
third century a gradual process of transformation began in the leadership and
organizational models of the Christian
churches. By the third century Christianity
was attracting members of the municipal
ruling elites, who were trained for public
life and experienced in city politics. Many
Christian communities welcomed these
aristocratic members, and they moved
quickly into leadership positions. These

men were schooled in the institutions of public life; their notions of authority, order, organization, and leadership came from the political life of the city. They brought into the churches new leadership models, models that had proved effective for governing large and diverse communities.

In the provinces of the Roman Empire, the clergy who collectively shared the tasks of leadership began to model themselves after city councils. As a consequence the concept of leadership began to shift subtly from ministry to governance. An important element of this transition was the growing divide between the clergy and the laity. The language in which this demarcation was cast echoed the division in city politics between the rulers and the subjects. In a liturgical prayer for the ordination of presbyters in the early third century, the presbyters were cast as rulers.[1] "Look upon this your servant and impart the spirit of grace and counsel, that he may share in the presbyterate and govern your people with a pure heart."[2] As the concept of leadership shifted from ministry to governance, advocates of the newer concept of leadership appealed to the Old Testament, for the leaders of the nation of Israel were indeed rulers. And as the church understood itself to be Israel's successor, the leadership patterns found in the Old Testament became useful.

Like the Jewish community, the Christian community stressed the importance of adjudicating disputes between members within the community. Both groups eschewed appeals to the political authorities of the empire. By the third century, the practice of adjudicating disputes within the community led to the establishment of the bishop's court. Like the Roman provincial governor, who had the judicial authority (*cognitio*) within his administrative area, the bishop's right to hear cases and to pronounce judgment rested simply on the authority of the office. When Constantine, in 306, became the first Christian emperor, he placed these bishops' courts on the same legal basis as the empire's municipal courts.

From the third to the fourth century the office of bishop became increasingly monarchical. The bishop's throne stood at the front and center of the worshiping community and was eventually placed on a raised dais. One writer advocating monarchical powers for the bishop urged the congregations to whom he was writing to "let them [bishops] be your rulers therefore and let them be accounted of by you as kings; and do you offer them tribute in service as to kings for by you they ought to be sustained and those who are with them."[3] In this new understanding of church office, the bishop ruled the congregation in God's stead. He or she was "God's mouth" and the "mediator of the word"; one who held the power of life and death.

By the fourth century, this shift in leadership models became evident in church architecture. The early Christian basilica, with its colonnaded aisles and recessed apse in the front, was patterned after Rome's great public basilicas, which served as formal halls in which an emperor or governor received dignitaries or sat in judgment. The Roman basilica's architecture manifested the dignity and the authority of the government. By the fourth century the church had become the "throne room" of God.

As the architectural space in which Christians worshiped became a more public space, and as the models for leadership were drawn increasingly from public life, women's leadership became more controversial. Because the public-versus-private gender ideology restricted women's activities in public life, the new leaders of the church were not as comfortable with women's leadership in the churches.

In the early years of the third century a strident voice disturbed the self-satisfied slumber of the African church. The important church father and theologian Tertullian intended to return African Christianity to its early moral rigor, passion for martyrdom, and discipline by the sheer power of his rhetoric. In Tertullian's vision for reform, women's behavior would again conform to the standards of a lost golden age—not, unfortunately, the golden age of the Jesus movement's radical egalitarianism but of Rome's codified restrictions on women's roles.

In the writings of Tertullian, a representative of this new class of leaders, we see a clear correlation between the insistence that the church was a public institution and the resistance to women's leadership.

## TERTULLIAN'S OPPOSITION TO WOMEN LEADERS

From Tertullian's hostility to women leaders we learn that in the congregations familiar to him women were teaching, baptizing, exorcising, and healing. One woman who incensed Tertullian because of her teaching on baptism was a leader of a gnostic congregation that called itself Cainite and a theologian in her own right. Her argument that baptism was useless since water as a material element could not confer spiritual power occupied Tertullian's rhetorical and exegetical skills for long stretches of his treatise *On Baptism*.[4] Tertullian was undoubtedly reacting to the fact that women of other congregations were teaching and debating (entering into public theological discussions).[5] Those women whose teaching activities focused on catechizing probably also assumed the responsibility for baptizing their catechumens.[6]

Tertullian's seething rhetoric reveals only too well his attitude toward women who exercised these ministries. Of women teachers he said: "The very women of these heretics, how wanton they are! For they are bold enough to teach, to dispute, to enact exorcism, to undertake cures—it may be even to baptize."[7] On women entering into public debates he protested that "it is not permitted to a *woman* to speak in church, but neither is it permitted her to teach, nor to baptize, nor to offer, nor to claim for herself a lot in any manly function not to say [in any] sacerdotal office."[8] Nor on the topic of women baptizing was Tertullian's sense of outraged propriety abated:

But the impudence of that woman who assumed the right to teach, surely she is not going to arrogate to herself the right to baptize as well—unless perhaps some new serpent appears, like that original one, so that as this woman abolished baptism, some other should on her own authority confer it.[9] But if certain Acts of Paul, which are falsely so named, claim the example of Thecla for allowing women to teach and to baptize, let men know that in Asia the presbyter who compiled that document, thinking to add of his own to Paul's reputation, was found out, and though he professed he had done it for love of Paul, was deposed from his position. How could we believe that Paul should give a female power to teach and to baptize, when he did not allow a woman even to learn by her own right? "Let them keep silence," he says, "and ask their husbands at home."[10]

Tertullian did, paradoxically, accept women prophesying in church and managed to reconcile this with his condemnation of women teaching, discussing, or asking questions by his interpretation of Paul's insistence on women's silence. Tertullian saw this passage as forbidding women not to teach but to engage in public discussions for the purpose of learning. He extrapolated from his interpretation that if women were forbidden to participate in public discussion, then they certainly would not have been allowed to do public teaching. Tertullian's interpretation of Paul's statement that women must learn at home fit naturally with his conviction that this was the proper sphere for women's activities. Thus, according to Tertullian, women were not to teach or to baptize nor were they to engage in any kind of public discourse, either debating a theological question or asking questions for their own instruction.[11]

Tertullian represents the attitude of the conservative Roman aristocracy that the only proper roles for women lay within the private sphere. And it is Tertullian's innovative vision of the church as a political body rather than a household or private association that made women's leadership roles in the church particularly odious to him.

His paradoxical positions resulted from his recasting of Latin Christianity into a juridical or political mold. Tertullian offered the first consistent articulation of Christianity to draw its language, metaphors, and paradigms from institutions of public political life. Tertullian's rejection of women's leadership in the church was therefore determined by Roman society's relegation of women's activities to the private domestic sphere and its insistence that the public woman was a promiscuous woman.

Tertullian's scathing condemnation of women's ministries among groups that he designated as heretical was part of a larger denunciation of the ecclesiastical conduct of those groups; they were "without gravity, without authority and without discipline."[12] By this he meant there were not clear enough distinctions between catechumens and baptized, between clergy and laity, between pagan visitors and believers. Tertullian reflected the heated dispute between church groups that were beginning to adopt institutional structures resembling those of the Roman government and those who persisted in the older organizational pattern modeled on the household and private associations. The traditionalists defended the lack of a rigidly maintained hierarchy between clergy and laity and between catechumens and the baptized by claiming it expressed "the simplicity of Christ." Tertullian called their simplicity "the destruction of discipline." These groups called concern for hierarchy (or what Tertullian called discipline) pandering, meaning that the concern for showing the proper honors to the proper rank was nothing other than un-Christian flattery and attempts to buy influence.

The groups whom Tertullian attacked in fact had the same offices, ranked the same way, as those of Tertullian's churches. They had the same rites of ordination by which people were installed into those offices. What Tertullian seems to be criticizing, therefore, is the lack of social distance between those of different ranks, the lack of formality in maintaining those distinctions. If the organizational structure of both groups was the same, what standard was Tertullian using for comparison? I suggest that Tertullian's standard was the dignity, gravity, and formality with which public affairs were conducted, the tone or mood found in the municipal assemblies or *curiae* (city councils).

## THE CHURCH AS A BODY POLITIC

In Tertullian we see more than a natural, unthinking appropriation of paradigms from the public political sphere. Tertullian was self-conscious, self-confident, and creative as he borrowed language and constructs from Roman political life to interpret the basic features of Christianity.[13] Tertullian's teachings on the inner Trinitarian relationships, on the relationship between God and humanity, and on the relationships between Christians within the church are all patterned on the relationships that existed in the public political sphere.

Tertullian's solution to the problem of expressing both the unity and multiplicity of the three Persons of the Trinity was to use the concept of political (monarchical) rule. The Trinitarian nature of God was described as a *monarchia,* a single and individual rule, which can be administered by others without impairing the unity of that rule.[14] Thus the Father exercises a single and sovereign rule that is administered by the Son and the Holy Spirit, who become representatives or deputies of the Father.[15] The unity of the Trinity is a political unity. The notion of Christ as the delegated viceroy (*vicarius*) of God opened the way to considering the bishop as the delegated viceroy (*vicarius*) of Christ and gave rise to the notion of a monarchical bishop.[16] In Tertullian's doctrine of sin, it is this imperial notion of God that frames the God–human relationship. Sin is a breach of the baptismal vows made to God. Sin becomes, then, an offense against a monarch, and its seriousness is measured by the honor and dignity of the one offended. As a public offense, equivalent to a crime, sin brings with it a penalty, as well as an obligation to make restitution.[17] The language and the concepts are taken from the sphere of law—the idea of restitution from civil law, and the idea of penalty from criminal law.

Tertullian's description of the Christian community dramatically marks the transition of the model of the church from the household or private associations to the body politic. With him the church became a legal body (*corpus* or *societas,* the term the

Romans used for the body politic) unified by a common law (*lex fidei*, "the law of faith") and a common discipline (*disciplina*, Christian morality).

For Tertullian the church, like Roman society, united a diversity of ethnic groups into one body under the rule of one law. Christian doctrines, which constituted the rule of faith, unified Christian society in the same way that Roman law unified Roman society. Tertullian borrowed the term *disciplina* from the military, in which the unity among the great ethnic diversity of soldiers was expressed through their submitting to the common rigors of military discipline.

Tertullian conceived the society of the church as analogous to Roman society, divided into distinct classes or ranks, which were distinguished from one another in terms of honor and authority. The clergy (*ordo ecclesiasticus*) formed a rank similar to the *ordo senatorius* (the ruling senatorial class); the laity formed the *ordo plebius* (the subject plebeian class). The clergy as the *ordo ecclesiasticus* represented and manifested the honor and authority of the church, therefore it was imperative that it exemplify the moral discipline of the church.[18]

By virtue of their rank clergy, like their counterparts the senators, possessed certain rights: the right to baptize (*ius dandi baptismi*), the right to teach (*ius docendi*), the right to offer the Eucharist (*ius offrendi*), and the right to restore to fellowship after penance (*ius delicta donandi*).[19] Tertullian was sensitive to the fact that what had once been ministries had become in fact legal rights and privileges. He noted that the clergy was not to exercise its privilege after the manner of an imperium, nor was it to claim any license on the ground of privilege of position.[20] Imperium was the authority vested in a high elective office of the Roman government.

According to Tertullian, the laity also possessed, in a latent way, the same rights as the clergy—the right to offer the Eucharist and the right to baptize; but laypeople could not exercise those rights when the clergy was present.[21] In gatherings of two or three, the laity could exercise those rights, but not in a duly constituted assembly. The right lay first and foremost with the bishop, because baptism was one of his specific functions; it was a right also, however, of presbyters, deacons, and even of the laity. Nonetheless the bishop had the preeminent right over baptism, and for the sake of the "honor" (dignity) of the church, the authority of the bishop had to be respected in all cases. When Tertullian insisted that women could not baptize, we see that in his mind women were excluded from both the clergy and the laity![22]

The term Tertullian used to designate the right of the clergy or the laity to exercise a ministry of the church was a legal term—*ius*. The laity, by virtue of baptism, possessed the right to baptize, as well as the rights to teach and to offer the Eucharist.[23] But women could exercise none of these ministries. Among the opening salvos of his attack on his female theological adversary was Tertullian's assertion that women did not possess the right to teach even sound doctrine, much less to create heresies. Here the term he used was *ius docendi* (the legal right to teach); as he concluded his treatise he returned to the Cainite leader again and called her a "wanton" woman who had "usurped" the right to teach.

In Tertullian's new vision of the church as a political body, the church's ministries had become legal rights to be exercised only by full members of the political body. Since according to the public-versus-private gender ideology, women could not hold office, participate in debate, or exercise any public functions, neither could they do any of these things in the body politic of the church, Tertullian reasoned. The right to minister was a right restricted not to the clergy but to citizens who were members of the body politic; and women could not be members of the body politic. Tertullian justified his prohibitions against women's leadership by labeling these functions "manly."[24]

Women's performance of public activities (i.e., exercising the *ius docendi, ius baptizandi,* etc.) meant that they had abandoned the domestic sphere, so again Tertullian described such women as wanton. When they exercised any public ministry, they were usurping rights that did not belong to them because they were women; legal rights could belong only to men.

## PUBLIC HONOR AND FEMALE SHAME

When Tertullian attacked women ministers as wanton, the sexual connotation was not inappropriate. The Latin term *procaces* (bold, shameless, and impudent) was applied to women when they were outside their proper sphere, that is, the household.[25] The women who were teaching, disputing, exorcising, and healing were wanton in Tertullian's thinking because they were functioning in male space. The now public sphere of the church thus required women to show in their comportment, dress, and grooming a respect for its public and male character.

Nowhere is the trauma of this transition from household space to public space more poignant than in Tertullian's passionate treatise *On the Veiling of Virgins.* "Young women," he scolded, "you wear your veils out on the streets [*in vicis*], so you should wear them in the church [*in ecclesia*], you wear them when you are among strangers [*extraneos*], then wear them among your brothers [*fratres*]."[26] "If you won't wear your veils in church, then I challenge you to go around in public without them."[27] But that is just the point: The church had been a private sphere; like a household, it was a place where women could come and go openly and freely. But Tertullian was insisting that the church was no longer a private sphere; it was now in fact no different from the marketplace. The rules of propriety for women that applied in the streets were now brought into the inner—once domestic—sanctum of the church.

Like Paul, Tertullian saw in the practice of veiling a way for women to manifest their concern for shame while holding positions of authority. Tertullian was concerned with the leadership and honor of the virgins in the African congregations. The virgins were part of the ecclesiastical order, part of the clergy, and sat in special seats reserved for them with the presbyters, widows, and bishops. Their number and their commitment to a life of chastity was one of the church's most esteemed emblems. These virgins signified their unmarried state by not wearing veils. For the church these young women, unveiled and dedicated to God, were like a public and visible offering, worthy of praise and manifesting God's glory.[28] Tertullian called this practice a "liberty" granted by the church to honor the virgin and her choice. As Tertullian formulated it, she was honored by being granted the right (*ius*) not to wear a veil. But it was this public honor, not so much the absence of veils, that most offended Tertullian. He argued that to grant a virgin dedicated to God the right not to wear a veil and to honor her with this right was the same as honoring her with the right to hold male office or rank. He stated flatly, "Nothing in the way of public honor is permitted to a virgin."[29]

The public honors bestowed on the virgins offended Tertullian's sense that femaleness was to be associated with submission, passivity, and sexual exclusivity. For Tertullian the vow of chastity itself was not enough to demonstrate a woman's concern for sexual exclusivity. There had to be a public, visible demonstration of the concern for modesty and chastity, which he thought could best be shown by the wearing of the veil. Otherwise, Tertullian warned, women who had taken the vow of virginity, "after being brought forward and elated by the public announcement of their good deed, laden by the brethren with every bounty and charitable gift," would no doubt become sexually active, since they were on public display. If they did not use the veil to signify their concern for shame (sexual exclusiveness) they would in the end become pregnant and add to their guilt by attempting abortions and by contriving to conceal their motherhood. For Tertullian a veiled virgin could continue in her position of prestige, authority, precedence, and honor because she was publicly demonstrating her concern for shame, for sexual exclusiveness.[30]

Tertullian's conviction that women had no place in any of the public aspects of the Christian assembly was also influenced by his culture's assumptions about honor and shame. When he wrote about women outside the context of Christian worship, he decried the lax standards for their behavior in pagan society and urged Christian women to repudiate them and to adopt the norms of an earlier, more conservative, culture to which Tertullian looked back with nostalgia.

The standards he set for women's use of makeup were observed only by the vestal virgins in Rome in his day.[31] His attitudes toward the influence of women on the state of moral decadence in the empire echoed his conservative predecessors. Livy, in his *History of Rome*, created a passionate speech for Cato on the occasion of the vote to repeal the Oppian law, which during a wartime emergency twenty years earlier had placed certain restrictions on women. They had been forbidden to wear more than half an ounce of gold or colored fabrics, and they couldn't ride in carriages in the city except for purposes of attending religious festivals. Livy described the day of the vote: "The matrons could not be kept at home by advice or modesty or their husbands' orders, but blocked all the streets and approaches to the Forum." They urged the men, who alone had the right to vote, to "restore to them their former distinctions," for ornaments and dress were to the women what political offices and honors were to men—the signs of their rank and dignity.[32]

In Cato's speech a few lines are spent on the shocking immodesty of women "running out into the city" and "speaking to other women's husbands." The greater outrage, however, is expended over the audacity of women to concern themselves with a matter of public law, which lay totally outside their sphere. "And yet, not even at home, if modesty would keep matrons within the limits of their proper rights, did it become you to concern yourselves with the question of what laws should be adopted in this place." What is worse, he persists, is that "we, Heaven help us, allow them now even to interfere in public affairs, yes, and to visit the Forum and our informal and formal sessions." The failure to restrict women's public behavior in the matter of wearing jewelry and fine fabrics and the worse failure to exclude them from involvement in public affairs would lead to the most frightening kind of moral and political decay: "Give loose rein to their uncontrollable nature and to this untamed creature and the result will be a women's revolt."[33]

For a conservative like Tertullian, in the context of Christian worship, this confinement to the domestic sphere could be achieved by excluding women from so-called public roles. Outside this context, Christian women's sense of shame had to be signaled by their clothes, hairstyle, and makeup.

In Tertullian's treatise on the personal grooming of women, he summarized the regimen for Christian women under two virtues: humility and chastity.[34] He condemned the wearing of jewelry—gold (bracelets and armlets were especially popular), silver, precious stones (anklets were fashionable among the racier women), and pearls (favorites for dangling earrings)—as incompatible with the Christian virtue of humility. His justifications are Christian, but he was expressing the values of many Latin writers on the display of wealth in women's jewelry.[35]

Tertullian condemned the use of skin creams to lighten the complexion and the application of rouge and mascara. He followed the general arguments of Latin moralists who asserted that a woman who wore makeup was presenting a false face: "How unworthy of the Christian name to wear a fictitious face, you on whom simplicity in every form is enjoined—to lie in your appearance."[36] But the major force of his argument was that a woman who used makeup could not maintain the virtue of chastity, because makeup, jewelry, and clothes gave a woman a public "identity." So Tertullian argues:

Moreover, what causes have you for appearing in public in excessive grandeur, removed as you are from the occasions which call for such exhibitions? For you neither make the circuit of the temples, nor demand [to be present at] public shows, nor have any acquaintance with the holy days of the Gentiles. Now it is for the sake of all these public gatherings, and of much seeing and being seen, that all pomps [of dress] are exhibited before the public eye; either for the purpose of transacting the trade of voluptuousness, or else of inflating "glory." You, however, have no cause of appearing in public, except such as is serious.[37]

He continued, "How much more provocative of blasphemy is it that you, who are called modesty's priestesses, should appear in public decked and painted out after the manner of the immodest?"[38] Avoiding makeup and staying at home were components of the virtue of chastity. Tertullian held Christian women to the conservative standards of an earlier day.[39] He continued in a bitter reminiscence:

If you don't go about in modest attire, what will separate you from your poor inferiors [pagan women], unhappy victims of the public lust, whom, although laws were formerly wont to restrain from the use of matrimonial and matronly decorations, now at all events, the daily increasing depravity of the age has raised so nearly to an equality with all the most honorable women, that the difficulty is to distinguish them.[40]

Tertullian's own views on the matter of women's behavior are clear from his treatises *De Cultu Feminarum, De Exhortatione Castitatis, De Virginibus Velandis*. But they also implicitly reveal Christian women's views on the matter of women's behavior and the likelihood of their being persuaded by Tertullian's theology or rhetoric.

It seems that women's definition of chastity was different from the male moralists'. Tertullian said, "For most women either from simple ignorance or else from dissimulation, have the hardihood so to behave as if modesty consisted only in the bare integrity of the flesh [i.e., keeping it covered] and in turning away from actual fornication."[41] Christian women shared this understanding of chastity with their pagan sisters, and Tertullian was at pains in his treatise to persuade them otherwise.

Tertullian's first line of argument was designed to convince Christian women that pagans did not really possess the virtue of chastity. He did this by creating a new definition of Christian chastity that made the Christian woman responsible for male sexuality: A Christian woman was not chaste unless she had no impact on male sexuality. Tertullian pressed this strange point so far as to say that a beautiful woman ought to obscure her beauty. By these standards pagan women did not measure up to Tertullian's definition of chastity.

Christian women, however, did not in fact feel responsible for male sexuality, nor were they particularly concerned to present an overwhelming appearance of chastity by abandoning personal grooming. Tertullian put the following protest in a woman's mouth: "To me it is not necessary to be approved by men; for I do not require the testimony of men; God is the inspector of the heart." Tertullian answered this imaginary woman opponent by saying, "To Christian modesty it is not enough to be so, but to seem so too."[42]

Christian women shared the pagan attitude toward woman's grooming—namely, that a woman should enhance her beauty in order to please her husband. Here Tertullian argued courageously that the Christian husband was not moved by his wife's beauty and that his chief concern was that she not be pleasing to others.[43] Women and men shared the view that beauty was a good in itself. In philosophical speculation it had a direct relationship to the Good, and Tertullian was careful not to seem to contradict this prevailing wisdom. But for Christian women, he argued, beauty was superfluous since it had nothing to do with salvation. "You may," he said to Christian women, "justly disdain it if you have it not, and neglect it if you have it."[44] The standards that Tertullian tried to set for women's behavior were those of a supposed lost "golden age" of moral integrity, when women quietly and chastely observed their domestic roles.

At each point Tertullian's concerns, like those of his predecessors, were that women's proper place be in the domestic sphere and that chastity be women's foremost concern. Participation in public life—whether the life of the city streets, market, and theater or the life of public institutions such as the church—either by receiving honors, exercising public functions, or participating in public debates was strictly forbidden because it was male territory. Tertullian, like the moralists before him, viewed the transgressing of the boundaries of women's proper sphere as a primary cause and example of the moral decadence of the third century.

Tertullian's genius and erudition contributed to his enormous influence in shaping Western Christianity. One historian calls him "clearly the luminary of his age," who "inaugurated the new and living form of Christian Latin literature."[45] Tertullian's creative achievement in pouring Christian thought into the mold of elegant Latin is paralleled by his achievement in recasting the structures and functions of church life in the mold of public life. In doing so he created a conceptual order for the rich diversity of ecclesiastical life. By virtue of his gender, social class, and professional training it happened to be a "public order" that excluded women.

## NOTES

1. On the monarchialization of the episcopacy, see Elisabeth Hermann, *Ecclesia in Re Publica* (Frankfurt am Main: Peter D. Lang, 1984), 21–29, for a description of the variety of Roman political institutions that served as models for church organization. See also Georg

Schoellgen, "Monoepiskopat und monarchischer Episkopat, Eine Bemerkung zur Terminologie," *Zeitschrift für die neutestamentliche Wissenschaft und die Kunde der älteren Kirche* 77, 1/2 (1986): 147–51.

2. *Apostolic Tradition* 7.

3. *Didascalia* 9.

4. Tertullian *De Baptismo* 1, 17.

5. Tertullian *De Praescriptione Haereticorum* 41.5.

6. Several scholars have interpreted passages on women leaders teaching and baptizing as indicating that women were involved in the process of evangelizing, catechizing, and then baptizing their converts. See Elisabeth Schüssler Fiorenza, *In Memory of Her: A Feminist Reconstruction of Christian Origins* (New York: Crossroad, 1983), 173; H. Achelis and J. Fleming, *Die syrische Didascalia übersetzt und erklärt, Texte und Untersuchungen,* 25, 2 (Leipzig, 1904).

7. *De Praescriptione Haereticorum* 41.5.

8. *De Virginibus Velandis* 9.1.

9. Tertullian is actually addressing this woman's teaching on baptism. She may or may not have been baptizing people herself. Tertullian apparently saw some kind of link between the two offenses, that of a woman teaching and a woman baptizing.

10. *De Baptismo* 17. While most scholars accept Tertullian's report on *The Acts of Paul* at face value, its reliability should be at least critically examined. Recent work on the *Acts of Paul and Thecla* suggests that many of the stories existed in the oral tradition before they were written down. The story of Thecla especially has the composite character of a story long in circulation. The alleged deposition of a presbyter for a putative forgery had evidently little effect on the circulation of the document, which has survived nearly nineteen centuries. See also Dennis MacDonald, *The Legend and the Apostle: The Battle for Paul in Story and Canon* (Philadelphia: Westminster Press, 1983).

11. *Adversus Marcionem* 5.8.11; *De Baptismo* 17.

12. *Adversus Marcionem* 5.8.11; *De Baptismo* 17.

13. Alexander Beck, in *Römisches Recht bei Tertullian und Cyprian* (Halle: Max Niemeyer, 1930), 39ff., tends to accept Eusebius's report that Tertullian was a famous jurist. Timothy Barnes, in *Tertullian, A Historical and Literary Study* (Oxford: Clarendon Press, 1971), 24, has argued persuasively that the Christian Tertullian of North Africa is not the famous lawyer (*jurisconsulti*) whose works appear in the Theodosian collection; Tertullian's use of legal terminology does not go beyond what might be expected from a well-educated rhetor, a man trained for public life.

14. Tertullian *Adversus Praxean* 3.

15. *Adversus Praxean* 24; *Adversus Marcionem* 3.6.

16. Beck, *Römisches Recht,* 70.

17. Beck, *Römisches Recht,* 46. In Greek thought the primary metaphor for sin was a sickness or wound that called for the services of a physician. See Joseph Trigg, "The Healing That Comes from God: The Alexandrian Response to the Third Century Penitential Crisis" (Ph.D. diss., Univ. of Chicago, 1978). Cf. Ignatius *Letter to Polycarp* 2.

18. On the church as *corpus* or *societas* see Herrmann, *Ecclesia in Re Publica,* 42. Beck, *Römisches Recht,* 58; on *lex fidei,* see Beck, 51; on *disciplina,* Beck, 54.

19. *Exhortatione Castitatis* 7; *De Monogamia* 12.

20. On *ius dandi baptismi* see *Exhortatione Castitatis* 17; on *ius docendi* see *De Baptismo* 1; on *ius offrendi* see *Exhortatione Castitatis* 7; on *ius delicta donandi* see *De Pudicitia.* 21.

21. *De Monogamia* 12.

22. *De Baptismo* 17.

23. *De Exhortatione Castitatis* 7.

24. *De Virginibus Velandis* 14.

25. The virtue of chastity is measured by three factors: appearing in public places, clothing and makeup, and sexual activity. See Livy XXXXIV.2. For this reason teaching can be associated with wantonness.

26. *De Virginibus Velandis* 13. The separation of public and private spheres and women's confinement to the private sphere was maintained by the practice of the veiling of women who needed to be present in public places. See Gerda Lerner, *The Creation of Patriarchy* (New York: Oxford Univ. Press, 1986), 123–40; Joachim Jeremias, *Jerusalem in the Time of Jesus* (Philadelphia: Fortress Press, 1969), 359ff.

27. *De Virginibus Velandis* 14.

28. *De Virginibus Velandis* 9.

29. *De Virginibus Velandis* 14.

30. Cf. chap. 5 of Tertullian, *On the Veiling of Virgins.*

31. *Digest of Justinian,* 34,2,25,10.

32. XXXIV.5-6 In a moving defense of the women's right to have the law repealed, Cato's opponent pleads, "No offices, no priesthoods, no triumphs, no decorations, no gifts, no spoils of war can come to them; elegance of appearance, adornment and apparel—these are the women's badges of honor" (Livy XXXIV.vii.10).

33. Livy XXXIV.ii.

34. *De Cultu Feminarum* I.4. See also Michel Spanneut, *Tertullien et les premiers moralistes africains* (Paris: Editions J. Cuculot, S. S. Gembloux, P. Lethiellieux, 1969), 32–40.

35. See Jean Claude Fredouille, *Tertullien et la conversion de la culture antique* (Etudes Augustiniennes 8, Paris, 1972), 49–57, for a comparison of Tertullian with the Latin moralists on women's virtues.

36. *De Cultu Feminarum* II.5.

37. *De Cultu Feminarum* II.11.

38. *De Cultu Feminarum* II.12.

39. *Digest* 34,2,25,10, and *Postumia* L.4.44.1f.

40. Referring to the Oppian law of 195 B.C.E.; *De Cultu Feminarum.* II.12.

41. *De Cultu Feminarum* II.1.

42. *De Cultu Feminarum* II.4.

43. *De Cultu Feminarum* II.3.

44. *De Cultu Feminarum* II.3.

45. Barnes, *Tertullian: A Historical and Literary Study*, 192.

Reclining men are entertained by topless
courtesans at a symposium. Attic red figure cup
attributed to the Tarquinia Painter, inv. Kä 415.
Antikenmuseum, Basel. (Claire Niggli.)

# 7

# The Penetrator and the Penetrated

■■■■

The Romans inherited their views about
the proper roles of men and women in
public and in private from ancient Greece.
Christianity, in turn, absorbed these views
from the Roman Empire, its cultural home.
As Christianity spread, it transmitted this
Greco-Roman gender system throughout
the West and succeeded in shaping cultural
attitudes about women and sexuality that
continue to prevail.

On the surface of things, however,
Western society may seem far from its
Greco-Roman cradle. The institutions of

slavery, prostitution, concubinage, and arranged marriages have been abolished. Respectable women come and go in public places. Many hold public office. Dozens of women's magazines reassure their subscribers that makeup, jewelry, and colorful clothing are appropriate expressions of female sexuality for "good" women.

Nevertheless the ancient Greek theory of the sexual self has had remarkable tenacity. It shows up today whenever women are said to be the weaker sex. It asserts itself again when we hear that women are prone to emotionalism and sentimentality and that this proclivity is less desirable than the masculine stiff upper lip and tearlessness. The openly sexual woman is still considered inappropriate and disagreeably masculine if she is sexually aggressive. When women are dismissed as irrational and men are presumed to be innately logical, we can be sure these conclusions are prompted by the persistent whisperings of long-dead Greek philosophers in society's ear.

By taking a close look at ancient Greek theories of the male and female self, we can begin to see what is at the root of the millennias-old claims for innate male superiority and the justification for female subordination.

## THE PHALLUS AND POWER

According to this early theory, the self has two sides: a superior, masculine self—rational, virile, masterful, and noble—and an inferior, feminine self that is irrational, sexual, animal, and potentially dangerous. Enshrined within this theory of the self are the gendered values of male honor and female shame. Masculinity, equated with sexual and political dominance, is designated "rational." By identifying the sexual, appetitive, and "dangerous" aspects of the self as irrational, the philosophers split off the "uncontrollable" parts of human nature and projected them onto a "lower female self." Through this gendering of the self, femaleness became the primary symbol for the irrational and uncontrollable. Women could then be labeled irrational, sensual, and dangerous because of the supposed dominance of their "lower" female nature and the weakness of their "higher" masculine self.

The notions of male honor and female shame had already given a set of cultural meanings to sexuality. Male sexuality was expected to be active and aggressive, because it demonstrated male honor. Female sexuality had to be controlled, because it represented danger and a threat to the male public order. Out-of-control female sexuality was dishonorable and shameless. When Greek intellectuals created theories about sexuality, they used aggressive male sexuality as the paradigm for all sexuality.

## AGGRESSIVE MALE SEXUALITY

One expert witness for the cultural meanings of sexuality in antiquity was the traveling Greek dream analyst Artemidorus Daldianus. In his view from the second century C.E., dream symbols conveyed meanings from the dreamer's waking world, and erotic dreams were especially portentous for predicting changes in wealth and social status.[1]

The penis is like a man's parents since it contains the generative code (*spermatikos logos*), but also like his children since it is their cause. It is like his wife and girlfriend since it is useful for sex. It is like his brothers and all blood relations since the meaning of the entire household depends on the penis. It signifies strength and the body's manhood, since it actually causes these: for this reason some people call it their "manhood" (*andreia*). It resembles reason and education since, like reason (*logos*), it is the most generative thing of all.[2]

When Artemidorus interpreted the dream symbolism of sexual intercourse, he paid close attention to who was penetrating (*peraineia,* active verb) and who was penetrated (*perainesthai,* passive verb). "To penetrate one's brother, whether older or younger, is good for the dreamer; for he will be above his brother and will look down on him."[3] Penetration symbolized dominance or superiority. If the one penetrating stands higher on the social ladder than the one being penetrated, the dream predicts good outcome: "To have sex with one's own female slave or male slave is good, for slaves are the dreamer's possessions, therefore taking pleasure in them signifies the dreamer's being pleased with his own possessions, most likely because of their increase in number or value."[4] But if the dreamer is penetrated by one below him on the social ladder, the dream bodes ill: "To be penetrated by one's house slave is not good. This signifies being despised or injured by the slave; the same applies to being penetrated by one's brother, whether younger or older, or a fortiori by one's enemy."[5] The same principle of interpretation extends to dreams of sexual relations with animals: "If the person dreams that he mounts the animal, he will receive a benefit from animals of that particular species, whatever it is. . . . If he is mounted, he will have some violent and awful experience."[6]

Artemidorus's categories for sexuality, a penetrator and a penetrated, are solely about *male* sexuality. A social profile of those who solicited Artemidorus's dream interpretations would show them to be men at the head of households, who ran trades or held public office in the city.[7] The freeborn citizen male stands at the center of Greek discourse on sexuality. The symbolism of the phallus and the multiple meanings of sexuality all derive from the sexual experience of the free male.

What is striking about all Greek discourses on sexuality, Artemidorus's among them, is that they conceptualize sexual experience as analogous to social experience. There are no long, introspective soliloquies about the experience of the erotic or reverent phenomenological descriptions of what transpires between the two partners. Rather the experience of sexual relations is fundamentally an experience of social relations. Classics scholar John Winkler, summarizing Artemidorus's analysis of dreams, offers a concise description of the way phallic penetration symbolized one's place and function in society: "To penetrate is not all of sex, but it is that aspect of sexual activity which was apt for expressing social relations of honor and shame, aggrandizement and loss, command and obedience, and so it is that aspect which figured most prominently in ancient schemes of sexual classification and moral judgement."[8]

The phallus figured as a symbol of male honor. The quest for male honor, the fear of shame, and the will to dominate—that ever-present system in antiquity—was the grid through which sexual experience was interpreted.

In democratic Athens, where the newly created social role of citizen was open only to freeborn males, masculinity was the consummate model for sexual relationships as well as political relationships. To be masculine in sexual relationships was to be socially dominant, the initiator, the active partner, the penetrator. To be masculine in political relationships meant to exercise autonomy, to be assertive, to maintain action.[9]

This equation of male sexual prowess and male political power attained literally monumental proportions during the formative period of the democratic city-state. A new kind of monument, the herm, proliferated during this period (sixth through fifth centuries B.C.E.). The herm was a solid rectangular block with two carved features, the bearded head of the generic adult male on top and an erect phallus below. The head represented the male citizen, emphasizing "the sameness of all male citizens," according to John Winkler, and disregarding distinctions of class or achievement.[10] The herm's phallus served to link male citizenship with male sexual prowess. When victorious Athenian generals were to be honored in 476 B.C.E., the generals insisted that no one of them be singled out by name, and therefore three herms were erected in their honor in the central marketplace. A herm stood at the entrance to the household of each Athenian citizen, symbolizing the household's incorporation into the polis through the figure of the male citizen.[11]

All power and honor hinged on a man's ability to maintain the appearance of masculinity. Any hint of vulnerability or passivity—of femininity—would mean that the man had forfeited his manliness and therefore his rights as a citizen. A wealthy and powerful male "could penetrate any other person without loss of social status," according to John Boswell, a historian of male sexuality. "But for the same male to be penetrated—by anyone—would incur disrespect if it were known and might even subject him to loss of civil privilege."[12]

For this reason a charge of prostitution (*kinaidos*) against a man was slanderous; he was accused of promiscuity, receiving payment, and passivity to another man's penetration.[13] This was a popular political accusation because it undermined the claim to political power, which had to be reinforced by demonstrations of sexual dominance. The loss of the public acknowledgment of one's masculinity was a profound form of dishonor (*atimia*), which meant that the individual was, in effect, socially degraded to a status equivalent to that of slaves and women. The sentiment appears in the oratory of a first-century rhetor, Rutilius Lupus:

> Nature has distinguished male and female so that each performs his/her own proper duty and office — and what if I were to show that this man has misused his own body in a feminine way? Surely Nature would be shocked and astonished that any man would not think it a most blessed gift for him to have been born a man and that he had spoiled Nature's kindness to him, hastening to transform himself into a woman.[14]

For a man to be used sexually like a woman was the ultimate shame.

Sexual intercourse between male and female provided the primary metaphor for political and social relationships. The Greeks conceptualized the sexual encounter in terms of an active partner who penetrates and a passive partner who is penetrated. To be active meant to dominate, master, and control; to be passive meant to be dominated or ruled and to obey. The sexual relationship was thought to mirror the social relationship between men and women. Without the influence of male dominance in social relations, the sexual act might have been described with different metaphors, such as the female engulfs the male, or the male is taken up or lost in the female. Greek philosophical treatises do speak of an erotic dimension to male-female sexual relations, but the dominative aspect of sexuality predominates.

The disturbing construction of sexuality as relationships of dominance and subjugation becomes more intelligible when we examine the pattern of sexual relationships for freeborn males.[15] Here we see a correlation between a variety of sexual relationships framed within a social hierarchy and an ideology of sexuality as social dominance. For the Greek citizen male, from whose vantage point the discourses on sexuality arise, the principal social setting for erotic sexuality was the symposium, a drinking party that followed a private dinner. A generous host would procure dancers, musicians, slave girls, and courtesans for entertainment as well as provide abundant wine. The revelers entered the household of their host through a vestibule, which led directly to a large dining room. This portion of the house, called the men's quarters, formed the boundary between public and private spheres in classical Greece. The guests coming in off the street had no access to the respectable wife and daughters of the household, nor did these women play any part in the revelry of the symposium.[16]

In contrast to the male guests, who represented the highest social class, the female guests, as slaves, prostitutes, and courtesans (professional sexual companions), belonged to a lower social class, lower in fact than the wives and daughters of the male guests. Secluded in the women's quarters, these matrons, unlike the "shameless" prostitutes, protected their honor by their absence from the male sphere of the symposium.

While sexual encounters during the symposium took place in the convivial public space of the dining room, marital sex was sequestered in the bedroom. In the iconography of vase paintings, marital relations were indicated by a half-open door, which signified entry into the women's quarters — an inner space that could be locked and sealed off from the public male world. The citizen's wife was confined not only by her seclusion in the women's quarters but also by the restrictions placed on her sexual activity. The privacy that enshrouded her signified that she was the exclusive sexual property of one man. Through its mores and laws, Greek society jealously guarded the virginity of the daughters of the citizen class and the sexual exclusivity of its wives. In the division of sexual labor between courtesans and wives, the erotic and procreative dimensions of sexuality became uncoupled. Since procreative sexuality was assigned to the wife, men pursued the erotic aspect of sex with a variety of other partners: slaves, prostitutes, and courtesans.

Another class of sexual relations that existed within the household is rarely commented on by ancient writers—that between the master and his female and male slaves. Nevertheless it was important to the Greek culture's construction of sexuality. Ownership of the physical body of a slave extended to sexual ownership. In fact, the use of the Greek word *soma* (body) for a slave was so widespread that it appears in Greek papyri found in Egypt. Slaves were to provide sexual service not only to their owners but also to others at their owners' behest, such as guests whom their masters were entertaining. In the larger households the slave entourage included trained musicians who offered sexual as well as musical entertainment.[17] The rights of ownership over the sexual body of the slave were so absolute that it wouldn't have occurred to Greek writers to include the slaves' perspective on sexuality. The voices of slaves—and of women, for that matter—are never heard in Greek descriptions of sexuality and sexual relations.

Among the sexual pairings at symposiums was the bearded male lover and the adolescent boy. Even though this relationship involved two males of the same social class, it was perceived in terms of active and passive. The boy's youthful beauty made him the object of desire—the smooth chin, the soft shoulders, the gracefulness of the body. The stimulus for the erotic lay in the drama of the pursuit, the challenge and pleasure of awakening the young man's imagination and intellect and the expectation of favors in exchange for these gifts.[18] In Greek an active participle of the verb *erao* (to love) *erastes* designates the older lover as the active partner, the one who desires, initiates, and courts. The passive participle *eranomos* names the boy as the object of erotic desire, the passive partner, the respondent. The adolescent was encouraged to prove his nobility by the dignity and restraint with which he received these attentions. Michel Foucault carefully dissects a typical speech addressed to a young man in order to understand how the "honor" of a citizen boy could be preserved while he was the passive object of another man's sexual desire. He concludes: "By not yielding, not submitting, remaining the strongest, triumphing over suitors and lovers through one's resistance, one's firmness, one's moderation (*sophrosune*), the young man proves his excellence in the sphere of love relations."[19]

The recurring passive-active polarity among all sexual relations of free males again portrays the penetrator as commanding the top position of the sexual hierarchy. The sexual dignity of the adolescent boy was in some sense preserved, because, as vase paintings of the time show, such noble homosexual intercourse was frontal, between the thighs. Dorsal or anal sex suggested the passive partner's social inferiority and was generally practiced only with slaves. One modern scholar suggests that the symposium provided the setting where the adolescent boys were initiated into heterosexual sex by anally penetrating a female slave prostitute. So while being passive and penetrated in relationship to the adult male lover, the adolescent was moving into the role of active penetrator with a lower-class female.[20]

### DANGEROUS FEMALE SEXUALITY

The gender system of Greek society gave this cultural construction of sexuality its peculiar stamp, polarizing public man and private woman, male honor and female shame. Central to these oppositions was the splitting of the sexual self into a male side and a female side—the male sexual self associated with honor and expressed through dominance; the female sexual self associated with shame and manifested by passivity.

The opposition between male honor and female shame was also the foundation of the Greek philosophical theory of the self. Although the symposium offered a congenial setting for sexual experience, the philosophers who reclined on their couches were as likely to seek pleasure from intelligent conversation with one another as by consorting with courtesans. Plato's most famous treatise, *The Symposium,* was composed as conversations among men sharing in the conviviality of the symposium. Not surprisingly in such settings discussions turned to the nature of sexual desire, not to the techniques of sexual practice but to what universal structures of the self that this desire might reveal. To this end they attempted to think abstractly about sexual desire:

The gods created in us the desire of sexual intercourse, contriving in man, one animated substance, and in woman another . . . and the seed having life and becoming endowed with respiration, produces in that part in which it respires a lively desire of emission, and thus creates in us the love of procreation. Wherefore also in men the organ of generation becoming rebellious and masterful, like an animal disobedient to reason, and maddened with the sting of lust, seeks to gain absolute sway and the same is the case with the so-called womb or matrix of women. The animal within them is desirous of procreating children.[21]

Philosophers typically viewed the sexual self—the one that appeared at drinking parties and consorted with prostitutes—as a kind of animal self. The animality of the sexual self was portrayed in the figure of the satyr, who possesses a human torso but animal ears, feet, and tail and has an erect penis. When he appears on vase paintings, he is usually stalking sexual prey, a maenad with loose, flowing hair and bare breasts.

In this speculation on the nature of sexual desire, the embryo of a philosophical concept of the self was being gestated. What we would now simply call sexual passion was then described as a wild animal residing in the sexual organs. While normally docile and obedient, this animal when stimulated would threaten to over-whelm its master, reason. The choice of the animal metaphor for sexuality implies that sexual passion existed in some conflict with what these philosophers conceived of as truly human. In the philos-opher's portrait of the self, a rational element rules over an irrational element—a sexual self potentially dangerous if allowed to rage out of control. What is at stake is the ability to rule oneself (*archein*), the ability to master oneself (*enkratein*). The use of the political terms *rule* and *mastery* reveals Greek assumptions about the rebellious and disorderly nature of the sexual self.

There are striking parallels in Greek literature between the descriptions of the irrational self and the characterizations of female nature, which were made explicit when the irrational, sexual part of the self came to be called female. To be controlled by sexual passions was to be a slave. Diogenes in his *Lives of the Philosophers*, Aristotle in his treatise *Politics*, and Xenophon in his *Oeconomicus* all stress the danger of being a slave to one's passions.[22] Self-control was a prerequisite for control over others. Plato judged the sexual self to be a particular danger to the stability of political order. In the uto-pian society proposed in *The Laws*, sexual intercourse would be limited to its procreative function alone:

This law of restricting pro-creative intercourse to its natural function [would operate] by abstention from congress with our own sex, with its deliberate murder of the race and its wasting of the seed of life on a stony and rocky soil, where it will never take root and bear its natural fruit, and equal abstention from any female field whence you would desire no harvest. Once this law [is] perpetual and effective the result will be untold good.[23]

It was a bold proposal and well before its time, as Plato himself knew. But in the fourth century of the Christian era, this proposal would be taken up again by Christian intellectuals like Augustine and would become a kind of law regulating the Christian community.

Plato discerned two forces at work in the self:

Well now, it is plain to everyone that love is some sort of desire . . . we must go on to observe that within each one of us there are two sorts of ruling or guiding principles that we follow. One is an innate desire for pleasure, the other an acquired judgment that aims at what is best. Sometimes these internal guides are in accord, sometimes at variance; now one gains the mastery, now the other. And when judgment guides us rationally toward what is best, and has the mastery, that mastery is called temperance [*sophrosynē*], but when desire drags us irrationally toward pleasure, and has come to rule within us, the name given to that rule is wantonness.[24]

Plato's reflection on the nature of sexual desire presupposes a divided self. Where the two forces of desire and judgment are in conflict, the struggle will be so intense, so unreconcilable, that whenever one wins, the other must lose. The relationship between these two forces cannot be negotiated; one must dominate the other.

The domination of judgment over desire produces the virtue of *sophrosynē* (temperance), while the domination of desire over judgment results in the vice of wantonness (*akolasia*).

The ferocity of this contest between temperance and desire is conveyed, appropriately, by the metaphors of military combat and athletic competition. Plato argued for the feasibility of his law restricting intercourse by showing that it could be done if the man's "physique was in good condition." He appealed to the famous athlete Iccus of Tarentum: "Such was his passion for victory, his pride in his calling, he combined fortitude and self-command of his character that, as the story goes, he never once came near a woman or a boy either, all time he was in training."[25] Just as the warrior learned courage through "fighting the cowardice within himself and vanquishing it," so also a man could not gain full mastery over the self "unless he fights a winning battle against the numerous pleasures and lusts which allure him to shamelessness and wrong, by the aid of precepts, practice and artifice, alike in his play and serious hours."[26] A man's mastery, ascendancy, or domination over the appetites could be celebrated as a victory as imposing as any won on the battlefield or in the arena, for every man was engaged in a private war with himself.[27]

Plato's construction of the doctrine of the complex self ultimately rests on a bedrock of Greek social structure. The hierarchical and dominative relations within the city-state became the model for the self. Plato's utopian state has three tiers—the rulers functioning like the rational self, the tradesmen like the spirited self, and the farmers like the appetitive self. The analogy that most interested Plato, however, was between the rational self in the soul and the role of rulers in the state. The rule of reason over passion and the bodily appetites was analogous to the rule of the state over society. Every individual was a replica of society in miniature. In the perfect man, reason would rule, with the spirited elements as its auxiliary over the appetites. Even though Plato envisions a tripartite model for the human person, he still organizes the parts as ruler and ruled.

In the reality of Plato's day, men were philosophers and rulers while women were concerned with the care of bodies and appetites. In the simplest sense, the ruling rational soul was identified with the male role of citizen in the polis, while the bodily self (or the passions) was identified with elements of the female role. Just as the relationship between the higher self and the lower self replicated the hierarchical relationships within the polis, so it also replicated the relationship between male and female in Greek society.

Only among the citizen class did these philosophers expect to find a man who had achieved mastery over his passions. Plato used the derogatory term *base mechanic* to describe a craftsman of the lower social class whose higher self was "naturally weak so that it cannot govern and control the brood of beasts within him but can only serve them and can learn nothing but ways to flatter them."[28] Because a tradesman was a member of the lower class, Plato considered the rational self of the tradesman to be naturally weak. Since only a well-developed higher self (the rational self) was capable of ruling and governing the lower self, members of the lower class needed to be placed under the authority of those whose rational self was capable of rule.

We say he ought to be the slave of that best man who has within himself the divine governing principle, not because we suppose . . . that the slave should be governed for his own harm, but on the ground that it is better for everyone to be governed by the divine and the intelligent, preferably indwelling and his own, but in default of that imposed from without.[29]

Just as children were guided in the development of virtue by being placed under the authority of a guardian, so virtue in the slave and the craftsman was dependent on the guiding authority of a ruler or head of household.

According to Plato, the rational self was to the whole person what the rulers were to the state. The rational part of the soul was the intelligent, deliberating, virtuous, and ruling member of the corporate self. Health and harmony within the self could be secured only when the control of reason over the spirited and appetitive parts of the self was achieved. In Plato's utopian vision, the rulers were that social class which had been carefully trained for abstract thought, deliberation, virtue, and authority. Plato's utopian society achieved perfection when the rulers' training in virtue was complete and their control over the body politic absolute.

A remarkable feature of Plato's vast thought experiment is that he envisioned women as well as men capable of becoming rulers. In effect his plan called for dismantling the private sphere (the traditional locus of female power) and assigning the rearing of children in common (wives would also be held in common). Women with special abilities would undergo the same educational process as men to prepare to be rulers.[30] Nevertheless, in the reality of contemporary Greek society, public man had already been divided from private woman and a great chasm lay between them. Political life, public speech, and the power to rule lay on the masculine side of that divide. Plato's theory of the self created a gendered self because the rational ruling element of the self corresponded to real social roles of citizen males in Athenian society.

But the hierarchical model of the self was constructed not only on male dominance in the polis. His role as head of the household was equally useful. In a dialogue of Xenophon's on household management from the fifth century B.C.E., the character Socrates warns that the passions idleness, moral cowardice, negligence, gluttony, and gambling are vicious rulers that will deplete the resources of a house. "So hard is the rule of these passions over every man who falls into their clutches," says Socrates, "that they force him to pay over all the profits of his toil, and to spend it on their own desires."[31] The mastery of the passions, therefore, is a necessary precondition for the effective management of a household. In the ideal state, a young man will start disciplining the passions early; by the time he is ready to marry and establish a household, he will possess a measure of self-mastery. In Xenophon's dialogue, Critobulus reassures Socrates that he is ready now to take up estate management: "You have told me quite enough about such passions as these, and when I examine myself I find, I think, that I have them fairly well under control, and therefore . . . advise me what I should do to increase my estate."[32]

The metaphors Xenophon uses are instructive. The appetites, which should be obedient slaves serving reason and judgment, have become illegitimate masters; Xenophon calls them tyrants and despots. When philosophers liken the appetites and the lower part of the self to slaves, they are making two points: first, that the appetites, like slaves, are intended to serve the interests of another; and second, that the appetites, like slaves, must be coerced by a superior authority to serve those higher interests rather than their own.

Xenophon's Socrates asks, "Then do you think that the man is free who is ruled by bodily pleasures?" The answer is a resounding "by no means."[33] To be free was to be under the authority of no one, while to be unfree was to stand beneath another's authority. Freedom required that one exercise self-mastery, be under no one's authority, and, by virtue of self-control, be able to exercise authority over others. As Foucault explains: "The person who, owing to his status, was under the authority of others was not expected to find the principle of his moderation [self-mastery] within himself; it would be enough for him to obey the orders and instructions he was given. Self-control, freedom and authority over social inferiors constituted a single complex whole."[34]

The rule of the male over his household had its counterpart in the rule of soul over body and intellect over appetite. As the physical body and passions were ruled by the male intellect, so also the household stood as an obedient and sentient body directed by the male citizen. In effect, the dominative relations of the household were projected onto the self and at the same time the hierarchical relationship within the self was used to legitimize relations of social dominance in the household.

Aristotle, in the generation after Plato, also produced a gendered definition of the self. His model for the higher, rational part of the self was the male head of household. His theory of the self, like Plato's, was based on gender roles in Greek society (and sustained them ideologically):

It is clear that the rule of the soul over the body, and of the mind and the rational element over the passionate, is natural and expedient; whereas the equality of the two or the rule of the inferior is always hurtful. Again the male is by nature superior, and the female inferior and the one rules, and the other is ruled; this principle of necessity extends to all mankind.[35]

Maryanne Cline Horowitz, a historian of science, asks, "Could it be instead that because Aristotle associated female with material activity (providing food and clothes) and males with the spiritual activity (scholarship and government) these distinctions became embodied in his embryology?"[36]

Male authority in the city-state and in the household was associated with the male virtue of self-control (*sophrosynē*), which Aristotle believed was less developed in women than in men. Therefore women's temperament was more influenced by the movement of the passions. He offered a catalog of animal behavior to show that the same gender differences prevailed among animals as among humans. This was his conclusion:

> The fact is, the nature of man is the most rounded off and complete, and consequently in the man the qualities or capacities referred to above are found in their perfection [in man]. Hence the woman is more compassionate than man, more easily moved to tears, at the same time is more jealous, more querulous, more apt to scold and to strike. She is, furthermore more prone to despondency, less hopeful than the man, more void of shame and self-respect, more false of speech, more deceptive, and of more retentive memory.[37]

According to Aristotle, woman's emotions, loves, fears, anger, and speech were undisciplined. In the male of the species, the emotions were more strictly regulated by the virtue of *sophrosynē*.

This philosophical theory of the self eventually became a valuable tool for excluding women, children, and slaves from political power, because their powers of reason and self-control were deemed weaker. In this passage from Aristotle, note how the arguments that woman is subordinate to man (a social fact in Athenian society) are blended with the arguments that woman *should* be subordinate to man through the use of a philosophical theory of the self:

> The free man rules over the slave after another manner from that in which the male rules over the female, or the man over the child, although the parts of the soul are present in all of them [both reason and passion], they are present in different degrees. For the slave has no deliberative faculty at all; the woman has, but it is without authority [*akuron*] and the [male] child has, but it is immature.[38]

*Akuron* signifies the lack of legitimate power or authority. That the male rules over the female is a statement of social arrangements. The notion that the male *should* rule over the female rests on the philosophical argument that although woman possesses the rational faculty, she does not possess it with authority.

The social hierarchy of the household has come at last to rest on a firm philosophical foundation: The diminished rational faculties of women, children, and slaves necessitate their subordinate position under the authority of a fully rational male. The same intellectual disability that subordinates women, children, and slaves within the household also excludes them from participation in the polis. Yet the rationality of the citizen male in its philosophical conception supports his two roles, as head of the household and as citizen. Philosophical conceptions of the rational self bore political and social consequences in the ancient world.

It is not difficult to see the implications that this has had for philosophical and theological discourse. The modern "scientific" heirs to Greek philosophy and Christian theology—biology and psychology—have taken over uncritically the ancient assumptions about male and female as a few recent quotes amply illustrate. From a French psychologist, "the average woman's judgment is never as good as the average man's—and when they pass the age of forty, their ability to reason seems to deteriorate quite rapidly,"[39] and an American biologist, "the undoubted superiority of the male sex in intellectual and creative achievement is related to their greater endowment of aggression. Even when women have been given the opportunity to cultivate the arts and sciences, remarkably few have produced original works of outstanding quality."[40] Nor have contemporary religious leaders been able to emancipate themselves from these older views. As an Anglican clergyman protested, "a woman offering up the communion offers the sight, the sound and the smell of perversion."[41]

NOTES

1. John Winkler, *The Constraints of Desire: The Anthropology of Sex and Gender in Ancient Greece* (New York: Routledge, 1990), 30.

2. Artemidorus, *Oneirokritika*, 1.45 as cited in Winkler, *Constraints of Desire*, 42.

3. Artemidorus, *Oneirokritika*, 1.78 as cited in Winkler, *Constraints of Desire*, 212.

4. Artemidorus, *Oneirokritika*, 1.78 as cited in Winkler, *Constraints of Desire*, 211.

5. Winkler, *Constraints of Desire*, 211.

6. Winkler, *Constraints of Desire*, 216.

7. Michel Foucault, *The Care of the Self* (New York: Random House, 1988), 7.

8. Winkler, *Constraints of Desire*, 40.

9. David Halperin, "The Democratic Body: Prostitution and Citizenship in Classical Athens," *Differences: A Journal of Feminist Studies* 2, 1 (1990): 12.

10. John Winkler, "Phallos Politikos: Representing the Body Politic in Athens," *Differences: A Journal of Feminist Studies* 2, 1 (1990): 35. The herm takes its name from the Greek god Hermes.

11. Winkler, "Phallos Politikos," 36.

12. John Boswell, "Concepts, Experience and Sexuality," *Differences: A Journal of Feminist Studies* 2, 1 (1990): 72.

13. Winkler, *Constraints of Desire*, 46.

14. Rutillus *Lupus* 2.6 as cited in Winkler, *Constraints of Desire*, 61.

15. The celebration of a dominative sexuality and its close ties with the prerogatives of citizenship provides a perspective for understanding the glorification of sexual violence in Greek mythology. Greek vase paintings celebrate the sexual exploits of the gods with scenes of their sexual pursuits of terrified mortals. Following the contours of a vase, a woman flees the pursuing god, who brandishes a thunderbolt or trident. According to Eva Keuls's interpretation, their weapons also symbolize the erect phallus and are often aimed at the crotch of their intended victims. What is being celebrated is the political and sexual power of males, not violence against women per se; but the medium for this celebration is, in fact, sexual violence against women. See Eva Keuls, *The Reign of the Phallus: Sexual Politics in Ancient Athens* (New York: Harper & Row, 1985), 33–64.

16. See Kathleen Corley's *Jesus, Woman and Meals in the Synoptic Gospels*, Claremont Ph.D., 1992, for a discussion of women at banquets.

17. Sarah Pomeroy, *Women in Hellenistic Egypt* (New York: Schocken Books, 1984), 142–43.

18. Michel Foucault, *The Use of Pleasure* (New York: Random House, 1985), 185–226.

19. Foucault, *Use of Pleasure*, 210.

20. Keuls, *Reign of the Phallus*, 174.

21. Plato *Timeaus* 91a-b, trans. Benjamin Jowett, *The Collected Dialogues of Plato,* ed. Edith Hamilton and Huntington Cairns (Princeton: Princeton Univ. Press, 1961).

22. Diogenes *Lives of the Philosophers,* VI.2.66, Aristotle *Politics* 1.5 and 13, Xenophon *Oeconomicus,* 1.1 and 22.

23. Plato *The Laws* 839a, trans. A. E. Taylor, *Collected Dialogues.*

24. Plato *Phaedrus* 237d-238a.

25. Plato *The Laws* 840a, trans. R. Hackforth, *Collected Dialogues.*

26. Plato *The Laws* 1, 6:47d.

27. Plato *The Laws* 1.626de; 8.840c. See also Michel Foucault, *Use of Pleasure,* 63-77.

28. Plato *Republic* 19.590c, trans. Paul Shorey, *Collected Dialogues.*

29. Plato *Republic* 10.590d.

30. Plato *Republic,* V. See also Jean Bethke Elshtain, *Public Man, Private Woman, Women in Social and Political Thought* (Princeton: Princeton Univ. Press, 1981), 19-54.

31. Xenophon *Oeconomicus* 1:19-20 and 22.

32. Xenophon *Oeconomicus* 2:1.

33. Xenophon *Memorabilia* 4:5, 2-3.

34. Foucault, *Use of Pleasure,* 80.

35. Aristotle *Politics* 1254b, trans. Richard McKeon. The *Basic Works of Aristotle* (New York: Random House, 1970).

36. Maryanne Cline Horowitz, "Aristotle and Woman," *Journal of the History of Biology* 9, 2 (Fall, 1976): 207.

37. Aristotle *The History of Animals,* trans. McKeon, 608b.

38. Aristotle *Politics* Bk. 1, chap. 13 (260b, 28-31).

39. Tama Starr, *The Natural Inferiority of Women. Outrageous Pronouncements by Misguided Males* (New York: Poseidon Press, 1991), 217.

40. Starr, *Natural Inferiority,* 221.

41. This was stated during the 1970s controversy over ordaining women in the Episcopalian church.

*The Penetrator and the Penetrated* ■■■■

*The Incubus: The Begetting of Merlin.* Throughout
history, thousands of women have been accused
of sin and heresy in the form of witchcraft
charges. Allegedly, these women gave themselves
sexually to the devil, thereby becoming
instruments for inflaming uncontrollable sexual
desire. Fourteenth-century French manuscript.
Courtesy of Bibliothèque Nationale, Paris.

# 8

# Sin Is a Sexually Communicable Disease

■■■■

Christianity inherited a troubled relationship to sexuality from the cultural world in which it first took shape. The values of male honor and female shame and the opposition between public man and private woman had a profound influence on the way Christian theologians came to view the sexual self. Through their assimilation into Christian institutions such as asceticism, monasticism, and clerical celibacy and into Christian doctrines about sexuality, sin, and human nature, the values of the Greco-Roman gender system shaped Western attitudes toward women and sexuality for nearly two millennia.

When Christianity made its first appearance among merchants, tradespeople, women, and slaves, the aristocrats of the empire were not much impressed. They knew that one could expect little more than superstition from such a crowd, and they thought it likely that Christian rites included immoral practices. Like other religious sects existing on the margins of Roman religions, Christians were plagued by rumors that they practiced incest and cannibalism in their rituals. During the first two centuries these rumors ignited the populace and resulted in an outbreak of persecutions.

The Neronian persecution of 67 C.E. was seared into the memory of the Christians of Rome. When the blame for an urban fire fell on the emperor Nero, because it occurred in the same quarter of the city where he had wanted to raze buildings in order to build his new Golden Palace, he scapegoated the Christians, accusing them of having started the fire out of a general hatred for humankind, since they refused to participate in public festivals that secured the benevolence of the gods. His accusations were not without a certain credibility, because rumor had it that Christians met secretly at night to hold orgies at which they practiced cannibalism and incest. He made a spectacle out of his punishment of the Christians by burning them as living torches during an evening garden party.

## THE POWER OF CHRISTIAN REASON

For the next two centuries, Christian intellectuals, fearful that at any time dangerous rumors of Christian cannibalism and incest could erupt into another wave of persecution, published open letters to the emperors defending Christian morality and religious rites. Far from being immoral and lawless, they protested, Christians were in fact the true philosophers. Judge for yourselves, they said. Look at Christian sexual practice: "Many men and women now in their sixties and seventies who have been disciples of Christ since childhood have preserved their purity [sexual abstinence]; and I am proud that I could point to such people in every nation [ethnic group]."[1] Justin Martyr, the second-century Christian apologist, reminded emperor Marcus Aurelius:

Just recently one of us submitted a petition to the Prefect Felix in Alexandria, asking that a physician be allowed to make him a eunuch. The physicians there said that they were not allowed to do this without the permission of the Prefect. When Felix would by no means agree to endorse [the petition] of the young man he remained single, satisfied with [the approval] of his own conscience and that of his fellow believers.[2]

The Roman state should understand, the apologists insisted, that Christians were in fact ideal citizens, virtuous in the ways that the Roman state understood virtue: In the moral life of Christians, reason ruled over the passions.

By the canons of Greek philosophy, only philosophers were in a position to achieve true mastery over the irrational self, because they alone had the leisure to cultivate rationality through the study of geometry, music, astronomy, rhetoric, and logic. These disciplines trained the mind, directed it away from the bodily life, and strengthened its authority over the passions. Nevertheless, second-century Christian apologists like Justin explained to a skeptical public that Christianity had succeeded where the philosophers had failed. What Plato had envisioned as possible only for the philosopher kings—a moral and intellectual discipline whereby reason gained mastery over the passions—was now possible for women, tradespeople, and slaves. Through conversion to Christianity those irrational masses, once incapable of controlling their passions, now through reason had become model citizens. In the third century Origen protested in defense of Christianity, "Why then is it outrageous if Jesus wanting to show mankind the extent of his ability to heal souls, chose infamous and most wicked men, and led them on so far that they were an example of the purest moral character?"[3]

In the process of defending Christians against damaging rumors and promoting Christian morality, Christian apologists created a new Christology. Christ, they explained, was actually an incarnation of universal Reason, the rational principle that ruled the cosmos. Furthermore Christ as universal Reason was present in the rational soul of every person. Christians therefore could bypass the lengthy process of cultivating virtue, which depended on education and social class, by conforming to Christ as the universal Reason already present in their consciousness. "We have been taught," wrote Justin Martyr,

that Christ is the first begotten of God, and have previously testified that he is the Reason of which every race of man partakes. Those who lived in accordance with Reason are Christians, even though they were called godless, such as, among the Greeks, Socrates and Heraclitus and others like them; So also those who lived without Reason were ungracious and enemies to Christ, and murderers of those who lived by Reason. But those who lived by Reason and those who live so now, are Christians, fearless and unperturbed.[4]

In one grand sweep of his new Christology, Justin transformed Christians into philosophers, and all virtuous men (like Socrates) who lived according to Reason, into Christians.

When the cool persuasion of the apologists failed to quench smoldering suspicions about Christian immorality, however, the martyrs provided an even more powerful argument that in Christians divine Reason had subdued the irrational passions. In the oft-recited accounts of Christian martyrdom, governors and crowds were overcome by awe at the amazing control Christians manifested over fear, pain, humiliation, and even death. The account of the martyrdom of Polycarp (Smyrna, 155 C.E.), which circulated among the churches of Asia Minor, opens with these lines:

Blessed and noble, indeed, are all the martyrdoms that have taken place according to God's will, . . . For who would not admire their nobility and patient endurance and love of their Master? Some of them, so torn by scourging that the anatomy of their flesh was visible as far as the inner veins and arteries, endured with such patience that even the bystanders took pity and wept; others achieved such heroism that not one of them uttered a cry or a groan.[5]

When Polycarp was led into the arena to be burned on a great pyre, he said to the soldier who was about to nail him to a stake, "Leave me as I am. For he who grants me to endure the fire will enable me also to remain on the pyre unmoved, without the security you desire from the nails."[6] So great was the power of the Christian spirit to control the passions of the body that Polycarp stood with quiet attention as the wall of flame engulfed his body. Two decades later in Lyons a group of martyrs were praised for "the sovereign liberty of their word against the Gentiles and their nobility of soul shown through their patient courage and fearlessness."[7] The very possibility of this degree of control over the passions was proof of the presence of the divine.

With the conversion of the emperor Constantine to Christianity in the fourth century, the persecutions ended, and with them, the experience of martyrdom. In the decades that followed, the new heroes of the faith were Egyptian and Syrian ascetics, who renounced property, family bonds, and household responsibilities to seek Christian perfection in the solitude of the desert. Central to their withdrawal from the world was the renunciation of sexuality. The Roman Christians of the Western empire were profoundly moved by the stories of these Eastern ascetics, and many adopted an ascetic lifestyle while living at home that included the renunciation of sexuality, the practice of fasting, and vigils. The Greek philosophers had celebrated the rule of reason over passion as the trademark of the aristocracy, the ruling class whose virtue legitimated their political power. By the fourth century, Christians celebrated the supreme victory of reason over passion in the lives of the ascetics. They became for the Western Church models of the highest expression of Christianity.[8]

The ascetic movement gained popularity through the publication of a popular novella, *The Life of Anthony,* by Athanasius, bishop of Alexandria. Athanasius told the story of a restless young man who at the age of twenty lost his parents through death and found himself at the head of a prosperous household. His conversion to a life of renunciation took place in the village church when he heard the Gospel reading "If you would be perfect, go and sell what you have and give to the poor." He sold the family acreage, disposed of the movable property, and distributed his patrimony to the poor. He then adopted the life of an ascetic, living on the outskirts of the village. As part of his training "he repressed the body and kept it in subjection" by eating only bread, water, and salt—and that, infrequently (once every fourth day). When he slept, he slept on the bare ground and often he would pass the night keeping a vigil of prayer. For, as Athanasius explains, "the fiber of the soul is sound when the pleasures of the body are diminished."[9] Conquest of the body opened the way for control of the mind. To continue his training Anthony retreated deep into the hostile desert and enclosed himself in an abandoned fort, where he pursued his ascetic training for twenty years. When he emerged, Athanasius declared, "his soul was free from blemish for it was neither contracted as if by grief, nor relaxed by pleasure, nor possessed by laughter or dejection. . . . He was altogether . . . guided by reason."[10]

An ascetic impulse had been present in the Christian movement from the beginning. Paul had written to the Christians at Corinth, "To the unmarried and the widows I say that it is well for them to remain unmarried as I do. But if they are not practicing self-control, they should marry" (1 Cor. 7:8–9). Women especially were attracted to the ascetic ideal. Since chastity was the supreme virtue for women, sexual abstinence seemed compatible with the essence of womanhood. On the other hand, when daughters and wives claimed the right to make decisions about their sexuality (to renounce sexual relations), a fundamental prerogative of males seemed under attack.

For many women the heroic figure of Thecla celebrated in the popular *Acts of Paul and Thecla*, a second-century collection of stories associated with Paul, embodied the ascetic ideal. For an aristocratic woman like Thecla, the renunciation of the world was summed up in the single act of renouncing an arranged marriage. In so doing she asserted her own autonomy—her right of disposal over her body and her sexuality. In the new context of the ascetic movement women were no longer valued for their reproductive sexuality, and a new ideal of womanhood was created—that of the consecrated virgin. Although the ideal of virginity enshrined the earlier values associated with womanhood, it also gave women a certain autonomy. By renouncing "the world," they gained control over their own sexuality.

Through her renunciation, a woman who embraced the ascetic ideal transcended the world of the body and sexuality. Fourth-century writers on asceticism envisioned the virgin lifestyle as a return to the original state of human life, before the fall, sin, and sexual intercourse, as illustrated by this reconstruction of the Edenic ideal from John Chrysostom:

> Adam and Eve remained apart from marriage, leading the sort of life in Paradise they would have led had they been in Heaven, luxuriating in their association with God. Desire for sexual relations, conception, labor pains, childbirth, and every form of corruptibility was removed from their soul. As a clear stream flows forth from a pure source, so in that place were they adorned with virginity.[11]

The inferiority of women and their subordination to men was directly linked to their reproductive sexuality and to their social role of care for bodily life.[12] By renouncing the body and sexuality and following the ascetic ideals, women in effect transcended their femaleness. The mastery of the passions and the body had long been a masculine enterprise. Now ascetic women who were able to sustain the physical rigors of fasting could be praised for demonstrating masculine virility. Female ascetics who repudiated both their reproductive sexuality and their social roles became, so to speak, "honorary" males.

Because the male constituted the ideal form of humanity, and the masculine virtues of courage and self-control represented the pinnacle of moral perfection, the only language these writers could find for expressing the excellence of women ascetics was the language of masculine perfection. John Chrysostom praised the ascetic Olympias thus: "Don't say 'woman' but 'what a man!' Because this is a man, despite her physical appearance."[13] Female excellence could be praised only by the use of masculine attributes. The fact that masculinity had become the symbol for excellence subverted the power of female achievement. Christian theologians failed to translate the excellence of female ascetic attainment into feminine symbols. (Even today the expression "what a woman!" evokes images of female sexuality rather than female achievement.) Instead of celebrating femaleness as providing a unique avenue of access to God, or seeing in femaleness a profound expression of the divine, Christianity left the traditional cultural meanings of femaleness and female sexuality unchanged. Rationality and self-control retained their masculine cast, while passion, sexuality, and body were particularly female.

After two centuries of the practice of sexual renunciation in the quest to know God, Augustine formulated a theology that identified sin with sexuality. The women who did not renounce sexuality were caught in the web of the new connections drawn between sin and sexuality. Since womanhood was so intricately connected to sexuality, it was woman's sexuality, erotic and seductive, that led both women and men away from God. Woman's body, since it was a stark proclamation of sexuality, was not in the image of God; it represented rather the pull of those forces that drew humanity away from God.

A theological doctrine is very much like a living organism. It begins in a germinative moment, grows to maturity in a favorable environment, and dies of natural causes. That germinative moment for a theological doctrine often lies in an individual's profound spiritual experience. The theological doctrine of an original sin inherent in human nature and passed across generations was formulated by an African intellectual, Augustine (354–430), whose enormous influence earned him the title of father of the Western church. Augustine's conversion was shaped by the popularity of the ascetic movement in fourth-century Christianity and the social institutions of his day—concubinage and arranged marriages among them—and spawned by a vigorous intellectual and spiritual quest. As a highly trained scholar and rhetorician, Augustine reflected on and analyzed his experiences in order to discern universal patterns within them. To this process he brought the categories of his intellectual formation, namely, the Greek philosophical concepts of the self and of the divine.

Augustine's *Confessions* chronicle his long and tortuous journey into the service of God. Much of this spiritual autobiography is devoted implicitly to issues of sexuality and sexual relations. To Augustine's mind, in fact, his conversion to Christianity was inseparable from his renunciation of sex. He traced the history of his sexual renunciation back to the moment of this sexual awakening. In his sixteenth year when his father saw him at the baths and noticed that he was becoming a man, Augustine reported that he "joyfully told my mother about it as if already looking forward to grandchildren." His mother, however, an ardent Christian, privately warned him "not to commit fornication; but above all things never defile another man's wife." His mother's advice struck the adolescent Augustine, he recalled, as nothing but "womanish counsels which I would blush to obey."[14] As a young man, Augustine endorsed pagan society's belief that manhood could be achieved only through sexual exploits.

A full exploration of his sexuality waited until he went to Carthage for his studies, where (as he remembered it) a "cauldron of unholy loves was seething and bubbling all around me. I was not in love as yet, but I was in love with love. . . . To love and to be loved were sweetened all the more when I gained the enjoyment of the body of the person I loved."[15] A year of sexual discovery was consummated when Augustine, at eighteen, took a concubine, with whom he lived for fifteen years. It was customary for a young man not to marry until his career was established, and for Augustine this stage was still fifteen years off. Like other young men of his social class, he took a concubine, a woman of a lower social class, whom for social reasons he could not marry. Such a relationship provided young men of the upper classes a companion, a sexual partner, and a household manager. Augustine was deeply attached to this unidentified woman, and together they raised a son, Adeodatus.

Unexpectedly in 384 Augustine was appointed to the prestigious chair of rhetoric in Milan, where members of the imperial court were in residence. This new position set the seal on Augustine's career, and he was ready to marry. His mother eagerly contracted a marriage for him with the daughter of a socially appropriate family. The girl (probably ten) was two years below the legal age for marriage according to Roman law, and Augustine was to wait for two years before taking her as his wife. Part of the contractual arrangement with the family required that Augustine send away his concubine, who was perceived as a potential rival of the wife-to-be. Augustine remembered:

> My mistress was torn from my side, as an impediment to my marriage, and my heart, which clung to her, was torn and wounded till it bled. And she went back to Africa, vowing to me never to know any other man and leaving with me my natural son by her. And I, unhappy as I was and weaker than a woman, could not bear the delay of the two years that should elapse before I could have taken the bride I sought. And so, since I was not a lover of wedlock so much as a slave of lust, I procured another mistress.[16]

The marriage never came to pass, for within those two years Augustine converted to Christianity and renounced sexual relations.

In adolescence Augustine had rejected the Christian faith of his mother. For him the Christian Scriptures read like a book written by uneducated and illiterate sorts, Christian doctrines appeared either confusing or incomprehensible, and they failed to answer the really basic questions about human life. Augustine's migration back to the faith of his mother had passed through a version of Manichaeism and a version of Platonism. By the time he was a professor of rhetoric in Milan, his intellectual questions had been adequately resolved, and in the person of Bishop Ambrose of Milan he found a Christian intellectual who enjoyed the respect of the aristocratic Roman elite. He was at last ready for conversion and baptism.

It was at this moment in his life that he had a chance encounter with *The Life of Anthony*. In his *Confessions* Augustine recalled receiving a visit from a fellow countryman from Africa named Ponticianus, who recounted the following story. Ponticianus and three companions in the emperor's service had wandered idly looking for diversion through the streets of Treves (in what is now Germany). Two of them chanced upon a small house, where they had occasion to read *The Life of Anthony*. A fire began to burn in one young man as he read about that passionate renunciation which seeks the kingdom of God. "'Tell me,' he exclaimed to his friend, 'what goal are we seeking in all these toils of ours? What is our motive in public service? Can our hopes in the court rise higher than to be friends of the emperor?'" "'But' he glowed, 'if I chose to become a friend of God, I can become one now.'" He immediately resolved "to enter into God's service," and his friend, loath to break the bonds of friendship, resolved to join him in this renunciation. The story ends with: "Both of them had affianced brides who, when they heard of this, likewise dedicated their virginity to you."[17] Sexual renunciation was the port of entry for God's service. While Ponticianus was finishing his story, Augustine felt "inward confusion and horrible shame." He turned to his friend Alypius, who had also listened to this story, and said, "'What is the matter with us? What is the meaning of this story? These men have none of our education, yet they stand up and storm the gates of heaven while we, for all our learning, lie here groveling in this world of flesh and blood!'"[18]

So began the vehement quarrel that raged within his soul, "a fiery struggle in which I was engaged with myself." He retreated to the garden of the house where he was staying. The battle was with himself; he tore his hair and hammered his forehead with his fists as he struggled toward the renunciation he longed to make. "Thus I was sick and tormented, reproaching myself more bitterly than ever, rolling and writhing in my chain till it should be utterly broken."[19] It takes ten pages for Augustine to re-create the full force of this internal storm. The conflict within which Augustine was locked was the conflict with his own sexuality—reason against passion. For Augustine to convert to Christianity meant to renounce sexual desire, but his will was not strong enough to achieve his resolve, and he fell back again and again. Then finally in "a mighty rain of tears" he gave vent to his despair.

Then suddenly, almost miraculously he found that the power to will was there. Words floated over the garden wall, "'Pick it up, read it, pick it up, read it.'" When he grasped a book of Paul's letters lying on a bench and opened it, his eyes fell on the passage "Make no provision for the flesh, to gratify its desires" (Rom. 13:14). "I wanted to read no further," wrote Augustine, "nor did I need to, for instantly after the sentence ended there was infused in my heart something like a light of full certainty, and all the gloom of doubt vanished away."[20] Through divine intervention he was able to make the renunciation.

The experience in the garden became paradigmatic when Augustine developed his doctrine of sin. He unfolded this doctrine by reflecting on the events that took place in another garden—the Garden of Eden—refracted through the prism of Platonic philosophy. Borrowing from the Greeks, Augustine saw inner conflict as staged in the divided self—the higher, rational part of the self ruling and governing the irrational part, the appetites and passions. The higher self was capable of knowledge of the abstract, unchanging, invisible world of the divine. The lower self was suited only for life in the unstable, changing world of sense, with its complexity and diversity.

In the original state of perfection, according to Augustine, human beings lived in harmony with themselves and with God. This was possible because the rational, ruling part of the self was completely absorbed in contemplation of God and therefore was able to order and direct the irrational aspects of the self perfectly. When Adam and Eve opted for autonomy and self-rule, apart from total contemplation of God and obedience to God's commands, they were punished by the crippling of the rational part of the soul, so that it could no longer govern the irrational passions. Where the Genesis narrative says, "They ate and the eyes of both were opened," Augustine asked, "Opened to what?" And he answered, to lust for each other as punishment for sin.[21]

The first sin of Adam and Eve was the sin of pride, which consisted in their rebelling against God and opting for self-rule or autonomy. The punishment for the sin of pride was the impotence of the rational mind. Augustine called this punishment concupiscence (desire that rages out of control). Lust is a good Anglo-Saxon translation for this latinate term. The rebellion against God resulted in a revolt of the passions; the punishment fit the crime. Adam's refusal to be controlled and governed by the will of God resulted in the refusal of his lower nature—the passions—to obey his higher, rational nature. It was no accident that Adam and Eve hid themselves after eating the forbidden fruit, for after the Fall "they felt a movement in their members of which they were ashamed," sexual stirrings unbidden by the rational mind, embarrassing it by exposing its lack of control.[22] The strategic placement of the fig leaf indicated the locus of the punishment for sin, the very place from which concupiscence arises.

The paradigm for this loss of control by the rational mind was sexuality. Augustine's own experience of his inability to master his sexual drives was for him an expression of the original crippling of human nature that resulted from the Fall. When Augustine speculated on the nature of sex in paradise before the Fall, he described it as a passionless, rational sexual experience.

> We move our hands and feet to perform their special functions when we so will. This involves no reluctance on their part and movements are performed with all the ease we observe in our own case and in that of others. . . . Why should we not believe that the sexual organs could have been the obedient servants of mankind at the bidding of the will in the same way as the other if there had been no lust which came in as the retribution for the sin of disobedience. Why should we not believe that except for the sin and its punishment of corruptibility the members of a man's body could have been the servants of man's will without any lust for the procreation of children. . . . Because he did not obey God, [man] could not obey himself.[23]

Augustine believed that this crippling of the ruling powers of the rational mind was sexually transmitted by each generation to the next, and so passed to the whole race. It was through sinful, irrational passion that the race was propagated; and it was through this sinful passion that each new generation was infected with this weakness in the rational, ruling portion of the self. Sin was a sexually communicable disease. According to Augustine's theory, the sinlessness of Jesus stemmed directly from his birth from a virgin. If Mary was impregnated by the Holy Spirit, then irrational sexual passion was not involved in the conception of Jesus, and therefore original sin was not passed on to him. Augustine followed the reproductive theory espoused by Aristotle, that the male of the species contributes the "form" to the embryo, carried by the male seed. The female provides only the matter, since she is not capable of producing the life-bearing seed.[24] Thus, in Augustine's view, the sperm transmits this original sin; because they did not produce seed, women were incapable of transmitting sin.

The passionate and irrational aspect of sexuality—which is what made it sinful—could be redeemed in marriage through the good of procreation and by limiting the sinfulness of sexuality to one partner. Because it was the lustful, passionate dimension of sexuality that made it sinful, any form of sexuality that did not aim at procreation was therefore sinful. For this reason Augustine asserted that "true marital chastity avoids intercourse with a menstruating or pregnant woman; indeed it refrains from any marital encounter where there is no longer any prospect of conception, as with older people."[25] In these contexts, Augustine believed, the only meaning that sexuality could have was the domination of desire over reason, which would reverse the control of reason over passion and hence place it in the category of sinful sex. This Augustinian understanding of sexuality still dominates Roman Catholic theology. The church's condemnation of birth control is built on the premise that sexual intercourse that does not aim at procreation is sinful lust. Although Vatican II reversed this fifteen-century-old tradition and declared that the purpose of sexuality was to create bonds of affection, it did not go so far as to allow birth control.

## SINFUL SEX AND THE FEMALE SELF

A system of ideas premised on the problematic character of sexuality was not new, of course. Centuries before Augustine the Greeks had designated female sexuality as a force to be controlled and dominated, a conceptualization of female sexuality that corresponded with women's subordinate roles as slaves, mistresses, and wives. The "lower" self—bodily, passionate, constantly threatening to rage out of control—was a source of shame. Honor could be achieved only through public demonstrations of mastery over this appetitive self. The body and its appetites, like woman, functioned as symbol for shame.

In the Augustinian system, however, the sexual self was transformed from a symbol of shame to a symbol of moral guilt. The bodily appetites were expressions of a sinful nature and deserved eternal punishment. In Augustine's view, God's universal judgment on humanity was justified by universal guilt embodied in sinful, sexual human nature. Only the sacramental waters of baptism could expunge the guilt inherent in the sinful nature of every newborn. The old confidence of the philosophers in the well-disciplined rational self was shattered by Augustine's notion of original sin. Only through the aid of divine grace would the crippled rational self be able to control the unruly desires of the lower self.

Initially it may appear that Augustine created gender equality in sin—not just women, but men too, possess a sinful, sexual nature. But the role of women in Roman society had not changed by Augustine's period. He, like the Greek philosophers, related to women primarily in their roles as concubines, wives, and slaves. When Augustine pondered the purpose of woman in his commentary in Genesis, he could not see beyond her role in procreation.

Now, if the woman was not made for the man to be his helper in begetting children, in what was she to help him? She was not to till the earth with him, for there was not any toil to make help necessary. If there were any such need a male helper would be better, and the same can be said of the comfort of another's presence if Adam were perhaps weary of solitude. How much more agreeably could two male friends, rather than a man and a woman enjoy companionship and conversation in a life shared together. And if they had to make an arrangement in their common life for one to command the other to obey, in order to make sure that opposing wills would not disrupt the peace of the household, there would have been proper rank to assure this, since one would be created first and the other second.[26]

Relegated to sexual functions only, the burden of guilt imposed by sinful sexuality rested more heavily on woman than man. For although men also possessed a sinful sexual nature, maleness was still equated with rationality. Women, in this view, were essentially nothing but sexual beings, limited to one dimension, one the Christian theology repudiated.

Here Augustine was again the uncritical heir of the Greek philosophical tradition. In Greek thought the sexual self was objectified as a collection of energies and drives that originated in the body. The rational self, sometimes called the soul, was the nonmaterial aspect of the self that the philosophers believed had a certain kinship with the realm of divine and unchanging realities. As Socrates, Plato's model philosopher, explained, "We are convinced that if we are ever to have pure knowledge of anything, we must get rid of the body and contemplate things by themselves with the soul by itself."[27] Plato believed that the desire to free the soul was found chiefly, if not only, in the philosophers. In fact the philosopher's occupation lay precisely in freeing and separating soul from body.[28] Because the soul belonged to the realm of the immortal, the soul possessed within itself knowledge of what was true, eternal, and unchanging. The soul "discerns justice, its very self, and likewise temperance and knowledge."[29] Virtue resided in the soul, not the body. The separation of the soul from the body was achieved through long practice, by constantly contesting the domination of those appetites rooted in the body. When finally the soul properly controlled and ordered the body and its passions, the virtuous life and harmony were simultaneously achieved.

The equation of woman with sexuality and body (representing the irrational and constantly changing material world) and the exclusion of sexuality and passion from the divine opened up a chasm between woman and God. Only by repudiating her sexual identity and renouncing femaleness could this chasm be bridged. The equation of woman with sexuality meant she was both subordinated to man and alienated from God.

In Augustine's clever resolution of an exegetical dilemma presented by two contradictory passages of Scripture, he gave a Christian baptism to this Greek theory of the self. The passage "God created humanity in his own image, in the image of God he created them male and female" (Gen. 1:27) declares that both male and female are in the image of God. Paul's insistence "for a man ought not to cover his head since he is the image and glory of God; but woman is the glory of man" (1 Cor. 11:7) shows that man is in the image of God but woman is not. Augustine reconciled the apparent contradiction by carefully arguing that male and female were indeed in the image of God, insofar as they both possessed a rational soul capable of contemplating God and ruling the passions. But this rational soul had two elements, a masculine element capable of contemplating God, and a feminine element that animated the body and was oriented toward bodily life.[30]

Although male and female were not differentiated on the level of soul, they were differentiated on the level of body. The male body reflected the superiority of the masculine element of the soul; the female body, however, expressed the feminine element in the soul. In the contortions of Augustine's reasoning, the female body, because it was created for sexual service, expressed the sexual aspect of human being, while male body expressed the rational aspect of human being. The male body thus reflected the image of God in a way that female body did not, since the female body reflected only sexual function. This reasoning underlies the statement in the Vatican declaration on the ordination of women that only the male body can represent Christ, because Christ represents God through the maleness of his body. Women cannot be ordained as priests because their bodies are capable of representing only their sexuality, not God.[31] "The priest is a sign," insists the Vatican, and "there would not be this 'natural resemblance' which must exist between Christ and his minister if the role of Christ were not taken by a man. . . . The incarnation of the Word took place according to the male sex."[32]

By equating sin and sexuality, Augustine only drew a theological conclusion from a long-standing Christian social practice. Generations of celibate ascetics had held the renunciation of sexuality to be the central spiritual discipline in the quest for the knowledge of God. This implied that sexuality could not lead to knowledge of God and that sexuality actually undermined the process of spiritual transformation. Augustine's doctrine of concupiscence as original sin took root in the Western church because so many people found his theological insights helpful in articulating their own experience—the clerics who practiced celibacy, the monks who struggled to control their sexual desires, and even the bishops who tried to govern troublesome congregations. Irrational, unruly desire buried deep in the human heart accounted for the struggles of those who were trying to exercise authority over themselves or over others.

From the fourth-century synod of Elvira, Spain, to the twelfth-century papal decrees, synods and councils struggled to impose celibacy on the clergy. As Christianity became a state religion and adopted the attitudes toward gender roles of Greco-Roman society, fewer women held church offices. Those insisting on the celibacy of male clerics and monks perceived female sexuality as a threatening and uncontrollable force. During the medieval period the papacy's struggle to assert its authority over the clergy led to a particularly perverse and destructive construction of female sexuality. Through the mechanism of the Inquisition a theory of sexuality was created that demonized sexuality by attributing the powers of sexuality to demons. This new ideology's creators drew heavily on the Augustinian doctrines of the sexual drives as a symbol of moral evil. The demonization of sexuality during the witchcraft persecutions fell far more heavily on women than on men. When sexuality was defined as demonic, a new concept of woman was invented—the medieval witch.

By the medieval period, the ascetic movement had produced a strong and vital social institution in monastic Christianity. Because monasteries were complete economic and social units in themselves, they proved to be an effective means for organizing communities of Christians in the wilderness of northern Europe following the collapse of urban civilization in the West with the fall of the Roman Empire. These monasteries were the bearers of the literary culture of Roman imperial Christianity, preserving the literary wealth of the Roman period by copying manuscripts, producing handbooks, and compiling anthologies. The spiritual authority of the monastic communities was based on their continuous cycle of liturgical prayers offered as service to God and on the self-denial inherent in the monastic way of life. A lifelong vow of celibacy was the principal requirement for entry into the community, thus again divorcing the practice of sexuality from the pursuit of God.

In Western Christendom priests were appointed to their offices by the nobility, who owned the churches erected on their lands and who collected the tithe (livings) that belonged to the churches. These livings were paid out as salaries to the clerics they appointed to serve the village churches. Motives other than the spiritual welfare of the peasants were often at work in the appointment of clerics. Friends or kin might be appointed to the more lucrative church offices. A cleric appointed to a sleepy village church might choose to live in the energetic city while still collecting his living, leaving his office vacant. If he was conscientious, he might hire a vicar to replace him. Sometimes church offices were simply sold for profit.

For many centuries there had been an attempt to make the authority of the clergy dependent on the practice of celibacy. Although the celibacy of the clergy had existed as an ideal since the fourth century, it had never become a universal practice. The papacy, which had been in the hands of Italian nobility, had shown no interest in enforcing celibacy. But by the thirteenth century the papacy had managed to extricate itself from control by powerful families. A period of internal reform of the office of the papacy followed, which eventually launched the papacy on a course that would lead to its enormous political power, competing with the monarchies of Europe. A central feature of this internal reform was the imposition of celibacy laws on the clergy. This was a means of reestablishing the spiritual authority of the papacy as well as a means for extricating the clergy from the control of the nobility. By threatening married priests with excommunication, the papacy became a more formidable power for clerics than the nobility, who possessed only the power of the purse.

In the eleventh century Pope Gregory VII convened a series of synods throughout Christian Europe and packed them with reform-minded bishops. He condemned priestly marriage and promoted celibacy as a standard for all ranks of the clergy. He then declared that married priests were guilty of the crime of fornication and ordered parishioners to boycott their masses. He threatened parishioners with excommunication should they take communion from a married priest. In 1139 Pope Innocent III laid the legal groundwork for persecuting wives of priests in a decree that declared all marriages after ordination invalid. Overnight, women who had been legal wives were now labeled concubines, whores, or adulteresses.

The attempt to enforce the celibacy laws, however, led to enormous social upheaval. Emissaries from the pope traveled from village to village preaching frightening sermons about the evils and dangers of female sexuality, calling the clergy to celibacy, and placing before them the choice of either losing their positions and livings or renouncing their mistresses and wives. The rhetoric required to bring about this social revolution prepared the ground for the demonization of female sexuality. An abbot refusing to accept jurisdictional responsibility for a convent of nuns wrote:

We, and our whole community of canons, recognizing that the wickedness of women is greater than all other wickedness of the world and that there is no anger like that of women, and that the poison of asps and dragons is more curable and less dangerous to men than the familiarity of women, have unanimously decreed for the safety of our souls, no less than for that of our bodies and goods, that we will on no account receive any more sisters to the increase of our perdition, but will avoid them like poisonous animals.[33]

The good abbot Conrad of Marchtal thought that the greatest danger to male celibacy was female sexuality. But the women he was referring to were celibate nuns!

The struggle to impose celibacy on the clergy took more than six centuries. While papal legates were raging against sexual passion, married clergy clung tenaciously to the satisfactions of domestic life. At Pointoise in 1074 when the abbot announced to the priests that he would impose clerical celibacy in his territory, the priests responded by spitting on him, beating him, and throwing him out. In the town of Rouen in the same year, a similar announcement was greeted with a hail of stones.[34] Again in Rouen in 1119, another attempt to impose priestly celibacy was greeted by fistfights in church.

A widespread tactic for overcoming the resistance of married clerics was to attack their wives. Pope Urban II in 1089 allowed that a wife could be enslaved if a subdeacon was unwilling to separate from her. The archbishop Manasse V of Rheims permitted the imprisonment of the wives of clerics. A synod in Valladolid in 1322 forbade church burial to the wives of priests. As late as 1651, clergy were still living with wives (now classified as concubines), and a synod of Osnabrück declared, "We shall . . . inspect the houses of those under suspicion night and day and have the shameful persons publicly branded by the hangman. And should the authorities be lax or negligent, they shall be punished by us."[35] In the same century the bishop of Bamberg appealed to the authority of the princes to "thrust its way into the rectories, fetch out the concubines, publicly whip them, and place them under arrest."[36]

It was a short step from the idea that female sexuality was dangerous and an instrument of the devil to the idea that female sexuality itself could be a demonic power. Folk religious beliefs about the magical powers of sorcerers and witches had persisted for many centuries among the peasants. Synods and councils had long insisted that these beliefs were superstitious and rejected the notion that any individuals possessed magical powers. The power of sexual desire to resist this new discipline of the church, however, appeared so great that it was easy to see the very power of the devil operating in it. A thirteenth-century theologian, Bonaventure, despaired, "Because the sexual act had been corrupted (through original sin) and has become, so to speak, stinking, and because human beings are for the most part too lustful, the devil has so much power and authority over them."[37] Thomas Aquinas made this same conviction a part of his systematic theology: "Catholic faith teaches us that the demons have some importance, that they can harm human beings and even prevent sexual relations."[38] Through the twelfth and the thirteenth centuries at synods from Salisbury to Mainz and Valencia to Ferrara, the church condemned sorceresses who put spells on married people so that they cannot engage in conjugal relations.[39]

But for celibate males, the danger was not attacks of impotence but, according to church authorities, the lure of female sexuality. In 1484 the pope's fiery zeal to quench sexual desire ignited into a frightening conflagration. In this year a papal bull of Innocent VIII, "The Witches' Bull," enlisted the Inquisition as a judicial process for prosecuting witches who had allegedly given themselves to the devil sexually and had thereby become his instruments for inflaming, controlling, and obstructing sexual desire. The fire he fanned consumed hundreds of thousands of women who were condemned as witches. Probably more than a million women were burned at the stake for the heresy of witchcraft as the Inquisition swept across Europe.

The workings of the Inquisition were complex: Denunciations came from the populace; papal inquisitors presided over the judicial proceedings; the questions of the prosecutor and the answers of the accused were duly recorded by a secretary. When the judicial proceedings were finished, the civil authorities presided over the executions, in which witches were burned at the stake. While the machinery of the Inquisition was in the hands of the papacy, it was dependent on the willingness of the populace to denounce and the willingness of the nobility to execute.

The German inquisitors Jakob Sprenger and Heinrich Institoris, appointed by Pope Innocent VIII, created the systematic theology that linked the threat of female sexuality with the folk belief in the magical powers of witches to control sexuality. Their scholarly discussion of witches in the *Malleus Maleficarum* (*The Witches' Hammer*), produced for the Inquisition, elaborated the finer points of this theory of witchcraft:

There is also, concerning witches who copulate with devils much difficulty in considering the methods by which such abominations are consummated. On the part of the devil: first, of what element the body is made that he assumes; secondly, whether the act is always accompanied by the injection of semen received from another; thirdly, as to time and place, whether he commits this act more frequently at one time than at another; fourthly, whether the act is visible to any who may be standing by. And on the part of the women it has to be inquired whether they who were themselves conceived in this filthy manner are often visited by devils; or secondly, whether it is those who are offered to devils by midwives at the time of their birth; and thirdly, whether the actual venereal delectation of such is of a weaker sort.[40]

Medieval beliefs provided some answers to these questions. The devil would take the form of a woman, have intercourse with a man, and thereby gather his semen. He would then take the form of a man, have intercourse with a woman, and deposit the semen that had been procured in the earlier transaction. The demon impersonating a woman was called a *succubus* (Latin *succubare*, "to lie under"), because she lay under the man; the demon taking the form of a man was an *incubus* (*incubare*, "the lie"), since he lay on top of the woman.[41] Although its speculations on human-demon coupling may invite our ridicule, this passage does express some dangerous beliefs. One is that female sexuality is dangerous, that is, susceptible to demonic control. Another is that women's sexual powers derived their potency from the devil.

"The Witches' Bull" identified the seven methods by which witches exercised their baleful influence over intercourse and conception, and the *Malleus Maleficarum* elaborated them. Both obsessive sexual desire and male impotence could be traced to witchcraft. Furthermore witches could prevent the flow of semen either by operating internally on the "motive force" that caused "flow of the vital essences" or by acting externally with the use of herbs or a cock's testicles. Witches were also known for removing the male organ altogether. One witch kept twenty or thirty such organs alive and fed them oats and corn. When one man sought to retrieve his, she generously offered him his choice. When he took a large one, however, the witch refused him that one saying it belonged to the parish priest.[42]

The witches were also alleged to be capable of changing men into beasts. They attacked women's reproductive potentiality by procuring abortions and by offering children to the devil. The *Malleus Maleficarum* presented such evidence as the following. A noblewoman had been warned by her midwife to avoid all contact with a "notorious witch" during her pregnancy. Forgetting that warning, the woman left her castle and chanced to meet the witch, who greeted her and placed her hand on the lady's stomach. "Suddenly she felt the child move in pain. When in great anxiety she returned to the castle and related to her midwife what had occurred, the midwife proclaimed she had lost the child. And indeed the child was aborted in pieces." The inquisitors concluded the story thus: "This great difficulty was permitted by God to punish her husband whose duty it was to bring witches to justice and avenge their injury to the creator."[43]

The inquisitors' campaign against witchcraft was a campaign against "the malice of women." The authors of the *Malleus Maleficarum* speculate that if the world were without women and their wickedness, it would be free of "innumerable dangers." These conclusions followed on the premise of the inquisitors that "all witchcraft comes from carnal lust which is in women insatiable." For this argument, they appealed to Proverbs 30: "'There are three things that are never satisfied, yea a fourth thing which says not, It is enough; that is, the mouth of the womb.' Wherefore for the sake of fulfilling their lust they even consort with devils." The persecution of an individual woman as a witch rested on the broader foundations of the cultural denigration of women in general. Here we hear familiar arguments about women's profligate sexuality, inferior intellect, and general deceitfulness.

There is a "natural reason" why woman is "more carnal than a man," and that is "a defect in the formation of the first woman, since she was formed from a bent rib, that is, a rib of the breast that is bent as it were in the contrary direction to a man's and since through this defect she is an imperfect animal, she always deceives."[44] Of course what carries the argument is not this unusual view of women's physiology but an appeal to the misogyny of the age, here embroidered with fantasies masquerading as science.

Eve, the mother of women, showed she had "little faith" in the word of God when she disobeyed the divine prohibition about eating from the tree of knowledge of good and evil, "and all this is indicated by the etymology of the word; for *Femina* [the Latin word for woman] comes from *Fe* (Faith) and *Minus* (Less) since she is ever weaker to hold and preserve the faith. And this as regards faith is of her very nature."[45] This ludicrous denigration clearly derives from the centuries-old belief in women's intellectual inferiority. The inquisitors insisted, "Since women are feebler both in mind and body, it is not surprising that they should come under the spell of witchcraft. For as regards intellect, or the understanding of spiritual things, they seem to be of a different nature from men."[46] The inquisitors concluded this section of their exposition with a pious thanksgiving for their own gender: "It is better called the heresy of witches than of wizards since the name is taken from the more powerful body. And blessed be the Highest who has so far preserved the male sex from so great a crime, for since He was willing to be born and to suffer for us, therefore He granted to men this privilege."[47]

The inquisitors' view of women's dangerous sexuality should come as no surprise. Female sexuality appeared dangerous because men believed they had to control women, and in the end they were not able to. What was new was the fusion with Augustine's theology of sexuality. Sexual passion was in itself rebellion against the higher authority of the rational soul, and a rebellion against the rational soul was like rebellion against God. Monastics and clerics renounced sexuality to be closer to God; to the males who were supposed to be denying sexual passions, female sexuality loomed frighteningly large and threatening. The Inquisition wove this fear of female sexuality together with popular beliefs about the activities of witches around conception and birth and created the elaborate edifice of a theology of witches who had carnal intercourse with demons. This theology served as the basis for a persecution of women, carried out through the cooperation of ecclesiastical and civil authorities, that lasted for more than four centuries.

### THE SACRALIZATION OF THE FAMILY AND
### THE RESTORATION OF SEXUALITY

By the sixteenth century there was a wide consensus that the monastic system, which had formed a basic structural element of medieval society, had become corrupt. The wealth of the large monasteries and the elegant lives of their abbots drew sharp criticism. The worldly power of the prince-bishops and the profligacy of the begging monks seemed to overshadow the genuine spirituality that had given birth to the system. The earliest treatises calling for reform of the church were biting in their criticisms of both the clergy and the monks. Wherever reformers gained governmental power, monasteries were officially disbanded. In Geneva the

Calvinist reform began with the dissolution of the monasteries by the city council. Under Cardinal Wolsey, Thomas Cromwell launched the English reformation with the dissolution of twenty-nine monasteries in 1525.

Out of this widespread disillusionment with monastic life there evolved a new theology of sexuality. Its most colorful proponent was the monk Martin Luther, who initiated the German Reformation in the early 1500s with a series of tracts written in German, addressed to the common people. Luther began to formulate this new theology of sexuality as he lectured on the Book of Genesis at the Wittenberg theological school. As Luther pondered Gen. 1:27, reading that male and female were both created in the image of God, he understood the phrase "male and female" to refer to male and female *bodies* since it is only the body that distinguishes male from female. If male and female are in the image of God, then the bodies of both male and female are in the image of God, and therefore the body is good since it also is a bearer of God's image. And if the body is good, then sexuality is good.[48]

And when Luther reflected on Gen. 1:28, God's command to the newly created male and female to "be fruitful and multiply," Luther understood that not only was sexuality good, but, more than that, it was a divine ordinance. In Luther's Nominalist theology a divine ordinance counted as a fundamental expression of God's will and the divine basis for human nature itself. God willed that human nature, created good even in its bodily existence, should be faithful to the divine ordinance and the divinely planted impulse to procreation.

Therefore, Luther argued, vows of celibacy, not sexuality, were actually sinful, since celibacy was contrary to human nature as it was divinely created and contrary to the will of God. To the beleaguered married priest, Luther proclaimed that the laws of man could not cancel the ordinances of God. Since marriage was an institution that had been ordained by God, the marriage of a priest and his wife could not be annulled. (It was a common practice for married priests to present their wives as resident housekeepers to papal investigators.)[49]

Luther's theology in effect provided theological legitimation for the sexual drives of men and women and affirmed the sexual rights of men and women within marriage. Nowhere is this conveyed more poignantly than in Luther's pastoral counseling of Philip of Hesse. The energetic young Philip had already proved to be a valuable ally for the German reformer. He had organized a defense league of Protestant princes in case the Catholic emperor tried to impose Catholic practice on Germany by force. Philip's marriage, contracted for political reasons, to a daughter of a duke from a neighboring territory had failed to provide any sexual satisfaction. Previously Philip had found satisfaction without difficulty outside the bonds of his marriage; however, the newly converted Philip had a guilty conscience over these other relationships and felt that he could not present himself at the Lord's table.

Since Luther disavowed divorce, except on the basis of adultery, a dissolution of his marriage was not possible in the Protestant sexual ethic. However, Luther acknowledged as legitimate Philip's sexual needs and proposed (on the basis of the Old Testament) that Philip contract a second marriage in which his legitimate sexual needs could be met within the bonds of marriage. There were grave problems to this solution, since bigamy was forbidden by imperial law. Luther also counseled keeping this second marriage secret. In the end, this proved to be impossible. When the story broke, Philip's life was in danger for the capital crime of bigamy. He had to gain pardon from the Catholic emperor by dissociating himself from the military alliance.[50] Although Luther's pastoral counseling was ill-advised, it does illuminate how seriously he took the fundamental human need for sexual partnership.

As Luther radically reworked the medieval theology of sexuality, he created a new theology of marriage. He argued on the basis of his exegesis of Genesis that men and women were created for marriage. A wife, he said in his sermon "On the Estate of Marriage," is a gift of God, and therefore everyone should pray for a spouse. Married love and familial love are the highest forms of love. Married love, he said, seeks the good of the other, in contrast to monastic life, which seeks only the good of the self.

Luther transformed marriage from being a hospital for those possessed by incurable lust to *the* institution best suited for salvation. According to Luther, marriage was the new form of monastic life. Medieval monasticism had been organized around the idea that individual acts of penance must be performed to expiate individual sins. The routines of monastic life were based on the penitential disciplines of fasting, renunciation of the world, and the daily recitation of the penitential psalms. Many monks undertook grander penitential work, such as the hardship and danger of pilgrimage to some holy site.

In Luther's new theology, marriage and child rearing offered the most direct route to the rewards of heaven. All that men and women did within marriage counted as acts of penance. Marriage was an even better sacrificial act than a pilgrimage. Because a child was a creation of God, God took pleasure in it, and therefore even the duty of washing diapers was a work pleasing to God and certainly superior to reciting the penitential psalms. Giving birth to a child was a noble deed and a service to God in no way inferior to the work that the clergy did. Parents were in fact clergy themselves; they were apostles and bishops to their children, for they were doing the work of saving souls.[51]

These new ideas on sexuality and marriage spread rapidly through Europe by tract, sermon, and gossip. The clash of the two theologies—one proclaiming celibacy, the other marriage—provoked intense and often traumatic social conflict. The Genevan reformer Guillaume Farrell, and his companion, Pierre Viret, with the additional support of civic officials, went to a Franciscan convent of nuns to preach the good news of marriage. The resistant prioress was forcibly removed from the room to make way for these important men of the city to address the nuns. When the preachers reached the topic of "carnal corruption" (the nuns' name for marriage), these celibate women screamed and shouted in order to drown out the offending sermon. Only one nun converted to the new teaching on marriage. She left the convent.

When this sister returned to request the provision of a dowry, she returned in the company of a woman who herself had once been an abbess but had converted to the new theology of marriage. This time a woman preached to the nuns the good news of marriage. An older member of this convent remembered that event:

In that company was one false abbess, wrinkled and of diabolical language, possessing a husband and child named Marie Déntiere of Picardy, who mixed herself up in preaching and in perverting the people from devotion. She placed herself among the sisters . . . But because of the desire she had of perverting someone, she did not take note of [their] reproaches and said, "Alas, poor creatures if only you knew how good it was to be next to a handsome husband and how God considered it pleasing. For a long time

I lived in those shadows of hypocrisy where you are, but God alone made me recognize the abuse of my pitiful life and I was brought to a light of truth. Considering with regret how I lived, for in these orders there is nothing but sanctimoniousness, mental corruption and idleness . . . I took about five hundred ducats [probably for a dowry] from the treasury of the abbey and I left that unhappiness. Thanks to God I have five handsome children and I live wholesomely." The sisters shrank back from these words of error and deceit, and they spat at her in hate.[52]

The teachings of the Reformers on sexuality were radical and liberating for women; the evil of their sexuality perceived as dangerous from the standpoint of clerical celibacy and male monasticism was transformed into a God-ordained good. But the good of female sexuality was securely anchored in the sheltered waters of the Reformation doctrine of marriage.

Although the Reformers affirmed the spiritual value of marriage and the goodness of woman as sexual partner, they did so without modifying the hierarchical structure of the institution of patriarchal marriage. Marriage was discussed from the male point of view, as an institution in which a man profited greatly from the aid and assistance of a woman. The service that a woman provided for her husband was expanded from that of sexual partnership to emotional companionship in which a man might find comfort and solace. Calvin, in his commentary on Genesis, explained:

Certainly, it cannot be denied, that the woman also, though in the second degree, was created in the image of God; whence it follows, that what was said in the creation of the man belongs to female sex. Now, since God assigned the woman as a help to the man, he not only prescribed to wives the rule of their vocation, to instruct them in their duty, but he also pronounces that marriage will really prove to men the best support of life. We may therefore conclude, that the order of nature implies that the woman be the helper of man. The vulgar proverb, indeed, is that she is a necessary evil; but the voice of God is rather to be heard, which declares that woman is given as a companion and an associate to man, to assist him to live well.[53]

Central to the Reformation theology of marriage was Gen. 2:18, where God said, "It is not good for man to be alone; I will make a helpmate for him." The role of woman as a helper to man in the context of marriage clearly subordinates her to him. This subordination of woman to man was given theological legitimation in the Reformation understanding of what the image of God in humanity is. The theologians of the Christian church—from the men trained in the Greek philosophical tradition through the theologians of the Middle Ages—understood the image of God in humanity to be located in the possession of reason or rationality. The Reformers stood on the other side of a revolution in the history of theology and philosophy. As heirs of the Nominalist tradition, they located the image of God in the will rather than in reason, and specifically in the ability to rule or exercise government and dominion. The key passage that connects the image of God with dominion is Gen. 1:28, where God after creating humanity in the divine image, said, "Let them have dominion over the fish of the sea and over the fowl of the air and over every living thing that moves upon the earth."

It is interesting that while the Genesis 1 account assigns the function of domination to both male and female, the Reformers were adamant that man was in the image of God in a primary sense, and woman, only in a secondary sense. For to man was committed the work of governing and ruling. Woman participated in the image of God and in the work of dominion only vicariously through man. Calvin, like Augustine, also struggled with the contradiction between Gen. 1:27 (male and female are in the image of God) and 1 Cor. 11:7 (only the male is in the image of God). In his commentary on Genesis, he asked,

> why Paul should deny the woman to be the image of God, when Moses honors both, indiscriminately, with this title. The solution is short; Paul there alludes to the domestic relation. He therefore restricts the image of God to *government,* in which the man has superiority over the wife, and certainly he means nothing more than that man is superior in the degree of honor. But here [referring to Gen. 1:27] the question is respecting that glory of God which peculiarly shines forth in human nature, where the mind, the will, and all the senses represent the divine order.[54]

In the period of the Reformation, then, women's nature was redeemed by a reevaluation of sexuality and marriage. But the redemption was only partial, for woman was still deemed inferior to man by nature. Commenting on Gen. 1:27 Luther said:

Moses includes each of the two sexes, for the woman appears to be a somewhat different being from the man, having different members and a much weaker nature. Although Eve was a most extraordinary creature—similar to Adam so far as the image of God is concerned, that is, in justice, wisdom, and happiness—she was nevertheless a woman. For as the sun is more excellent than the moon (although the moon, too, is a very excellent body), so the woman, although she was a most beautiful work of God, nevertheless was not the equal of the male in glory and prestige.[55]

When the Protestant reformers abolished the monasteries and with them the older Augustinian views on sexuality, they enshrined in its place the sanctity of marital sexuality. Sexual desire was the gift of God, sexual drives "to multiply and replenish the earth" were an ordinance of God. The new ideal of womanhood became domestic womanhood. The authority and the autonomy of the nun following the religious vocation were undermined. The only true religious role open to a woman of the Reformation was as a helpmate to a man.

The reaffirmation of sexuality by the reformers did not restore woman to a position of equality with man. And although sexual drives were now judged to be the good creation of a good God, God remained alienated from sexuality. Sexuality was a distant creation but not an expression of God's nature or life or creativity. Woman too remained distant from God, almost in the image of God, but not quite. God had more in common with man than he did with her.

## NOTES

1. Justin *First Apology* 15, trans. Cyril Richardson, *Early Christian Fathers,* ed. Richardson (Toronto: Macmillan, 1950), 250.

2. Justin *First Apology* 29, trans. Richardson, 260.

3. Origen *Contra Celsum* I.63., trans. Henry Chadwick (Cambridge: Cambridge Univ. Press, 1953).

4. Justin *First Apology* 46, trans. Richardson, 272.

5. *The Martyrdom of Saint Polycarp* 2, trans. Richardson, 149.

6. *The Martyrdom of Saint Polycarp* 13, trans. Richardson, 154.

7. *The Martyrs of Lyons,* Eusebius *Church History,* vols. 1 to 3

8. Peter Brown, *The Body and Society: Men, Women and Spiritual Renunciation* (New York: Columbia Univ. Press, 1988).

9. Athanasius *The Life of Anthony* 2.7, trans. H. Ellershaw, *NPNF*, vol. 4 (Grand Rapids, MI: Eerdmans, 1957).

10. *The Life of Anthony* 2.7.

11. Chrysostom *On Virginity* 14.3, trans. Elizabeth Clark, *Women in the Early Church*, ed. Clark (Wilmington, DE: Michael Glazier, 1983), 122–23.

12. Rosemary Radford Ruether, "Misogynism and Virginal Feminism in the Fathers of the Church," in *Religion and Sexism*, ed. Rosemary Radford Ruether (New York: Simon & Schuster, 1974), 150–83.

13. *Life of Olympias*, 3; see also Elizabeth Castelli, "Virginity and Its Meaning for Women's Sexuality in Early Christianity," in *Journal of Feminist Studies in Religion* (Spr. 1986), 75.

14. Augustine *Confessions* II.3, trans. Edward B. Pusey (New York: Washington Square Press, 1964).

15. *Confessions* III.1.

16. *Confessions* VI.15.

17. *Confessions* VIII.6.

18. *Confessions* VIII.8.

19. *Confessions* VIII.11.

20. *Confessions* VIII.12.

21. Augustine *On the Literal Meaning of Genesis, Ancient Christian Writers*, vol. 42, trans. John Hummond Taylor (Neuman Press, 1982).

22. Augustine *On the Literal Meaning of Genesis* XI.34.

23. Augustine *The City of God* 14:24; see also Uta Ranke-Heinemann, *Eunuchs for the Kingdom of Heaven: Women, Sexuality and the Catholic Church* (New York: Doubleday, 1990), 89.

24. Augustine *On the Literal Meaning of Genesis* X.20; see also Kari Børresen, *Subordination and Equivalence* (Washington, DC: Univ. Press of America, 1981), 66–68.

25. Augustine *Against Julian* III.21. Fathers of the Church, vol. 35, trans. Matthew Schumacher (New York: Fathers of the Church, Inc., 1987).

26. Augustine *On the Literal Meaning of Genesis* IX.56.

27. Plato *Phaedrus* 66c–d.

28. *Phaedrus* 66c.

29. *Phaedrus* 247d.

30. Børresen, *Subordination*, 21–31.

31. Augustine *On the Literal Meaning of Genesis* III.22; also VII.7; X.2.

32. Sacred Congregation for the Doctrine of the Faith, "Declaration on the Question of the Admission of Women to the Ministerial Priesthood," in *Women Priests: A Catholic Commentary on the Vatican Declaration,* ed. Leonard Swidler and Arlene Swidler (New York: Paulist Press, 1977).

33. A. Erens, "Les Soeurs dans l'ordre Prémontre, analect Praemontratensia," 1929, v. 6–26, trans. R. W. Southern, *Western Society and the Church in the Middle Ages* (New York: Penguin, 1970), 314.

34. Ranke-Heinemann, *Eunuchs for the Kingdom,* 109.

35. Ranke-Heinemann, *Eunuchs for the Kingdom,* 115–16.

36. Ranke-Heinemann, *Eunuchs for the Kingdom,* 116.

37. Bonaventure, *Commentary on the Sentences,* d. 34.a.2q.q. See also Ranke-Heinemann, *Eunuchs for the Kingdom,* 226–72.

38. Thomas Aquinas *Quaestiones de Quodlibet* X.g 9a.10.

39. Ranke-Heinemann, *Eunuchs for the Kingdom,* 229.

40. *Malleus Maleficarum,* part 1, question 6, trans. Rev. Montague Summers (New York: Benjamin Blom, repr. 1970).

41. See Thomas Aquinas *Summa Theologicae,* I.Q51.83.

42. *Malleus Maleficarum,* part 2, question 1.6–7.

43. *Malleus Maleficarum,* part 2, question 1.6.

44. *Malleus Maleficarum,* part 1, question 1.6.

45. *Malleus Maleficarum,* part 1, question 1.6.

46. *Malleus Maleficarum,* part 1, question 6.

47. *Malleus Maleficarum,* part 1, question 6.

48. Luther *Lectures on Genesis,* 1:26–28, trans. G. V. Schick, and "The Estate of Marriage" in *Luther's Works,* vols. 1 and 45 (St. Louis, MO: Concordia Publishing, 1958).

49. Ranke-Heinemann, *Eunuchs for the Kingdom,* 115.

50. Roland Bainton, *Here I Stand: A Life of Martin Luther* (New York: Abingdon Cokesbury, 1950), 373–75.

51. Luther "The Estate of Marriage," *Luther's Works,* vol. 45.

52. Jean de Jussie, Le levain du Calvinisme, ou commencement de l'heresie de Geneve, cited in Tom Head, "The Religion of the Femmelettes: Ideals and Experience Among Women in Sixteenth-Century France" (unpublished paper).

53. Calvin *Commentaries on the First Book of Moses called Genesis* 1.2.18, vol. 1, trans. John King (Grand Rapids, MI: Eerdmans, 1963).

54. Calvin *Commentaries on the First Book* 1.2.18.

55. Luther *Lectures on Genesis* 1:27.

*Venus of Laussel.* A goddess of old Europe, representing the power of life through the metaphor of female sexual generativity, was gradually subordinated to male gods in the development of Greek religion. Paleolithic. Musée des Antiquités Nationales, St. Germain en Laye. (Giraudon/Art Resource, NY.)

# 9

# What If God Had Breasts?

■ ■ ■ ■

The gendered values of honor and shame
and the notions of the subordination of
woman and the passivity of female sexuality
exercised a pervasive influence not only on
Greek society, but also on Greek theories of
reproduction, cosmology, and the divine.
When examined closely, Greek theories about
the universe and human biology reveal
more than simple scientific speculation. They
also convey encoded messages about the
supposed superiority of male over female.

The ancient descriptions of natural biological processes represented cultural beliefs about male honor and female shame, male rationality and female passivity.

Aristotle, for example, attempted to place cultural beliefs about the potency of male sexuality and the passivity of female sexual functions on a scientific footing in his treatises on the *Generation of Animals* and the *Parts of Animals*: "The male and the female are distinguished by a certain ability and inability. Male is that which is able to concoct, to cause to take shape, and to discharge semen, possessing the 'principle' of the 'form.' . . . Female is that which receives the semen, but is unable to cause the semen to take shape or to discharge it."[1] According to prevailing medical theory, males were able to produce sperm through "cooking" ordinary blood to coagulation, because their bodies were hotter. Since women's colder bodies were incapable of raising their menstrual blood to the necessary temperature, Greek intellectuals argued that only male semen had the power of life within itself. Aristotle's statement that semen possesses the "principle" of the "form" refers to its power not only to create life but also to order and form a new organism (a role analogous to that of the citizen male in the Greek polis). The semen contains in itself the principle of activity and effective organization for the developing embryo:

> In those animals in which these two functions are separate, the body—that is to say the physical nature—of the active partner and of the passive must be different. Thus, if the male is the active partner, the one which originates the movement, and the female qua female is the passive one, surely what the female contributes to the semen of the male will be not semen but material.[2]

Since the male semen has the power to generate in itself, the female egg cannot not have the same power.[3] The Greek active-versus-passive ideology of sexuality had become entrenched in the science of biology.[4] Although Aristotle developed his theories about male and female principles through the study of animal reproduction, he borrowed concepts from agriculture. Male semen was like seed planted in the earth; the female womb was like the fertile soil that provides the nutrients. Men produced seed; women were the plowed field in which the seed was sown.

Neither philosophers nor scientists do their speculative thinking in a vacuum. The gender hierarchy of Greek society was the lens through which philosophers viewed human reproduction. And their reproductive theories in turn functioned to legitimate the equation of males with honor and females with shame. By attributing awesome powers to the male seed and at the same time reducing women's role in reproduction to supplying raw materials, the honor due to maleness was enhanced and the supposed deficiency of femaleness was given a scientific explanation.

## COSMOLOGY

Notions of maleness and femaleness, sexual energy and creativity, and the mysterious process of reproduction provided the raw material from which most cosmologies were constructed. Although Hesiod's poetic cosmology, the *Theogony*, was created in the eighth century B.C.E., and Plato's philosophical cosmology in fourth-century B.C.E. Athenian culture, they have in common the use of metaphors taken from gender relations in society and from the social construction of sexuality. In Hesiod's creation myth, the voluptuous Earth is an active and effective creatrix, giving birth to her own consort and then with him producing the world to be inhabited and the pantheon of gods and goddesses.

First of all, the chaos came into being, next broad-bosomed Earth, the solid and eternal home of all, and Eros [Desire] the most beautiful of the immortal gods, who in every man and every god softens the sinews and overpowers the prudent purpose of the mind. Out of Void came Darkness and black Night, and out of Night came Light and Day, her children conceived after union in love with Darkness. Earth first produced starry Sky, equal in size with herself, to cover her on all sides. Next she produced the tall mountains, the pleasant haunts of the gods, and also gave birth to the barren waters, sea with its raging surges — all this without the passion of love. Thereafter she lay with Sky and gave birth to Ocean with its deep current.[5]

Although Plato abandoned the traditional gender hierarchy of his society in his utopian vision in the *Republic,* he reintroduced it in his philosophical cosmology. In Plato's myth of creation, female passivity attains cosmic proportions. He conceived of the creation of the cosmos as an interaction between male and female principles: "The mother and receptacle of all created and visible and in any way sensible things is not to be termed earth or air or fire or water, or any of their compounds, but is an invisible and formless being which receives all things and in some mysterious way partakes of the intelligible, and is most incomprehensible."[6] The Mother Receptacle is totally passive: "She is the natural recipient of all impressions, and is stirred and informed by them." It is the cosmic Father who is the cause of all things, specifically of the Forms, "which enter into and go out of her and are the likeness of eternal realities."[7] The male principle produces the eternal, unchanging patterns for all things in the cosmos; these Forms have in themselves the power to order and shape unformed matter. Plato's Forms are able to do in the Mother Receptacle what male sperm can do in the passive womb. Since Plato used reproduction as a primary metaphor for cosmological processes, the values of male honor, expressed in male agency, and female shame, as a correlate of female passivity, became a part of the very structure of cosmos.

The language of philosophical abstractions and religious myths is a borrowed language. The world philosophers wish to speak of cannot be empirically observed and therefore can be described only metaphorically. What makes metaphors and symbols effective in describing such invisible realms is that they are rooted in the concrete and particular details of social life. The most potent metaphors are those that draw on the more powerful determinants of social experience, such as birth, sexual intercourse, masculinity, and femininity. When the Greeks set out to describe the divine, they looked to these metaphors, just as they had when they theorized about human reproduction and the cosmos. The Greek ideology of sexuality was therefore the framework. As a result, the Greek notion of the divine is built on an opposition between male honor, rationality, agency, and rule and female shame, irrationality, passivity, and obedience. The divine, consequently, has a distinctly masculine character.

This poses a dilemma for a critical evaluation of the concept of the divine in both Western philosophy and theology. Contemporary Western societies have constructed their visions of themselves by drawing on political and philosophical traditions that go back to classical Greece. The authority of many political institutions, civic values, philosophical concepts, and theological doctrines rests on their historical connection to ancient Greek culture.

Cultural anthropologist and archaeologist Marija Gimbutas raises a question that is pressing for many women today: Are these traditions adequate? Because historians have made hierarchical political organization, social stratification, and a military class the primary characteristics of civilization, they begin the history of European civilization with classical Greece. This notion of "civilization" needs to be reexamined, asserts Gimbutas. She suggests that modern society look behind Greek culture to the European civilization of the Neolithic period that predated the Greeks, which she calls Old Europe (6500–3500), for more useful political, social, and religious traditions.

Archaeological excavations by Gimbutas and James Mellaart in the region that extends north from Turkey through the present-day European countries have uncovered developed agricultural societies in which there was a surprising absence of military classes and class hierarchies. Archaeologists find in burial sites telling evidence for the patterns of social organization. For example, the social importance of the Celtic warrior chieftain was signaled in burial sites that featured elaborate mounds and long passageways and by the golden ornaments that symbolically conveyed the importance of the warrior. The shield, the bow, and the highly decorated dagger, along with slaughtering tools, indicate that a chieftain was a master in the arts of death. The burial sites of Old Europe, by contrast, revealed a striking absence of weapons of war. They also failed to produce any evidence for a class hierarchy. Archaeologists found little variation either in the sizes of the burial sites or in the kinds of artifacts buried with each individual. In the layout of the town at Çatal Hüyük, Turkey, there was little evidence of social stratification. Nearly all of the residences had a floor plan of about twenty-five square meters.

James Mellaart's excavations at Çatal Hüyük show that these societies were organized around a religion that was not centralized in a temple but represented in numerous shrines interspersed throughout the residential settlement. Shrines seem to account for nearly one-third of the total number of residences. Homes and shrines were laid out in the same way, but the shrines were more highly decorated. In the corners of the central room were raised sleeping platforms, which also served as burial sites. The largest and most central sleeping platform, located on the east side of houses and shrines, belonged to the woman of the household.[8] The other sleeping platforms, slightly smaller in size, were used by the husband and children. Women and men lived together as a household in the shrines and functioned as priestesses and priests. Burial sites within the shrine provide evidence for the symbols of priesthood— women were buried with obsidian mirrors; men, with belt fasteners of polished bone.

The focal point of religious rites was the goddess, who represented the power of life through the metaphor of female sexual generativity. The representations of the goddess show her in stylized form with large breasts, sometimes pregnant, sometimes delivering. The generativity of the goddess stood for all the life powers in nature that nourished and nurtured human society.[9] Although the goddess was often accompanied by animals, such as leopards, and her shrines were highly decorated with the horns of the bull, no animals were sacrificed to her. She was honored by offerings of burnt grain. Both homes and shrines contained clay ovens with rounded openings. Models of these clay ovens bearing the features of the goddess—the open mouth of the stove representing the open mouth of the goddess—show that the work of preparing bread and the bread itself were sacred to the goddess.[10]

The life force of the goddess was sculpted into myriad images by her devotees in Old European society. The goddess figures have highly stylized breasts, buttocks, or vulva. The life powers of nature were also represented in a human form. In other figures the same features of female anatomy are joined to the head or neck of a bird to form the bird goddess, signifying life-giving powers. The snake goddess was associated with the primordial waters, and her creative powers were symbolized in the coils of the snake or abstract spirals. The powers of death, part of the cycle of life, were also symbolized as powers of the goddess. The powers of regeneration so evident in the world of nature were symbolized by joining the female form with that of a frog, hedgehog, or fish.[11]

The powers to produce life inherent in female sexuality provided the most potent symbols for the divine in the societies of Old Europe. In an agricultural society without a gender hierarchy and a warrior class, sexuality was symbolic not of relations of domination but of the powers of life and creativity.

The transition from the goddess cultures of Old Europe to ancient Greek culture is obscure. But it seems that Greeks were descendants of a group of nomadic warriors called the Kurgans, who swept in waves off the Asian steppes and overran the peaceful civilizations of Old Europe, in part destroying them and in part assimilating them. The Kurgans, pastoralists who had domesticated the horse, discovered and adopted the metallurgy of Old European society and swiftly adapted it to the production of weapons: daggers, halberds, mace heads, and battle-axes, often set with semiprecious stones. In Kurgan burial sites, archaeologists have discovered sharp distinctions in class. The burial site of the warrior chieftain was much larger and accommodated a rich collection of funerary gifts. The most disturbing evidence for social hierarchies was the presence in the warriors' graves of the bodies of women and children sacrificed at the time of the warrior's death and buried with him. They were probably individuals owned by the warrior. There are indications that the Kurgans killed the men of Old European towns and kept the women and children as concubines and slaves.

The Kurgans brought with them warrior sky gods, powerful and fierce, who presided over death. These gods were often represented in the form of a weapon or a male figure coupled with a weapon—a god, for instance, whose arms were replaced by axe-heads. Marija Gimbutas compares the symbols of the two cultures:

The Kurgan ideology, as known from comparative Indo-European mythology, exalted virile, heroic warrior gods of the shining and thunderous sky. Weapons are non-existent in Old European imagery; whereas the dagger and battle axe are dominant symbols of the Kurgan who like all historically known Indo-Europeans glorified the lethal power of the blade.[12]

The principal Kurgan god was the thunder god, portrayed carrying axe, mace, and bow. A sun god, or the god of the shining sky, who appeared with his animals, the stag and horse, and often with a vehicle, was also portrayed with dagger and sword. The weapons themselves were believed to transmit power. The blow of the axe blade delivered to the earth the fecundity of the thunder god. The Kurgan concept of the divine was a projection of the warrior elite—a virile male god whose power, like theirs, resided in his weapons.[13]

By the third millennium B.C.E. Kurgan culture was well established on the Greek peninsula. Traditional Kurgan burial mounds have been found throughout Greece in which chieftain and warriors were buried with women, weapons, and animal bones.[14] There are no records of the transition from the goddess religion of Old Europe to Greek religion. Nevertheless some scholars find in Aeschylus's famous trilogy of plays, *Oresteia* (458 B.C.E.), a dim memory of a time when female sexuality was honored. Orestes was on trial for the serious charge of matricide. Defending him were Apollo and the rest of the Greek sky gods. Ranged against him were the Erinyes, or Furies, ancient female goddesses associated with the earth. Orestes had killed his mother to avenge the death of his father, Agamemnon. Orestes' mother had killed her husband, Orestes' father, in vengeance because Agamemnon had arranged the sacrifice of their daughter to secure a victory in battle. The Furies argue in chorus against Apollo: "You plead for his acquittal: Have you asked yourself how one who poured out on the ground his mother's blood will live henceforth in Argos, in his father's house? Shall he, at public altars, share in sacrifice? Shall holy water lave his hands at tribal feasts?"[15]

The trial turns on new evidence submitted by Apollo that the mother is not the true parent of the child. For, he argues, it is the father's seed that carries the generative power of life and that produces new life when planted in the womb of the female. Apollo addresses the jury:

This, too, I answer; mark the truth of what I say. The mother is not the true parent of the child which is called hers. She is a nurse who tends the growth of a young seed planted by its true parent, the male. So, if Fate spares the child, she keeps it, as one might keep for some friend a growing plant. And of this truth, that father without mother may beget, we have present, as proof, the daughter of Olympian

Zeus: one never nursed in the dark cradle of the womb; yet such a being no god will beget again.[16]

It is male sexuality, not female sexuality, that is generative, according to Apollo. Matricide is therefore a crime of less seriousness than patricide. Orestes is acquitted. The powers of generativity, once expressed through reproductive sexuality that the societies of Old Europe reverenced in the female, had in patriarchal Greek society passed to the male.

In the development of Greek religion, the goddess gradually became subordinated to the male god. She was portrayed as a consort, a daughter, a wife.[17] Gimbutas notes that in Kurgan religion, the female goddess appeared as the wife of the male god rather than as an independent creator, as the she had been in Old Europe.[18]

Gerda Lerner traces the subordination of women and the demise of the goddess to political changes in the third millennium, when a society based on kinship ties gave way to the archaic state. In the wake of this sociopolitical transformation, the figure of the goddess was supplanted by a pantheon of gods and goddesses.[19] By the time of the emergence of monotheism, the male gods had come to dominate.[20] The principle of male generativity was retained as monotheistic religions arose from polytheistic religions, but the sexual metaphors for generativity drawn from natural processes were replaced by metaphors of rule and order borrowed from the processes of ordering society. Lerner observes a shift in symbolism in creation stones from the third to the second millennium B.C.E. Symbols for the universal powers of generativity changed from the "vulva of the goddess to the seed of man." Moreover, the tree of life as a naturalistic symbol for the creativity of nature was supplanted by the tree of knowledge. In addition, the centrality of the rituals of sacred marriage, which ensured the productivity of the land and society, were replaced by the symbol of covenant, a verbal contract.[21] The sexual generativity associated with life-giving powers in Old European and Greek religions was transformed into a male verbal and rational creativity in the monotheistic religions. In the creation story of the Hebrews (early monotheists), a male God creates life by his word and command alone. "And God said, 'Let the earth bring forth living creatures,'" and "God said, 'And let the waters bring forth swarms of living creatures.'" God created and ordered this thriving world of life. "God divided the light from the darkness," "the waters from the dry land," and "God created two lights, the greater to rule the day, the lesser to rule the night." And the creating and ordering were done by God's *word*. God's power, his ability to create life and sustain it, is expressed in his word and command. The potency of the creative word is analogous to the potency of a royal command. This new metaphor for creative power, the word, is a metaphor of political authority rather than of life forces, as the sexual reproduction metaphor is.

Many female symbols have survived, however, although submerged by successive waves of masculine symbols created as patriarchal societies became dominant. The Christian ritual of baptism, for instance, draws its meaning from women's work of giving birth. In some of the earliest baptismal rites, converts entered the waters naked, like the baby in the womb. After being immersed, they came forth from the water as people who had been born again. The first food these "newborn" converts received was in fact made of milk and honey—an imitation of breast milk—signifying their entrance into the Christian community as babes. Symbols drawn from natural creative processes, especially maternal ones, possess a certain power that has defied continuous attempts to suppress them, as a close examination of the Hebrew Scriptures shows.

## THE FEMININE FACE OF GOD

There is a feminine face of God in the Hebrew Scriptures — images and metaphors for God and God's activities that are drawn from the world of women's experience.[22] The Hebrew word for one of the most important attributes of God is *rahum,* generally translated "compassion." However, the literal meaning is "womb love." *Rahum* carries with it the idea of a yearning for the new life present in the womb. This same Hebrew term is the basis for the word *rahamim,* generally translated as "mercies." Yahweh says to her people, "Can a woman forget her nursing child or show no compassion for the child of her womb? Even these may forget, yet I will not forget you" (Jer. 49:15).

In Deut. 32:11, Yahweh says to her people, "As an eagle stirs up [her] nest and hovers over [her] young, and spreads [her] wings, takes them up and bears them aloft on her wings, so the Lord alone guided him [Jacob]." This beautiful image portrays God as the mother eagle who not only nurtures and protects her young in the nest but scoops them up on her enormous wing, carries them aloft, and then tips them off so they can learn to fly. In Psalm 22 the psalmist grieves over his tribulation and tries to reconcile his suffering with the knowledge he has of God's love for him. This God seems like a midwife. "Yet, it was you who took me from the womb, you kept me safe on my mother's breast, placed me on your lap from birth, and since my mother bore me you have been my God" (vv. 9–10).

Another powerful image compares Yahweh's anger with that of a mother bear robbed of her cubs. "I will fall on them, like a bear robbed of her cubs and will tear the flesh around their heart" (Hos. 13:8). If God's anger can take female form, then perhaps the anger of women need not be suppressed.

There are numerous images of God as a mother hen. "Thus says the Lord Almighty, have I not entreated you as a father entreats his sons, or as a mother her daughters, and a nurse her children so that you should be my people and I would be your God, that you should be my children, and I should be your father? I gather you as a hen gathers her chicks under her wings" The psalmist often speaks of God hiding us under the shadow of her wings (Ps. 17.8; 36.7; 91.4). Jesus borrowed this image of God for himself when he prayed on the mountaintop overlooking the city of Jerusalem, "Jerusalem, Jerusalem, the city that kills the prophets and stones those who are sent to it! How often have I desired to gather your children together as a hen gathers her brood under her wings, and you were not willing" (Lk. 13.34–35).

## SOPHIA—DIVINE WISDOM

One fascinating expression of the feminine face of God is found in the figure of Sophia (Wisdom), whose many appearances can be traced from Jewish theology into Christian theology.[23] Sophia appears as the teacher of Wisdom. She calls to those in the marketplace and promises them instruction: "I have good advice and sound wisdom, I have insight. I have strength. By me kings reign, and rulers decree what is just; . . . I love those who love me" (Prov. 8:14–17). She sets her teachings forth like a banquet of many courses and promises life to those who follow her teachings. "Whoever finds me finds life" (Prov. 8:35).

Sophia also appears as a creator-redeemer figure in the Wisdom of Solomon. She is the Mother whose protective presence guides the unfolding of the whole history of salvation. She was in the garden protecting Adam. Sophia delivered Noah from his ark, rescued Lot, and brought the children of Israel out of Egypt, working through her servant Moses. "She brought them over the Red Sea, and led them through the deep waters; but she drowned their enemies, and cast them up from the depth of the sea" (Wisd. of Sol. 10:18-19).

Sophia also appears at God's side before the birth of the cosmos. When there were no deep waters and before the mountains were settled, Sophia worked at God's side "like a master workman." God delighted in her, she herself was a woman of play and delighted in the new cosmos and in the newly created human race (Prov. 8:22-31). In the fourth-century debates over the full deity of Christ, theologians appealed to this passage as evidence that Christ was the firstborn of creation. Christ has long been associated with Sophia.

Sophia figured prominently as those in the Jesus movement tried to explain who he was and why he was important. Jesus, like John, was first presented as an emissary and then an incarnation of Sophia (the feminine face of God). It is Sophia who gathers to herself the outcasts and then claims them. Sometimes Jesus is portrayed as Sophia herself speaking and as doing Sophia's works in preaching to the poor and healing the suffering.[24]

Matthew presents the strongest Sophia Christology; for him, Jesus is Sophia incarnate. In the first chapter of his Gospel, John took a hymn of Sophia and transferred the titles of Sophia to Jesus. "In the beginning was the Word and the Word was with God and the Word was God" (John 1:1). In attempting to express the idea that the human person Jesus was also divine and preexistent, John cast him in the role of the divine Sophia.

Paul, too, in explaining that Jesus was more than a human being, applied to Jesus what was said of Sophia. Like Sophia, Jesus is the one from whom all things are, through whom all things were created both in heaven and on earth, and through whom all things continue in existence. Paul's Christological hymn in Col. 1:15 puts it succinctly: "He is the image of the invisible God, the firstborn of all creation."

## WHEN GOD BECOMES SHE

There exists a long tradition of divine figures who speak in the female voice. But we are less prepared today to hear divinity speak with anything but a masculine voice, to appear as anything other than male. What happens today when God is called she? In order to begin to see what possibilities this holds, let's suppose the parable of the prodigal son were written in the female voice. Here is the story of the prodigal daughter and the forgiving mother.

There was a woman who had two daughters, and the younger of them said to her mother, "Mother, give me the share of property that falls to me." And she divided her living between them. Not many days later the younger daughter gathered all she had and took her journey into a far country, and there she squandered her property on parties and loose living. And when she had spent everything a great famine arose in that country and she began to be in want. So she went and joined herself to one of the property owners of that country who sent her into her fields to feed swine. And she would gladly have fed on the pods that the swine ate; and no one gave her anything. But when she came to herself she said, "How many of my mother's hired servants have bread enough and to spare, but I perish with hunger? I will arise and go to my mother and say, Mother, I have sinned against heaven and before you; I am no longer worthy to be called your daughter; treat me as one of your hired servants."

And she arose and came to her mother. But while she was yet at a distance, her mother saw her and ran and embraced and kissed her. And the daughter said to her, "Mother, I have sinned against heaven and before you; I am no longer worthy to be called your daughter." But the mother said to her servants, "Bring quickly the best robe and put it on her, and put a ring on her hand and shoes on her feet, and bring the fatted calf and kill it and let us eat and make merry; for this my daughter was dead, and is alive again; she was lost, and is found." And they began to make merry.

Now the elder daughter was in the field; and as she came and drew near to the house she heard music and dancing. And she called to one of the servants and asked what this meant. And she said to her, "Your sister has come and your mother has killed the fatted calf because she received her safe and sound." But she was angry and refused to go in. Her mother came out and entreated her, but she answered her mother, "Oh, these many years I have served you and I never disobeyed your command, yet you never gave me a kid that I might make merry with my friends. But when this daughter of yours comes, who devoured your living on parties, you killed for her the fatted calf!" And she said, "Daughter, you are always with me, and all that is mine is yours. It is fitting to make merry and be glad, for this your sister was dead and is alive, she was lost and is found."

*What If God Had Breasts?* ■ ■ ■ ■

This story will strike us as being different in a number of ways from the one we know so well, and there will be a variety of responses to this truly "revised version." Let's reflect on the differences. First consider the figure of the prodigal daughter. In this story a young woman stands before us as a model for all humanity. She is both the sinner and the forgiven one. In this version she represents what is truly human. Our view of womanhood is changed by seeing her play for us that paradigmatic role. She is at center stage, the principal actor. She is the agent, the one who sets things in motion, the one who creates, the one who changes, the one who has power. Accepting a woman in this role transforms our image of woman as passive, as victim, and as respondent.

Let us now consider God as the forgiving mother. The message of forgiveness remains the same, but the tones, nuances, and colors are changed, however subtly. When we imagine God as the forgiving mother, we gather into that image the feelings and experiences and longings that we associate with the idea of mother. The story presents a mother-daughter relationship, with all of its complexities, tensions, strengths, and ambiguities. For some this makes the message of forgiveness more moving and compelling. For some it also affirms the goodness of being female. If the idea of God can be expressed with the metaphor of mother, then women are in the image of God. Women's ways of being in the world mirror God's ways of being in the world. Women's experiences of mothering, nurturing, and caring, mourning, grieving, and loving can also be used to describe the heart of God.

If this were the way the story was told in Scripture, then women's experience would clearly be a basis from which to do theology. Women's experience would be paradigmatic for reflecting on the nature of God and God's relationship to us. If this were the Gospel version, then women's experience would also be paradigmatic for preaching. A sermon centered on such a story would evoke the emotional depths of women's relationships.

The idea of God as mother has a rich and long tradition in Christian spirituality. In the fourteenth century, a woman theologian, Dame Julian of Norwich, recorded her visions of God in a book, *Revelations of Divine Love.*

> In the same showing, suddenly the Trinity filled full my heart with the utmost joy. For the Trinity is God, and God is the Trinity. The Trinity is our Maker. The Trinity is our Keeper. Trinity is our everlasting Lover. And then I saw that God rejoices that he is our Father; and God rejoices that he is our Mother; and God rejoices that he is our true Spouse, and that our soul is his beloved wife. And Christ rejoices that he is our Brother; and Jesus rejoices that he is our Savior. These are the five high joys.[25]

In Julian's understanding of God as Mother, she unveils a new dimension of God's love—that God rejoices in us, takes pleasure in us, delights in us, that we bring joy to God just by being ourselves. She does not speak of our joy in God, our response to God, our pleasure in God, but rather God's pleasure and delight in us. The concept of God Julian evokes is God the Mother delighting in her child, drawing deep pleasure from her child's smile or laugh or touch—a deep joy that springs from the child's simply being who she is.

Since women have not been defined as fully human, their being and experience have not been used to provide primary metaphors and symbols for God. There is always an underground connection between our metaphors and the social experience that enlivens them. Consequently female images for the divine can sometimes be reassuring when they evoke a mothering God or disturbing when they juxtapose God and the female body. The metaphorical character of the way we talk and think about God becomes much clearer when we use more than one metaphor.[26]

The emotional turbulence surrounding the use of a maternal metaphor is heightened when the eroticized parts of the female body are used to symbol the divine. Nonetheless, according to the theology of the last two millennia, women cannot symbolize God because they are not made in the image of God, and they are not made in the image of God, specifically, because of their association with sexuality rather than rationality. In the same way, women's sexuality cannot image God because it has been excluded from both the Greek philosophical and Christian theological notions of God. Women's sexuality as symbol or metaphor represents birth, the fragility and vulnerability of life, mortality, and contingency—the opposite of male rationality and control. To bring the female into the realm of the divine is to bring sexuality back into the realm of the divine, from which it has been banished since the advent of monotheism.

A beautiful hymn to the Holy Spirit from the fourth-century church in Syria images God as having breasts.[27]

> A cup of milk was offered to me,
> and I drank it in the sweetness of the Lord's kindness.
>
> The Son is the cup,
> and the Father is He who was milked;
> And the Holy Spirit is She who milked Him;
> Because His breasts were full,

And it was undesirable that His milk should be
ineffectually released.

The Holy Spirit opened Her bosom,
And mixed the milk of the two breasts of the Father.

Then She gave the mixture to the generation without
their knowing
And those who have received it are in the perfection
of the right hand.

The womb of the Virgin took it,
And she received conception and gave birth.
So the Virgin became a mother with great mercies.

In this hymn, the mystery of the shared life of the Trinity is expressed with metaphors of female sexuality. The life-generating
power of the Trinitarian God is symbolized by a nursing mother's
milk. This life is carried by the Holy Spirit, a female figure. Then
the Holy Spirit planted this life-giving substance in the womb of
Mary, who brought forth the Redeemer and Savior.

Julian of Norwich called Jesus Mother and superimposed
over the image of the crucifix the image of a woman in hard labor
about to give birth:

> We know that all our mothers bear us for pain and
> for death. Oh, what is that? But our true Mother Jesus, he alone bears us
> for joy and for endless life, blessed may he be. So he carries us within in
> love and travail, until the full time when he wanted to suffer the sharpest
> thorns and cruel pains that ever were or will be. . . . The mother can give
> her child to suck of her milk, but our precious Mother Jesus can feed us
> with himself.[28]

Images not only of nurture but also of suffering were transposed into a female key by mystics and poets seeking to express the depth of their insights.

Despite these occasional spontaneous bursts of inspiration unencumbered by masculine metaphors, Christianity has for the most part been mired in the limited symbol system it inherited from patriarchal societies. But hierarchic patriarchy is not intrinsic to Christianity, to its message, to its eschatological vision of the social order, or to its countercultural origins. Neither are gender hierarchy and the denigration of sexuality necessary components of authentic Western religion. Knowing about our roots in the earth-centered religion of Old Europe, with its Mother goddess and its kin-centered culture, can augment our efforts to reclaim the non-violence and egalitarianism of the new order announced by Jesus.

It is crucial to acknowledge at long last that women were and can be Christian leaders, that there is nothing debased about being female or sexual. The contemporary controversy over women's ordination has striking similarities with the conflict over slavery. In the nineteenth century Christianity was involved in a profound moral struggle that pitted Christian tradition against the essential message of the Christian gospel. Slavery was a recognized and legitimate social institution in the societies that produced the Old and New Testaments. At the end of this struggle the "good news" of Jesus' authentic Christian message that salvation is extended to all and therefore that all are equal prevailed; the social institution of slavery was not only not essential for the ordering of Christian society, but contrary to true Christian values. Contemporary Christian theologians need to undertake the same task of extricating the essential teachings of the Christian gospel from the patriarchal gender system in which it is embedded. Christian churches need to return to their own authentic heritage, reject the patriarchal norms of the Greco-Roman gender system, and restore women to equal partnership in the leadership of the church and participation in Christian life.

## NOTES

1. *On the Generation of Animals* 765b.

2. *On the Generation of Animals* 729a.

3. Maryanne Cline Horowitz, "Aristotle and Woman," *Journal of the History of Biology* 9, 2 (Fall, 1976): 195. Aristotle supports his conclusion that the female principle is passive from his observation that the unfertilized egg of the female bird failed to produce a fledgling.

4. Although the reproductive theory of the pre-Socratic philosophers Empedocles, Axagoras, and Democritus argued for both male and female seed, their views were rejected by Aristotle. On the basis of dissections, Galen posited again a two-seed theory of reproduction. Nevertheless the Aristotelian theory dominated Western thought up until the eighteenth century. See Thomas Laqueur, *Making Sex: The Body and Gender from the Greeks to Freud* (Cambridge: Harvard Univ. Press, 1990).

5. Hesiod *Theogony*, trans. Rosemary Ruether, *WomenGuides* (Boston: Beacon Press, 1985).

6. Plato *Timaeus* 51.a–b, trans. Benjamin Jowett, *The Collected Dialogues of Plato,* ed. Edith Hamilton and Huntington Cairns (Princeton: Princeton Univ. Press, 1961).

7. Plato *Timaeus* 50c.

8. J. Mellaart, *Çatal Hüyük* (New York: McGraw-Hill, 1967), 77–203.

9. Marija Gimbutas, *The Civilization of the Goddess: The World of Old Europe* (San Francisco: HarperSanFrancisco, 1991), 221–306.

*What If God Had Breasts?*  ■■■■

10. Marija Gimbutas, *The Language of the Goddess* (San Francisco: Harper & Row, 1989), 147–48.

11. Gimbutas, *Language of the Goddess*, 187–213.

12. Marija Gimbutas, "The First Wave of Eurasian Steppe Pastoralists into Copper-Age Europe," *Journal of Indo-European Studies* 5 (Winter 1977): 281.

13. Gimbutas, *Civilization of the Goddess*, 351–403.

14. Gimbutas, *Civilization of the Goddess*, 387–89.

15. Aeschylus *Oresteia: The Eumenides*, trans. Philip Vellecott (Baltimore: Penguin Books, 1964).

16. Aeschylus *Oresteia*.

17. Gerda Lerner, *The Creation of Patriarchy* (New York: Oxford Univ. Press, 1986), 149.

18. Gimbutas, *Civilization of the Goddess*, 389. There is evidence in other civilizations for divine females creating parthogenically. The Egyptian goddess Nun, associated with the primeval ocean, created the sky god and the rest of the universe without a male consort. Similarly, the Sumerian goddess Nammu, also without a male consort, created the sky god and the earth goddess.

19. Tikva Frymer Kensky places the transition a millennium later when larger city-states became nation-states (second millennium). The decline of the goddesses followed the eclipse of the role of women in public life (*In the Wake of the Goddess* [New York: Macmillan, 1992], 70–82).

20. Lerner, *The Creation of Patriarchy*, 199–211.

21. Lerner, *The Creation of Patriarchy*, 146.

22. For discussions of the presence of goddess figures in the Hebrew Scriptures, see Kensky, *In the Wake of the Goddess;* Raphael Patai, *The Hebrew Goddess* (Detroit: Wayne State Univ. Press, 1967); Virginia R. Mollencott, *The Divine Feminine* (New York: Crossroads, 1984).

23. See Susan Cady, Marcia Ronan, and Hal Taussig, *Wisdom's Feast: Sophia in Study and Celebration* (San Francisco: HarperSanFrancisco, 1990).

24. Elizabeth Johnson, "Jesus, the Wisdom of God," in *Ephemerides Theologicae Lovanienses* 61, 4 (December 1985): 276–89.

25. Julian of Norwich, *Showings,* trans. Edmund College, O.S.A., and James Walsh, S.J. (New York: Paulist Press, 1978), 279. See Newman Press ed., 1952.

26. Sallie McFague, *Metaphorical Theology* (Philadelphia: Fortress Press, 1982).

27. Rosemary Radford Ruether, *WomanGuides* (Boston: Beacon Press, 1985), 29–31. See *Odes of Solomon,* ed. James Charlesworth (Oxford: Clarendondon Press, 1973), 82–83, 216–17.

28. Julian of Norwich, *Showings,* trans. College and Walsh, 297–98.

# Index